This book offers a trenchant analysis of the politics of social policy in an era of austerity and conservative governance. Focusing on the administrations of Ronald Reagan and Margaret Thatcher, Pierson provides a compelling explanation for the welfare state's durability and for the few occasions in which each government was able to achieve significant cutbacks. Pierson's account draws on recent work in "historical institutionalism" and rational-choice theory to fashion an important argument about contemporary policy-making. The politics of retrenchment, he argues, is fundamentally different from that of welfare state expansion. The programs of the modern welfare state – the "policy legacies" of previous governments – generally proved resistant to reform. Hemmed in by the political supports that have developed around mature social programs, conservative opponents of the welfare state were successful only when they were able to divide the supporters of social programs, compensate those negatively affected, or hide what they were doing from potential critics. This book will be of interest to those in the fields of comparative public policy and political economy as well as to those concerned with the development of the modern welfare state.

DISMANTLING THE WELFARE STATE?

This series publishes comparative research that seeks to explain important, cross-national domestic political phenomena. Based on a broad conception of comparative politics, it hopes to promote critical dialogue among different approaches. While encouraging contributions from diverse theoretical perspectives, the series will particularly emphasize work on domestic institutions and work that examines the relative roles of historical structures and constraints, of individual or organizational choice, and of strategic interaction in explaining political actions and outcomes. This focus includes an interest in the mechanisms through which historical factors impinge on contemporary political choices and outcomes.

Works on all parts of the world are welcomed, and priority will be given to studies that cross traditional area boundaries and that treat the United States in comparative perspective. Many of the books in the series are expected to be comparative, drawing on material from more than one national case, but studies devoted to single countries will also be considered, especially those that pose their problem and analysis in such a way that they make a direct contribution to comparative analysis and theory.

DISMANTLING THE WELFARE STATE?

REAGAN, THATCHER, AND THE POLITICS OF RETRENCHMENT

PAUL PIERSON
Harvard University

CAMBRIDGE
UNIVERSITY PRESS

Published by the Press Syndicate of the University of Cambridge
The Pitt Building, Trumpington Street, Cambridge CB2 1RP
40 West 20th Street, New York, NY 10011-4211, USA
10 Stamford Road, Oakleigh, Melbourne 3166, Australia

© Cambridge University Press 1994

First published 1994
First paperback edition 1995
Reprinted 1996

Printed in the United States of America

Library of Congress Cataloging-in-Publication Data is available

A catalogue record for this book is available from the British Library

ISBN 0-521-40382-0 hardback
ISBN 0-521-55570-1 paperback

Contents

Acknowledgments

This manuscript has been "forthcoming" for some time, and it is a pleasure to finally be able to offer my thanks in print to the many people who have helped me with their comments, criticisms, and support. I have had the good luck to draw on the insights and advice of a great many people who agreed to be interviewed for this project. Although they have been promised anonymity, I want to express in a general way my appreciation for their help in introducing a nonspecialist to the complex politics of social policy. I am especially grateful to the participants in British policy networks who took the time to give me a better sense of the environment in which they were working.

Pulling together a list of those deserving thanks reminds one that the academy, at its best, is indeed a "community." For research assistance, I want to thank Michelle Tully and, especially, Peter Rutledge, who provided me with useful criticisms and steady encouragement as well as a constant stream of information. Among those providing detailed suggestions – most of which I have tried to follow – were Keith Banting, David Cameron, Patricia Craig, Tony Daley, Danny Goldhagen, Janet Gornick, Ian Gough, Ron Jepperson, Stephan Leibfried, Charles Lindblom, Andy Martin, Cathie Martin, Jerry Mashaw, David Miliband, Paul Peterson, Kit Pierson, David Plotke, Peter Taylor-Gooby, Rick Valelly, Margaret Weir, and Joe White. Chris Howell, Elizabeth Kier, Jonathan Mercer, and Miriam Smith provided careful readings of the entire manuscript's final draft as well as encouragement and friendship along the way. Whether through wisdom or luck, Tracey Goldberg missed most of the process, but I am very glad that she was there to offer the right mix of support and gentle prodding at the end.

In traveling the considerable distance from a draft of a dissertation prospectus to a completed book, I have benefited enormously from the guidance of a number of individuals who have combined a strong commitment to their own scholarship with a tremendous generosity in helping other researchers. Ted Marmor sparked my interest in the welfare state. Without his influence, this book would never have been written. He provided vigorous but sympathetic supervision of the dissertation that provided the initial outlines of this study, and has been steadfast in reminding me that "social policy" is not simply a set of dependent variables for social scientists but rather a range of activities with tremendous consequences for millions of people. Kent Weaver was enormously supportive of this project at a time when I was ostensibly his research assistant. His encouragement has been invaluable, and his theoretical insights have been of such help to me that this book would undoubtedly look far different without his contributions. At Harvard, Peter Hall and Theda Skocpol have provided the right balance of support and critique. Each has contributed significantly to the development of my views, and been sympathetic to my efforts to both build on and, occasionally, criticize aspects of their own work.

I am grateful for my association with Cambridge University Press. Peter Lange, general editor for the studies in comparative politics series at Cambridge, has been tremendously helpful. His incisive reading of the book's first draft had a substantial impact on my thinking. If the final product represents an improvement, his interventions deserve a large part of the credit. I thank also Herbert Gilbert, Cary Groner, Alex Holzman, and Emily Loose for their help in turning the manuscript into a book.

I want to acknowledge the considerable institutional support that has made this project possible. For research funding to speed the completion of this book, I wish to thank the Council for European Studies, the Concilium for International and Area Studies of Yale University, the Mellon Foundation, Oberlin College, the Brookings Institution, and Harvard University. I received much-needed assistance from the library staffs of a number of institutions, including those at Nuffield College, Oxford, the London School of Economics and Political Science, Yale University, the Brookings Institution, and Harvard University. I must single out for special thanks the Center for European Studies at Harvard, where this project was completed. I am enormously grateful to Abby Collins, Guido Goldman, and Stanley Hoffmann, who have overcome the atomistic tendencies of academia and succeeded in building and sustaining an extraordinarily stimulating and humane institution.

Portions of this book have appeared elsewhere, and I appreciate the willingness of their publishers to allow the publication of revised versions here. Chapter 3 appeared in slightly different form in *Studies in American Political Development* (1992). Parts of Chapter 2 were published in *World Politics* (1993).

This book is dedicated to my parents, in the hope that it reveals some small part of what I have learned from them.

Introduction: conservatives and the welfare state

We live in an age of big government. With the enormous postwar expansion of programs providing income maintenance, health care, and housing, the welfare state became an integral part of all the advanced industrial democracies. However, whereas the development of modern welfare states modified the workings of the market, poor economic performance in the past two decades reaffirmed the tight link between the health of the private economy and the political status of social programs. High unemployment slowed revenue growth while fueling pressures for higher spending. Persistent fiscal strain dramatically altered the welfare state's position. If until recently observers sought to explain the welfare state's inexorable expansion, the question now is how welfare states are adapting to an atmosphere of austerity.

For some governments, this adjustment was a painful necessity. Others, however, saw a contraction of the welfare state as an end in itself. In many countries a conservative resurgence accompanied the economic turmoil of the late 1970s. Conservative parties gained strength, and within these parties leadership shifted to those most critical of the postwar consensus on social and economic policy. These newly ascendant conservatives viewed the welfare state as a large part of the problem. They argued that social programs generated massive inefficiencies, and that financing them required incentive-sapping levels of taxation and inflationary budget deficits. In short, conservatives viewed retrenchment not as a necessary evil but as a necessary good.

This study investigates the new politics of the welfare state. It focuses on the United States and Great Britain, where the ideological and political assaults on social spending have been most intense and sustained. In both countries, the election of politicians promising to curb social expenditure generated expectations of radical reform. How successful were the Reagan and Thatcher administrations' retrenchment efforts? Why have some programs proven to be more vulnerable than others? What accounts for any major divergences between the outcomes in the two countries? Finally, what do the events of the past decade suggest about the future of the welfare state? These questions are the main concerns of this book.

My central thesis is that retrenchment is a distinctive and difficult political enterprise. It is in no sense a simple mirror image of welfare state expansion, in which actors translate (in the view of competing theories) a favorable balance of class "power resources" or institutional advantages into political success. Retrenchment advocates must operate on a terrain that the welfare state itself has fundamentally transformed.

Welfare states have created their own constituencies. If citizens dislike paying taxes, they nonetheless remain fiercely attached to public social provision. That social programs provide concentrated and direct benefits while imposing diffuse and often indirect costs is an important source of their continuing political viability. Voters' tendency to react more strongly to losses than to equivalent gains also gives these programs strength.

Retrenchment advocates thus have their work cut out for them. Almost always, retrenchment is an exercise in blame avoidance rather than in credit claiming.[1] Even a government like Margaret Thatcher's, possessing centralized political authority and confronting a weak and divided opposition, had to acknowledge the potential for widespread popular disapproval of significant reforms. The Reagan administration, operating from what was in most respects a weaker institutional position, faced even greater difficulties.

On the whole, the challenge proved to be too much for both administrations. Although for different reasons both supporters and opponents of retrenchment have had cause to exaggerate the success of conservative reformers, the reality is a messy, mixed picture of welfare states beset by genuine pressures but not by fundamental crises. The fear of popular opposition to radical spending cuts repeatedly forced each administration to retreat. Only on the infrequent occasions when it was possible to design reforms that defused such opposition did radical retrenchment occur. I will suggest that the characteristics of existing social programs, which have a significant influence on the prospects for mobilizing retrenchment opponents, now have a critical impact on the prospects for change.

The theoretical framework that guides this analysis of retrenchment will be presented in Chapters 1 and 2, whereas the empirical support appears in the following four chapters. The remainder of this introduction provides an overview of the political and economic context for conservative retrenchment efforts, a brief summary of the Reagan and Thatcher records, and a preview of the argument to follow.

FROM THE "GOLDEN ERA" TO CONSERVATIVE RESURGENCE

In all the advanced industrial democracies, the welfare state was a central part of the postwar settlement that ushered in a quarter century of unprecedented prosperity. The welfare state's contribution was both economic and political. Social expenditure was a key instrument of macroeconomic and microeconomic policy. The welfare state was considered a powerful countercyclical tool, producing deficits during recessionary periods and (at least in theory) surpluses during boom times. At a microeconomic level, social-welfare programs served to partially offset important market failures. Decent health care, housing, and a modicum of economic security can all contribute to the productive potential of workers, yet firms often view these factors as public goods. Welfare states offset the private sector's tendency to underinvest in its own work force.

The political role of the welfare state has been equally significant. Promises of social protection enhanced the legitimacy of Western democracies. Guarantees of social benefits helped workers adapt to changing market conditions and encouraged wage restraint. More generally, the expanded scope of government activity generated a range of linkages between state and society. The massive stakes associated with government policy-making helped fuel a growth of groups seeking to protect their members' interests. To take the most dramatic example, the American Association of Retired People (AARP), chartered in 1958, had a membership of 28 million and a staff of 1,300 (including a legislative staff of more than 100) by the late 1980s.[2]

Like other components of the postwar order, the welfare state came under mounting pressure following the first oil shock. The major source of stress was fiscal. The budgetary burdens associated with the welfare state mounted after 1973. This strain partly reflected the welfare state's maturation. As social provision accounted for an increasing share of gross national product (GNP), rates of expenditure growth that were well in excess of overall economic expansion could not possibly be sustained.[3] Demographic changes associated with an aging population also intensified pressures on pension and health-care systems. However, continuing slow economic growth and high unemployment were most important in creating an imbalance between revenues and expenditures.

Poor economic performance undermined both the budgetary foundations of welfare states and Keynesian faith in the virtuous links between public spending and economic growth. It helped generate an electoral reaction that propelled the conservative critics of the welfare state to power. However, the initial burden of responding to these pressures fell primarily on left-of-center governments. It may be difficult to remember that as recently as the mid-1970s left parties were increasingly seen as the natural "parties of government," not only in the Social Democratic strongholds of Scandinavia but also in countries such as Britain and West Germany.[4] In the United States, the Democratic Party strengthened its already-firm hold on Congress after Watergate, and recaptured the White House in 1976. Thus, the first politicians forced to cope with fiscal stress were inclined to see the economic disruptions as temporary aberrations and had little desire to challenge the main features of postwar domestic policy.

This changed by the end of the decade. The failure of President Carter's effort to organize a coordinated reflation of the major economies, the second oil shock of the late 1970s, and the spread of the "stagflationary" combination of high inflation and unemployment prompted a vigorous challenge to politics as usual. By 1979, the incomes policy of James Callaghan's Labour government lay in ruins following the wave of unpopular public-sector strikes that marked

Britain's "winter of discontent." Margaret Thatcher's Conservatives swept into office on a platform that, if short on specifics, clearly promised a new direction for economic management. In the United States, foreign-policy setbacks and a disastrously timed recession ruined Carter's reelection prospects. Ronald Reagan, advocating a major retreat from government activism, won a stunning victory in the 1980 election that also produced the Republicans' first Senate majority since 1954.

For the first time since before World War II, political executives in Britain and the United States were now openly critical of central features of social policy. For Reagan and Thatcher, the welfare state was not simply a victim of poor economic performance but one of its principal causes. They argued that the high tax requirements of mature welfare states discouraged work and investment. The countercyclical consequences of social expenditures were seen as inflationary rather than reflationary, destabilizing rather than stabilizing. Similarly, the cushioning effects of social programs for individual employees were now seen as an impediment to rapid economic adjustment, leading workers to sustain unrealistic wage demands that hampered competitiveness and increased structural unemployment.

Significant reform of the welfare state was unquestionably a high priority for both administrations. Across the board, existing social policies faced unprecedented scrutiny as a new group of policymakers searched for openings that might allow cutbacks or the substitution of private alternatives for public provision. These administrations' experiences thus constitute a crucial test of the welfare state's status in the "post-Keynesian" era. The confrontation between committed reform administrations and well-established social programs also sheds light on the nature and limits of the conservative resurgence of the 1980s.

THE REAGAN AND THATCHER RECORDS

Asked what her government had changed, Margaret Thatcher once confidently replied, "Everything." American conservatives were equally bold in proclaiming a "Reagan Revolution." That such hyperbolic claims could even be advanced suggests the strong reformist ambitions of both administrations. Each could take credit for striking departures from the status quo in a number of arenas. Much of this book is devoted to understanding why the welfare state, on the whole, was not one of them.

The examination of retrenchment outcomes offered in this book supports three broad conclusions. First, the success of direct attacks on social programs (what I will call "programmatic retrenchment") generally has been limited. Despite fluctuations that have largely echoed the business cycle, social expenditure has roughly maintained its share of economic output in both countries. These figures provide only very partial evidence, but they are nonetheless suggestive. My efforts to scrutinize policy reforms to identify long-term implications confirm the basic conclusion that although the welfare state has been battered, its main components remain intact.

This judgment will doubtless be controversial. To avoid any misunderstanding, I wish to distance myself at the outset from any claim that the Reagan and Thatcher administrations had little impact on the distribution of income. Indeed, the opposite is the case: Income inequality increased sharply in both countries in the 1980s, and public policy played an important role in this process.[5] However, this study is not about inequality but the narrower (though related) question of changes in social programs. Changes in the welfare state itself have in most cases been less significant than the substantial continuities in policy.

In a sense, measuring the extent of retrenchment is a half-empty/half-full question. It is important not to trivialize the changes that have taken place. Signs of austerity are evident in both countries, especially to those who rely on government programs and those who work with them. In many cases, services have become more threadbare, benefits have been cut, and eligibility rules have been tightened. By a number of measures, however, claims of a conservative revolution in social policy are suspect. Compared with reforms engineered in other arenas (e.g., macroeconomic policy, industrial relations, or regulatory and industrial policy) the welfare state stands out as an island of relative stability.[6] Compared with the preceding decades, moreover, the 1980s did not bring particularly radical change in social policy. Over any decade there are bound to be notable shifts in policy, but this was as true of the 1960s and 1970s – when new programs were regularly introduced and old programs scrapped or seriously overhauled – as it was of the 1980s. Any attempt to understand the politics of welfare state retrenchment must start from a recognition that social policy remains the most resilient component of the postwar order.

My second major conclusion is that the results of programmatic-retrenchment efforts have varied significantly, both within and across policy arenas. Although overall change has been limited, some programs have proven far more vulnerable than others. Housing programs and unemployment-insurance benefits have undergone extensive retrenchment in both countries. In Britain, the state pensions system has also been radically reformed. Retrenchment has been less extensive in other income-transfer programs and in health care. In addition to these important differences in outcomes among programs, there have also been important divergences among outcomes *within* particular arenas. Even programs that experienced substantial retrenchment were often able to ward off some government initiatives. This raises the question of why these programs were vulnerable to some retrenchment strategies but not to others.

The extent of programmatic variation deserves emphasis. It suggests that there are significant dangers in generalizing about "the welfare state," which is, after all, a concept covering a range of disparate public policies. Understanding the politics of retrenchment requires that we make sense of the differing success of conservative reformers in reference to distinct programs. One of the problems with theories of welfare state development is that they generally fail to disaggregate these discrete policies. System-level variables, such as the structure of political institutions or the strength of the political left, cannot alone explain variations *within* the system.

Analysts have generally failed to investigate the characteristics of individual programs that might affect their durability, beyond restating the widely held view that universal programs will be more durable than "means-tested" programs that are restricted to low-income groups.[7] In fact, the standard expectation that the broader electoral appeal of nontargeted programs will make them politically stable, while means-tested programs can easily be whittled away, does not withstand close scrutiny. In both countries, some means-tested programs have been vulnerable; others have not. The same has been true for universal programs. The durability of programs turns on factors more complex than whether or not they are designed to benefit the poor.

Several reasons for the lack of a straightforward relationship between targeting and political vulnerability will be examined in the chapters to follow. First, the weakness of means-tested programs is already reflected in their size, and there is no reason to assume that their targeted status will explain changes in that size. Second, one must recall that an ideologically committed and consistent conservative government would object most strongly to governmental provision for the middle class. If conservatives could design their ideal welfare state, it would consist of *nothing but* means-tested programs. Third, conservatives are very concerned with reducing spending, and it is hard to squeeze much spending out of residual, means-tested programs. Much as Willie Sutton felt compelled to rob banks because "that's where they keep the money," budget cutters find their attention drawn to universal programs. Fourth, beyond a certain point, cutting means-tested programs tends to produce significant policy problems, increasing bureaucratization and worsening work incentives. Finally, conservatives have had to worry about the "fairness issue." Although clearly not reluctant to increase inequality, conservative administrations generally preferred to do so in less visible ways than through vigorous attacks on poverty programs. Thus, in many cases, retrenchment advocates would gain little from sharp cuts in means-tested programs, whereas the political costs were often considerable.

As I discuss shortly, the vulnerability of programs has turned on whether or not the two administrations could identify substantial reforms that would not generate a major public outcry. Retrenchment occurred where supporting interest groups were weak, or where the government found ways to prevent the mobilization of these groups' supporters. The empirical chapters of this study provide a detailed investigation of individual policy arenas that indicates the program characteristics most likely to encourage or impede retrenchment efforts.

The third general conclusion concerns those policy changes that may increase the prospect for future cutbacks (what I will call "systemic retrenchment"). If the Reagan and Thatcher administrations had limited success in fashioning direct reforms of the welfare state, perhaps they were more successful in pursuing indirect strategies whose consequences will be felt only in the long term. Examples would include institutional reforms that strengthen the hands of budget cutters, policies that weaken the government's revenue base, and efforts to undermine the position of pro-welfare state interest groups. For the most part, neither the Reagan nor the Thatcher government appears to have been particularly effective in engineering such reforms. Institutional changes have been limited, and where there has been change, the implications for the welfare state have often been ambiguous. Organized labor – an important contributor to welfare state expansion – has been weakened in both countries; yet other social bases of political support remain strong, and one of the main findings of this study concerns the declining importance of the labor movement for the political status of the welfare state.

The most important example of successful systemic retrenchment has been the Reagan administration's partial "defunding" of the American welfare state. Tax reforms enacted in 1981 and 1986 have weakened the federal government's ability to finance social programs. These changes will put continuing pressure on the welfare state. Although conservative administrations had occasional minor successes in other areas, the real puzzles lie in explaining why overall systemic retrenchment has been limited, and why financial constraints have been imposed in the United States but not in Great Britain.

UNDERSTANDING THE POLITICS OF RETRENCHMENT

Both governments' accomplishments fell far short of their aspirations, and of what they were able to engineer in a range of other policy domains. This is puzzling. Writing on welfare state retrenchment remains sparse, but a reading of the literature on welfare state development suggests that these governments – especially Thatcher's – should have been well placed to bring about significant change. As I will discuss in detail in Chapter 2, there is significant controversy over the roots of welfare state expansion between those emphasizing the "power resources" of left parties and labor movements and those stressing the importance of political institutions. Either emphasis, however, suggests that the Thatcher government in particular should have been operating in a very favorable environment. British politics is distinguished by the concentration of power in the executive. The opposition Labour Party, shaken by a debilitating split with its right wing and engaged in a fratricidal conflict with its left, was in its weakest political position in decades.[8] The union movement was hamstrung by new legislation and enfeebled by very high unemployment. If the concentration of institutional authority in the hands of retrenchment advocates and the weakness of leftist opponents were crucial to achieving retrenchment, Thatcher's government should have been in a formidable position.

The Reagan administration's advantages were more limited but nonetheless considerable. Like Thatcher, retrenchment advocates in the United States faced a weakened opposition. The political clout of an already anemic union movement continued to deteriorate, and Democrats were reeling from a major electoral setback. The lack of party discipline in Congress opened opportunities for bringing conservative Southern Democrats – long suspicious of social programs – into the Reagan coalition. Nevertheless, the institutional fragmentation of the American political system confers fewer resources on a triumphant party, particularly one that fails to capture both the executive and legislative branches. Reagan thus seemed to be in a strong position, although weaker than Thatcher's.

In fact, these features of the political environment turn out to be less crucial than one might suspect. My analysis starts from the claim that retrenchment is a distinctive process, and that the assumption it will follow the rules of development that operated during the long phase of welfare state expansion is likely to be misplaced. There are two fundamental problems with an assertion that policy change in an era of retrenchment will mirror processes of expansion. First, the political goals of policymakers have changed. There is a fundamental difference between a government seeking to extend benefits to large numbers of people and one seeking to take those benefits away. The first process is one of political credit claiming, in which reformers need only overcome diffuse concern about tax rates (which governments often found they could mask through reliance on indirect taxes and social insurance "contributions") and the frequently important pressures of well-entrenched interests. The second process is more treacherous, requiring the imposition of concrete losses on a concentrated group of voters in return for diffuse and uncertain gains. Retrenchment involves a delicate effort to transform programmatic change into an electorally attractive proposition, or at least to minimize the political costs involved. Retrenchment advocates must persuade wavering allies that the price of reform is manageable – a task that a substantial public outcry makes almost impossible.

Equally important to this change in goals is the change in political context. The most important such change is the development of the welfare state itself. Large public social programs are now central features of the political landscape, and with them have come dense networks of interest groups and strong popular attachments to particular policies. The structure of these programs shapes the prospects for reform. As I argue in Chapter 2, to a far greater extent than in earlier periods, social scientists interested in contemporary political development must treat public policies not only as dependent variables but also as independent ones.

The result of these conditions – changed goals and a changed context – is a new kind of politics, in which efforts to minimize the development of widespread opposition are crucial. Divide-and-conquer strategies, and provisions that compensate potential losers, are often major elements in successful retrenchment initiatives. Even more important are efforts to hide what is happening by fashioning proposals that lower the visibility of changes or obscure responsibility for those changes. Far more than in the era of welfare state expansion, struggles over social policy become struggles over information about the causes and consequences of policy change.

The strength of left-wing parties and labor movements are not irrelevant to the retrenchment process, but they do not play the central roles they played in welfare state expansion. The structure of political institutions remains important, but in new and more complex ways. New factors emerge as highly consequential, especially aspects of existing welfare state structures. "Policy feedback" from previous periods frames current decision-making, influencing the prospects for executing strategies that can make retrenchment initiatives successful. In most cases this feedback creates strong coalitions of program supporters that effectively protect existing arrangements. In a few cases, feedback creates significant opportunities for reform.

In stressing the role of policy feedback, my argument represents part of a growing effort to incorporate historical analysis into the study of contemporary politics.[9] At the same time, it cautions against the hazards of drawing on history in the wrong way. There are significant dangers in using historical *analogies* to study contemporary change. In this case, the factors that have been central to welfare state expansion provide a dubious guide, because both the goals of social-policy reformers and the context in which they operate have changed dramatically. Instead of turning to history for analogous processes, historically grounded analysis should be based upon a recognition that social-policy change unfolds over time. The emphasis on the impact of inherited policy structures illustrates this point. A historical perspective highlights the fact that today's policymakers must operate in an environment fundamentally conditioned by policies inherited from the past. These policy structures influence the resources available to both retrenchment advocates and opponents, and also the prospects for shaping viable political strategies. The choices of Reagan and Thatcher's predecessors had a substantial impact on the successes of retrenchment advocates as well as on their more frequent failures.

I
Analytical foundations

I
The logic of retrenchment

The next two chapters provide a framework for the study of retrenchment, setting the stage for a detailed examination of the Reagan and Thatcher records. To be persuasive, accounts of welfare state change must combine microscopic and macroscopic analysis. They must consider both the goals and incentives of the central political actors and how the institutional rules of the game and the distribution of political resources structure their choices.

This chapter outlines the peculiar nature of retrenchment as a political project. For politicians eager to win reelection, seeking cutbacks in social programs raises considerable risks. Such cutbacks impose concentrated costs in return for diffuse benefits, and there is substantial reason to believe that concentrated interests possess marked advantages in political conflicts. To make matters even more difficult, retrenchment advocates must contend with an imbalance in voters' reactions to losses and gains; transfers of resources tend to induce more resentment from losers than gratitude from winners.

An understanding of retrenchment politics must start from an appreciation of this distinctive political problem. This chapter will focus on the nature of this distinctiveness and the strategic options available to retrenchment advocates that may make their problems more tractable. The following chapter will consider how the broader context – patterns of interest-group representation, institutional structures, and preexisting policy designs – influences the prospects for implementing these strategies.

As a preface, however, I discuss the concept of retrenchment itself. This is crucial, because fuzzy conceptions of retrenchment have encouraged confusion about exactly what has happened to these welfare states. Without understanding what retrenchment is and without specifying how it can best be measured, one cannot get a firm grip on what has happened, much less determine why.

CONCEPTUALIZING AND MEASURING RETRENCHMENT

Retrenchment is one of those cases in which identifying what is to be explained is almost as difficult as formulating persuasive explanations for it. There is little agreement about what kinds of policy changes are important or how they might be measured. As a result, discussions of the recent experience of welfare states have often floundered before even reaching the issue of causation. The few available studies of welfare cutbacks have generally used social-expenditure trends as a proxy for retrenchment success.[1] Although such trends are important, they provide an inadequate measure. Such figures indicate only short-term spending patterns, ignoring programmatic changes that produce long-term rather than immediate cutbacks. Furthermore, they focus attention exclusively on changes in the size of welfare state programs while ignoring changes in program structure. Finally, social-expenditure patterns say little or nothing about broader policy changes that may have important consequences for welfare state development.

These three points establish some basic ground rules for the study of retrenchment:

1. Examine long-term as well as short-term spending cuts. This ground rule is the most straightforward. Governments interested in curtailing social programs may enact policies that cut spending immediately; they may also enact changes to be phased in over time, the full effects of which may not be felt for many years. For example, a change in indexation rules may only reduce expenditures by 1 or 2 percent in the first year, but this "decremental" cutback will gradually grow in scope. Benefit or eligibility restrictions may exempt current recipients, affecting only new beneficiaries. Cutbacks in housing-construction programs may have little impact on the availability of low-income housing for a decade. An analysis of current spending levels will completely miss some of the most important cuts in social programs. This is a particularly important point in light of the propensity, discussed later in this section, of retrenchment advocates to pursue strategies that hide the magnitude of cuts by minimizing short-term negative consequences.

2. Examine program structure as well as program spending. Long-term expenditure trends still provide an insufficient basis for evaluating welfare state change. Gøsta Esping-Andersen has offered a telling critique of the preoccupation of comparative welfare state research with expenditure levels.[2] Spending levels are simple, quantifiable indicators that are ideal for cross-national statistical analyses. However, because expenditures reveal only size and not content, they provide an incomplete description of a country's welfare state. Welfare states intervene in markets to different degrees and in different ways. They also diverge on a variety of important dimensions, including their use of state-provided services, reliance on means-tested benefits, tax progressivity, commitment to full employment, promotion of private alternatives to state benefits, segmentation of recipients by status group, and willingness to loosen workers' dependence on wages.

The social and political role of the welfare state depends as much on these various dimensions of policy choice as it does on spending levels. Each can vary independently of total expenditure. Consequently, countries can maintain high spending levels without producing substantial redistribution or social solidarity among different groups.[3] Richard Titmuss captured this situation in his distinction between "institutional" and "residual" welfare states. Institutional welfare states rely mainly on comprehensive programs, utilize public provision of major services, attempt to reduce distinctions between different classes or status groups, and generally operate to partially restrict the market's impact on life chances. Residual welfare states are more reluctant to interfere with market mechanisms; they reject comprehensive services, and prefer state subsidization of private services to public provision. The goal is to provide a "safety net," usually based on a means test, while reinforcing market-produced patterns of social stratification.[4]

A study of welfare state change must focus on structure as well as size. To discuss retrenchment rather than cuts is to analyze political conflicts over the character of the welfare state. As Esping-Andersen has put it, "It is difficult to imagine that anyone struggled for spending *per se*."[5] Just as organized labor and left-of-center parties once pushed not just for higher spending but also for more extensive modifications of market outcomes, conservatives work to encourage market-oriented reforms as well as lower spending. Retrenchment should be seen as a process of shifting social provision in a more residualist direction, not just as a matter of budget cuts.

3. Study systemic retrenchment as well as programmatic retrenchment. Programmatic retrenchment results from spending cuts or a reshaping of welfare state programs. However, policy changes that alter the broader political economy and consequently alter welfare state politics may also promote retrenchment. Welfare state programs do not exist in a vacuum. Their shape is determined by the complex interplay of such factors as budgetary pressures, the structure of political institutions, and the strength and priorities of interest groups. Policy changes that alter the context for future spending decisions – what can be termed systemic retrenchment – may be as important for the welfare state as changes in spending or program structure "within" the welfare state itself.

Systemic retrenchment can take four forms. First, a government can attempt to defund the welfare state by constraining the flow of revenues to future administrations. Revenues provide the underpinning for a vast range of government activity. Welfare states require revenues: Where there is no money there can be no programs. Ronald Reagan recognized this when he compared big government to an unruly child, arguing that the way to discipline children's "extravagance" was "by simply reducing their allowances."[6]

A number of mechanisms can produce defunding. The simplest is to cut taxes or reduce the ease with which governments can raise taxes in the future. Just as I will argue that a government pursuing retrenchment will seek to diminish the visibility of unpopular program cuts, it may try to increase the visibility of taxation as a way to restrict the resource base for welfare state initiatives. For example, inflation-induced "bracket creep," which moves people into higher tax brackets, was traditionally a quiet way to increase revenues in the United States. Eliminating bracket creep would thus remove one of the most effective techniques for generating government revenues without creating a political outcry. Alternatively, a government could diminish future financial capacities by shifting to unsustainable sources of finance such as asset sales. Heavy deficit financing is another option. Although maintainable for limited periods of time, such financing would eventually leave governments with the unpalatable choice of raising taxes or further squeezing public expenditure.

Finally, a government might seek to increase non-welfare state expenditures (e.g., those for defense). Like the other approaches, this tactic is based on the reasonable expectation that any restriction of resources available for social programs will eventually result in increased pressures to check expenditures. A government that succeeded in these defunding efforts would have created a significant level of systemic retrenchment, even if the structure of social programs remained relatively constant in the short run.

A second type of systemic retrenchment would be a policy-induced change in public opinion, weakening popular attachments to public social provision. Public attitudes may affect the long-term position of the welfare state. If government policies increase public preferences for private provision, growing hostility toward public social programs could be expected to facilitate retrenchment. Thatcher's efforts to foster an "enterprise culture" by encouraging private social provision, and through other privatization initiatives (substitution of private for public employment in industry or increased share ownership, for example), provide a good example of this kind of strategy.[7] Whether such strategies actually have a substantial impact on popular attitudes toward public programs will be considered in Chapter 6.

Systemic retrenchment might also take the form of modifications in political institutions, changing the way decision making about the welfare state is carried out, and thus potentially changing policy outcomes. The "rules of the game" can have a tremendous impact on the construction of political interests and on the capacities of competing interests to exert influence within the political process. Although political scientists have recently shown renewed interest in the impact of political institutions, the consequences of institutional design for social-policy development remain a subject of controversy.[8] This issue is taken up in detail in Chapter 2. For now, it is necessary to note only that retrenchment advocates possess two strategic options that might make institutional conditions more conducive to the pursuit of cutbacks: They may try to centralize political authority, hoping to increase their capacity to implement their own policy preferences; alternatively, they might pursue a decentralizing strategy, transferring authority over social policy to local governments. Decentralization could facilitate retrenchment, primarily because economic competition among local jurisdictions often makes it difficult for them to pursue redistributive policies. Interest groups supporting the welfare state may also be weaker in more decentralized political arenas. Finally, decentralizing efforts may allow national advocates of retrenchment to shift the blame for cutbacks to local officials.

The fourth type of systemic retrenchment would be a weakening of pro-welfare state interest groups. The impact of an administration dedicated to retrenchment is likely to depend in part on the political strength of welfare state supporters. Groups offering such support include organizations of beneficiaries, producer interests with a stake in either the provision of specific services (e.g., housing or education) or in a pattern of public intervention in the marketplace (such as labor unions), and advocacy organizations dedicated to advancing programs for the underprivileged and underrepresented.

Governments seeking cutbacks will try to weaken these opponents. Whether governments have the capacity to achieve this goal is likely to depend significantly on the characteristics of particular groups. Those dependent on government financing are likely to be highly vulnerable. In some instances, governments may be able to bring about reforms that make it more difficult for groups to organize or pursue political action. For example, rules covering collective bargaining have a significant impact on labor-union strength. Tax changes, for that matter, may impede a group's ability to raise money.

Governments may also pursue more indirect strategies. Restrictive economic policies that raise unemployment rates, for instance, tend to undermine organized labor's political position. Thus, governments have a range of possible tools for attacking the organized interests supporting social programs.

The failure to develop a convincing conceptualization of retrenchment has greatly impeded research on the recent history of the welfare state. Far from being simply a matter of immediate cuts in public spending, retrenchment is a complex, multifaceted phenomenon. This discussion provides a basis for identifying the relevant dimensions of policy change.

Retrenchment can be defined to include policy changes that either cut social expenditure, restructure welfare state programs to conform more closely to the residual welfare state model, or alter the political environment in ways that enhance the probability of such outcomes in the future. To determine the success or failure of Reagan and Thatcher's efforts all three of these dimensions must be considered.

THE HAZARDS OF IMPOSING LOSSES

Government leaders want to advance their policy agendas, and they want to be reelected. If at all possible, they will seek to make these two goals mutually reinforcing. There is no need to assume that governments consider only electoral implications in formulating policies; it is enough for this analysis that such concerns are a central consideration, if only because failure to consider electoral consequences can jeopardize policymakers' long-term prospects for implementing their preferred policies.

Given the desire to reconcile policy initiatives with electoral considerations, governments favoring retrenchment are likely to face a dilemma. Cutbacks in social programs usually raise the risk of electoral retribution. There are two distinct reasons that retrenchment is generally an exercise in blame avoidance rather than "credit claiming."[9] First, the costs of retrenchment are concentrated, whereas the benefits are not. Second, there is considerable evidence that voters exhibit a "negativity bias," remembering losses more than gains. As a result, retrenchment initiatives are extremely treacherous. The unpopularity of almost all efforts to curtail public social provision creates a sizable danger that policy goals and electoral ambitions will conflict.

Cutbacks generally impose immediate pain on specific groups, usually in return for diffuse, long-term, and uncertain benefits.[10] That concentrated interests will be in a stronger political position than diffuse ones is a standard proposition in political science.[11] As interests become more concentrated, the prospect that individuals will find it worth their while to engage in collective action improves. Dairy farmers whose livelihood depends on government subsidies have far more reason to organize than the consumers who may pay a few cents more at the store. Furthermore, concentrated interests are more likely to be linked to organizational networks that keep them well informed of what their interests are, and how policymakers may affect them. These informational networks also facilitate political action. I will have more to say about the role of information in these matters shortly.

The well-documented imbalance between the way that voters react to losses and gains further enhances the political position of retrenchment opponents. Extensive experiments in social psychology have demonstrated that individuals respond differently to positive and negative risks; individuals tend to be risk-averse with respect to gains, but they are risk-seeking with respect to losses.[12] That is to say, individuals will take more chances – seeking conflict and accepting the possibility of even greater losses – to prevent any worsening of their current position. Studies of electoral behavior confirm the findings of psychologists. Negative attitudes toward candidates are more strongly linked with a range of behaviors (e.g., turnout or a desertion from the voter's usual party choice) than positive attitudes are.[13]

Why this "negativity bias" exists is unclear.[14] For current purposes what is important is the constraint that the asymmetry in reaction to losses and gains creates for policymakers. When added to the general imbalance between concentrated and diffuse interests, the message for retrenchment advocates is clear. A simple "redistributive" transfer of resources from program beneficiaries to taxpayers, engineered through cuts in social programs, is likely to be a losing proposition. The concentrated beneficiary groups are more likely to be cognizant of the change, are easier to mobilize, and because they are experiencing losses rather than gains will be more likely to consider the change in their voting calculations. In short, retrenchment advocates face a difficult clash between their policy preferences and their electoral ambitions.

A recognition that the political goal of loss imposition has a distinctive character is critical to an analysis of retrenchment politics. The struggles over social policy discussed in the following chapters all reveal the Reagan and Thatcher governments' sensitivity to the perilous nature of their reform agendas. Marked by this consciousness of potential political hazard, retrenchment politics has a quality quite different from that of the period of welfare state expansion, when political rivals often eagerly outbid each other in the quest to receive credit for government action.[15]

STRATEGIES FOR MINIMIZING COSTS

Confronting these harsh political realities, conservative governments might be expected to back away from attacks on social programs. Instead of throwing up their hands, however, retrenchment advocates may try to find ways to overcome the obstacles they face. A government determined to pursue a retrenchment agenda could try to ease the resulting dilemma by maximizing its electoral margin of safety. The less danger there is of losing the next election, the more political capital governments can afford to spend in pursuit of desired but electorally costly policies.[16]

There are, however, a number of problems with this approach. Many of the factors influencing a government's electoral position are largely beyond its control. Furthermore, government popularity often fluctuates unpredictably, making calculations of safety margins a hazardous undertaking at best.[17]

The second option is to try to reduce the political repercussions of retrenchment actions by minimizing the mobilization of the opposition. Strong opposition to particular political reformers is not a given; on the contrary, opponents must be successfully mobilized to pose a real threat to politicians.

There are three broad strategies that retrenchment advocates can use to minimize political resistance: obfuscation, division, and compensation. They may seek to manipulate information flows to decrease public awareness of their actions or of the negative consequences of them. Alternatively, they may endeavor to divide their potential opponents. Finally, retrenchment advocates may offer "side payments" to compensate some of those adversely affected by proposed changes. This represents a limited but potentially powerful repertoire. The Reagan and Thatcher records reveal instances in which each strategy was used to considerable effect, allowing substantial retrenchment to occur with surprisingly modest political costs.

Strategies of obfuscation

Of these three strategies, obfuscation, which involves efforts to manipulate information concerning policy changes, is the most important. As James Kuklinski has recently written, "The idea of information has overtaken political scientists."[18] In research on welfare state development, for example, this theme has been prominent in Hugh Heclo's analysis of how "political learning" occurs as policymakers adapt their understandings and design new initiatives based on the knowledge gained from past policy initiatives.[19] Heclo argues that policy development is as much a matter of puzzling over what to do in a complex social environment as it is a matter of power struggles among competing interests.

In contrast to Heclo's stress on the uncertainties facing government decision makers, I wish to emphasize the ways in which knowledge contributes to the exercise of power. Information is a scarce and valuable political resource. Political actions must be based on understanding, but our understandings are necessarily constrained by the sheer complexity of the social world and our own limitations of time and cognitive capacity. That policymakers can make it more difficult for the electorate to get information may make retrenchment initiatives less politically hazardous. All social actors possess imperfect information about issues relevant to their interests. Furthermore, the distribution of information is usually highly unequal.[20] In this context, it may be possible for policymakers to lower the political costs of retrenchment actions by making it more difficult for possible opponents to obtain relevant information about policy reforms.

Douglas Arnold has argued persuasively that voters endeavoring to reward or punish politicians are engaged in an effort to reconstruct "causal chains" linking negative or positive events to particular policy choices, and those choices in turn to the actions of specific politicians.[21] How voters actually construct these causal chains remains somewhat unclear. Arnold acknowledges that it is a subjective process, the details of which are likely to be highly complex and culturally contingent.[22] Despite this complexity, the implications for policymakers are relatively straightforward. Those engaged in efforts to initiate unpopular policies will try to lower the visibility of their reforms by complicating the reconstruction of causal chains that would allow voters to exact retribution.

Three possible sites of obfuscation, related to different parts of these causal chains, should be distinguished. First, retrenchment advocates can try to lower the salience of negative consequences. Not all negative events are equally apparent. Anything that makes it harder to detect the negative consequences of policy reforms will decrease political mobilization against them. Negative consequences are less likely to be observed if they are spread widely rather than concentrated, and if they are diffused over time rather than delivered in a single shot.

Thus, a frequent tactic used to lower the visibility of negative effects is decrementalism. Social programs operate within a changing economic context marked by rising prices and (generally) rising incomes. Retrenchment advocates may be able to achieve their goals with limited political exposure, then, by freezing a program within a growing economy.

Decrementalism can take two forms. Most obviously, a failure to adjust for higher prices lowers the real value of benefits. Less widely noted but more often pursued is the tactic of "implicit privatization," in which benefits retain their real value but play a diminishing role in an expanding economy. With public benefits frozen, social provision is shifted increasingly toward the private sector, and because change thus occurs very slowly it is less likely to attract attention. Decrementalism also hinders the development of opposition because retrenchment advocates need only achieve a single policy shift (e.g., a changed indexation method) to produce a flow of annual cutbacks.

The second link in Arnold's causal chain is between negative events and public policies. Even when voters are aware that their circumstances have worsened, they may have trouble connecting that to shifts in government policy. Sometimes, of course, the link is obvious. Someone who learns that his or her job has been eliminated, or that this month's pension check has been slashed, is unlikely to be puzzled for long. Nevertheless, the connections between policy and adverse events can be obscure. Politicians can reduce the visibility of their actions by making the effects of reforms indirect. As economists have long observed, there is often a difference between the de jure and de facto incidence of taxes. Political scientists have observed that because the use of indirect taxes obscures the links between policy and negative events, it leads to greater public tolerance for high taxes.[23] To take an example from the politics of retrenchment, cutbacks in health care might be imposed on hospitals or doctors, who then pass the cost on to consumers through higher prices. The visibility of effects can also be diminished by increasing the complexity of reforms. The consequences of simple cuts are easy to identify, but even though elaborate rule changes may ultimately have the same or even greater effects, that impact is often harder to detect. Washington lobbyists term this the "Dan Rather test": Reforms are less likely to generate a popular outcry if television reporters cannot explain the implications of the new policies in fifteen seconds or less.

Finally, as an alternative or supplement to efforts to lower the salience of negative consequences and their connection to policy change, policymakers can try to diminish public awareness of their own responsibility for those effects. Arnold calls this part of the chain the "traceability" of policy change. Since it is the fear of being held accountable for unpopular actions that constrains policymakers, they are likely to seek means of covering their tracks. R. Kent Weaver has discussed in detail some possible strategies of blame avoidance.[24] One option is burden shifting, that is, passing responsibility for imposing cutbacks to local officials, who may then attract some of the blame. This tactic obviously requires a program structure that allows central government to separate itself from the actual imposition of cutbacks. An alternative is to make cutbacks automatic. Changes in indexation rules, for example, lead to annual reductions without requiring repeated, visible actions on the part of policymakers. Deficit-reduction mechanisms, like the Gramm-Rudmann budget reforms in the United States, may be designed to operate the same way.[25]

A powerful tactic to diminish traceability is to delay the implementation of cutbacks. Opposition is easier to mobilize when retrenchment policies impose immediate losses on program recipients. Postponing such effects decreases the prominence of the cutbacks. This tactic has proven particularly effective in hous-

Table 1.1. *Obfuscation strategies and the reconstruction of causal chains*

Stage of causal chain	Obfuscation technique
Identification of negative effects	Decrementalism
Linking of negative effects to policies	Indirect incidence
Linking of policies to decision makers	Burden shifting, automaticity, lagged cutbacks

ing policy in both the United States and Britain, where a cut in public-housing construction has no impact on current recipients. The effects are concentrated on potential future recipients, who are unlikely to see their current interests as closely linked to the fate of public housing and are by their very nature unidentifiable and therefore impossible to organize. In any event, by the time the negative repercussions of policy changes begin to be felt, the political decisions responsible will be buried in the distant past.

"Never be seen to do harm." Often cited as the first maxim of electoral politics, this folk wisdom has not been well integrated into theories of policy development.[26] By obscuring negative outcomes, the connection between them and public policies, or one's responsibility for those policies, politicians can dramatically lower the political price they pay for pursuing a retrenchment agenda. Table 1.1 offers a summary of some techniques that retrenchment advocates can use to hide potentially unpopular activities. The chapters to follow are full of instances in which retrenchment advocates used obfuscation to achieve their goals. Information is a crucial resource, distributed in a highly unequal way. Its importance in political struggles has been vastly underrated.

Strategies of division

Although the potential for organized opposition in a particular policy area may be large, it is sometimes possible to isolate subgroups within that opposition. "Divide and conquer" is an obvious political ploy, but that need not render it any less effective. The constituencies of all public programs are to some extent heterogeneous. In the case of income-transfer programs, a wide range of distinctions can be exploited, including differences in household composition, income level, age, geographic location and gender, to name but a few. Although race rarely constitutes a legally permissible basis for distinguishing among recipients, there may be ways of activating this division as well. The consumers of publicly provided services (e.g., housing and health care) will have the same internal divisions.

Cutbacks may be designed so that they affect some benefit recipients but not others. The easiest way to do this is by pursuing retrenchment through tightened eligibility rules. Both the Reagan and the Thatcher administrations lowered income ceilings for some means-tested programs. Examples include housing assistance in both countries, and both Aid for Families with Dependent Children (AFDC) and food stamps in the United States. New eligibility rules may also exclude specific categories of recipients from benefits (e.g., excluding strikers from unemployment benefits in Britain and from food stamps in the United States, and barring British students from income support during school vacations).

Programs that provide services create an additional potential cleavage between service consumers and service producers. Retrenchment advocates may design reforms in such a way that they divide consumers of a particular service from producers. Again, housing provides a prominent example, where construction cutbacks had immediate repercussions for producer groups but not for consumers. Similarly, divisions between health-care producers and consumers in the United States have facilitated retrenchment in Medicare.

Where retrenchment is widely anticipated, targeting cutbacks on particular subgroups within a beneficiary population will minimize the size of the potential opposition to proposed reforms.[27] Benefit recipients who are spared the axe may feel quietly grateful that the burden has fallen on someone else. In any event, they are unlikely to mobilize effectively against such retrenchment efforts. Of course, next time it may be their group that finds itself singled out for attention. As a result, a common dynamic of retrenchment struggles involves competing efforts of governments to play one group off against another while program supporters attempt to "circle the wagons."

Strategies of compensation

Offering something positive to the victims of retrenchment policies will diminish prospects for heated opposition. Given the existence of "negativity biases" it is often very helpful to have some plausible way of making the case that beneficiaries will not be hurt. Compensation may be offered to groups most likely to mobilize against retrenchment, or to those most likely to garner public sympathy. "Grandfather clauses" may be introduced so that current recipients are excluded from the impact of policy changes. Losses are then restricted to an unspecified, and probably unorganizable, group of future recipients.

Alternatively, a government may attempt to offer compensation for public-sector retrenchment by expanding private benefits. Attractive private-sector options may mute opposition to the curtailment of public provision. Given the preference of retrenchment advocates for market solutions, privatization options – even when they require some kind of government subsidy – are likely to receive serious consideration wherever they appear to be viable.

Successfully mobilized, program supporters represent a threat that politicians seeking reelection are unlikely to ignore; the gains from retrenchment then appear too limited and uncertain to justify the political risk. Nevertheless, successful mobilization is the key, and there may be ways to prevent it. Obfuscation, division, and compensation: These three techniques have given conservative

Table 1.2. *Limitations of retrenchment strategies*

Strategy	Range of application	Drawbacks
Obfuscation		
Decrementalism	non- or poorly indexed transfer programs	Reversible
Division		
Tightened eligibility	Service and transfer programs	Policy irrationalities
Split consumer-producer coalitions	Service programs	Alienation of supporters
Compensation		
Provision of transitional benefits	Service and transfer programs	Cost, policy irrationalities
Expansion of private benefits	Most universal programs	Cost, policy irrationalities

critics reason to think that the welfare state's strong political position might not be unchallengeable.

Limitations of retrenchment strategies

Although a range of opportunities exist to hinder the development of a strong opposition, applying such strategies is no simple solution to the precarious enterprise of retrenchment. Each approach also possesses important drawbacks. Their range of application may be limited, and they produce political costs as well as benefits. To understand the role of retrenchment strategies in welfare state politics these limitations need to be considered.

The most obvious limitation is that even if these tactics can be used, they provide no guarantee of success. The reduction of political opposition must be sufficient in relation to the potential returns to the government to justify proceeding. Thus, retrenchment is most likely to occur when a variety of these approaches can be combined.

In addition, each tactic poses distinct problems. Table 1.2 provides an overview of the limitations of the various retrenchment strategies just outlined. Almost all of the possible approaches have restricted ranges of application. Programs have to possess particular characteristics to make each tactic applicable. For example, delaying cutbacks is possible where future expenditures are linked to current capital outlays (housing) or entitlements are based on long periods of contributions (pensions). Such strategies are inapplicable where there are no long lags between current policies and the actual distribution of benefits. The role of program characteristics raises a theme that will be pursued at length in Chapter 2, namely the ways in which the specific design choices made by preceding policymakers "feed back" into contemporary politics, constraining the options of retrenchment advocates.

Even where strategies can be applied, they may have negative consequences that offset their advantages for retrenchment advocates. Obfuscation strategies, for example, often have considerable drawbacks. The techniques that allow governments to limit their political exposure may also weaken their control over policy. Decremental approaches are extremely slow. Although this lowers visibility, it also lowers immediate payoffs (which may be of greatest interest to the ruling government) and increases the opportunities for future administrations to reverse the direction of policy. Burden shifting lowers the central government's political exposure, but it also reduces its control over policy. Thus, the Thatcher government generally rejected opportunities to shift responsibilities to local governments because of a desire to enhance its own power.

Efforts to divide potential opponents also have drawbacks. If an administration succeeds in splitting consumers and producers, it is also likely to anger producer groups (e.g., health-care providers, or construction and development interests) that are often supportive of conservative politicians. In some cases, strategies of division can generate significant program irrationalities. Dividing opposition by tightening eligibility rules, for example, can worsen the work-incentive problems prevalent in means-tested programs and increase the complexity of bureaucracy. Even a government unconcerned about producing effective policies must pay attention to such implications, because they can provide powerful ammunition for critics. As a result, this approach tends to yield quickly diminishing returns.

The final strategy, compensating losers, offers the greatest political protection to retrenchment advocates. However, it too entails substantial costs. The main limitation of compensation strategies is that they tend to cannibalize the policy results that retrenchment advocates seek. If substantial resources are poured into efforts to buy off opponents, potential budgetary savings dry up. Offering transitional benefits and expanding private alternatives is generally expensive. For administrations committed to short-term cost cutting as well as long-term retrenchment, this has generally proven to be a fundamental impediment. Cost constraints helped derail the "New Federalism" initiative in the United States (see Chapter 5) and proposals for radical pension reform and the expansion of private health care in Britain (Chapters 3 and 6). As a result, compensatory initiatives work best as a supplement to other strategies. Skillfully applied, they may effectively blunt the opposition while leaving the bulk of a retrenchment initiative in place. Compensation can be used alongside a strategy of division, with losses being offset for only some of those affected. It can also be part of an obfuscation strategy, with protection offered to those most immediately damaged, but not to those for whom costs are more distant.

Furthermore, compensation strategies also can precipitate program irrationalities. Offering transitional benefits softens the blow to current recipients, but it also creates bureaucratic complications as parallel systems have to be developed for old and new beneficiaries.[28] If the divergence between the two groups is clearly visible, the result can be an outcry against unequal treatment that heightens rather than lowers the level of political opposition. In the United States, transitional benefits were offered to pensioners to soften the impact when a flawed indexation system was revised in 1977. Those just below the cutoff for the transitional benefits (dubbed the "notch babies") have become an increasingly militant group favoring an extension of these transitional benefits.[29]

Similarly, expanding private alternatives can produce policy irrationalities. Because regressive tax expenditures usually subsidize privatization initiatives, the distributional consequences are difficult to justify. Tax breaks also produce economic distortions, artificially stimulating investment in subsidized activities. In some cases, private alternatives appear to be clearly inferior. For example, the Thatcher government's retreat from private health care seems to have partly reflected a recognition that the private sector was no match for the National Health Service in providing "value for money."

In short, identifying retrenchment strategies offers no panacea for conservative governments. All strategies to diminish the political vulnerability of retrenchment advocates have significant limitations. Governments must carefully weigh the advantages of these techniques for limiting the mobilization of opponents against their considerable weaknesses.

This chapter has outlined the microfoundations of retrenchment politics. Advocates of retrenchment confront a difficult task: The goals they pursue are likely to be unpopular, yet at some point they must subject their records to public scrutiny. They also possess some tactical options that may make this dilemma more tractable. Nevertheless, although it is useful to stress that retrenchment advocates face certain challenges and possess definite resources, this tells us little about what these policymakers are likely to do in specific situations, or how successful their efforts may be. The preferences and strategic repertoires of these actors must be linked to the constraints within which they operate. What determines whether those seeking retrenchment can successfully apply these strategies? Chapter 2 takes up this question.

2

Interests, institutions, and policy feedback

Politicians pursuing retrenchment face a difficult challenge; just how difficult will depend on the political context in which they operate. These actors seek their goals within specific environments. The distribution of political resources and the institutional rules of the game help to determine the prospects for successfully pursuing various strategies, as well as the benefits and costs associated with particular outcomes. This chapter considers the aspects of this broader context that are most relevant for retrenchment politics.

Existing scholarship offers only limited help in this effort. The recent shift in the welfare state's fortunes has been widely noted, but so far there have been few attempts to explain retrenchment outcomes. This absence stands in stark contrast to the flourishing literature on the origins and development of welfare states. A wealth of detailed research has generated clear analytical perspectives on the main factors contributing to or retarding welfare state expansion.[1] Two such theories have been particularly influential. One emphasizes the power resources of labor movements, whereas the other focuses on the role of institutions.

There is a natural inclination to turn directly to those theories to explain contemporary welfare state politics. In a study of retrenchment, however, these arguments need to be carefully reappraised. As I have already noted, there is little reason to assume that theories designed to explain outcomes in a particular context and involving the pursuit of particular goals will still apply once the environment and the goals of key actors have changed. Because both the context and goals associated with retrenchment are distinctive, whether theories of welfare state expansion offer insights into the retrenchment process must be considered an open question. I will argue that some factors heretofore critical to processes of program enactment and expansion, such as the role of organized labor, are of declining importance. Others, such as the design of political institutions, are of continuing significance but have different consequences because of the distinctive character of retrenchment politics. Finally, some previously peripheral factors move to center stage. Among these, the policy feedback from previous political choices are most important.

ORGANIZED LABOR, PROGRAM CONSTITUENCIES, AND THE WELFARE STATE

Because retrenchment politics generally involves efforts to prevent the formation of active opposition, the organizational capacities of welfare state supporters matter. In this respect, retrenchment resembles welfare state expansion, with the interests of important societal actors playing a part in determining political outcomes. In critical ways, however, the role of such actors in retrenchment represents a substantial change from the welfare state politics of the past.

In particular, the impact of organized labor has decreased considerably. This is a dramatic occurrence, for labor movements have long been seen as central to welfare state development. During the past decade the power-resources perspective, which attributes cross-national variations in social provision largely to differences in the distribution of political resources among classes, has been the leading approach in comparative politics to explaining patterns of welfare state expansion.[2] Class-based struggle over social provision may be intense, it is argued, because social programs have a significant impact on the bargaining position of workers and employers in the marketplace. Many social programs limit the economic vulnerability of wage earners and increase worker solidarity. According to power-resources theorists, encompassing, centralized unions, strong parties of the left, and weak or fragmented conservative parties all contribute to the expansion of these programs.

Given the consequences of many social-policy initiatives, the argument that their development turns on the balance of organizational power between representatives of labor and capital has great plausibility. Indeed, the power-resources approach has had considerable success in accounting for cross-national variations in social provision during the three decades following World War II. Furthermore, the replacement of crude social expenditure data with more fine-grained distinctions among patterns of social provision has greatly improved the explanatory power of the model.[3]

Nevertheless, a power-resources perspective cannot explain patterns of retrenchment in the United States and Great Britain. Reagan and Thatcher's records reveal two key features: Their overall impact has been modest and their success has varied widely across programs. A power-resources perspective would predict neither of these outcomes. In both countries, the political and economic resources of the left have diminished considerably. Rates of unionization have plummeted; left-of-center parties have been weakened. Although power-resource arguments suggest that this shift should have sharply altered the character of the welfare state, this has not been the case. There have been changes, but most programs remain largely intact.

Furthermore, the variation among program outcomes in each country has been extensive. This intrasystem variation suggests important limits to the explanatory power of systemic variables, including power resources. An across-the-board diminution in labor strength cannot account for major differences in the vulnerability of individual programs. The resilience of many elements of the welfare state suggests that although unions and left-of-center parties may play a key role in welfare state development, programs may be sustainable even where that support weakens.[4] In short, the Thatcher and Reagan records of mixed and limited success raise serious questions about the applicability of the dominant paradigm for studying welfare state development to the study of retrenchment.

The challenge to the power-resources approach advanced here needs to be carefully qualified. This analysis compares two unabashedly conservative administrations; both inherited what Esping-Andersen would call liberal welfare state regimes. In part, this selection of cases bypasses key issues raised by power-resources analysts. In a comparison of, say, the United States and Sweden, the strength of left parties and labor movements might well have emerged as more important.[5] In addition, just as the application of arguments derived from studies of expansion to problems of retrenchment is a questionable practice, the reverse warning should also apply: The current analysis may shed little light on earlier chapters in the history of the welfare state.

Caveats aside, this analysis suggests limitations in the power-resources approach. Even where power resources are held relatively constant, important differences in outcomes remain to be explained, especially when one examines individual programs. The power-resources argument, which focuses on system-level variables, is unlikely to account for such variations. And given that Thatcher and Reagan each faced severely weakened unions and left-of-center parties, a power-resources perspective would imply much more dramatic changes than have actually occurred. *Problem with this claim is in Reagan admin.*

Esping-Andersen has argued that "a theory that seeks to explain welfare-state growth should also be able to understand its retrenchment or decline."[6] On the contrary, power-resources arguments have limited relevance because welfare states are now mature and retrenchment is not simply the mirror image of welfare state expansion. In a context where public social provision is just emerging, the existence of broad organizations pushing a social-policy agenda is likely to be crucial. However, the unpopularity of program cutbacks will give politicians pause even where unions and left-of-center parties are weak. Equally important, maturing social programs develop new bases of organized support that have substantial autonomy from the labor movement. This shifting base of support may have consequences for the dynamics of policy development, but it is clear that the weakening of the labor movement does not translate automatically into a commensurate weakening of the welfare state.

Analysis of the contemporary welfare state's supporters must shift from organized labor to the more varied constituencies of individual programs. Interest groups linked to particular social policies are now prominent political actors. As I will argue in detail later in this section, the rise of interest groups is one of the clearest examples of how policy feedback from previous political choices can influence contemporary political struggles. Interest groups did not build the

compare war controlled by Democrats

welfare state, but the welfare state contributed mightily to the development of an "interest-group society." As Jack Walker noted in his detailed investigation of interest groups in the United States, "the steady expansion of the federal government figures as one of the major causes of the recent growth of new organizational devices for linking citizens with their government."[7]

By the time a politics of austerity began to emerge in the mid-1970s, most social programs in both Britain and the United States were connected to extensive networks of organized social support. The recipients of various benefits – pensioners, the disabled, and health-care consumers – were the most prominent of these. There were also, however, a range of public-interest organizations seeking to protect the position of the unorganized. Finally, the providers of public services had a large stake in sustaining levels of social expenditure. In this respect, organized labor (public employee unions) continued to be of significance. Their interests, however, were now linked primarily to the employment-generating effects of specific public programs rather than to the broad consequences of generous public provision for the bargaining position of workers, and their power was exerted more through individual unions than through broad union confederations.

The analysis offered in Chapter 1 suggests that these groups will continue to play an important role in welfare state politics. A strong and effectively mobilized opposition is likely to be able to face down even determined retrenchment advocates. This effectiveness, however, is open to challenge. Interest-group strength depends not simply on formal properties like the size of membership, but on the ability of the group's leadership to convince policymakers that the membership can actually be "delivered." This is especially true in the case of the mass organizations that support social policies. Unlike some groups (e.g., business associations), their power depends less on financial resources (over which leaders may have direct control) than on the ability to offer or withhold electoral support. Influence on policy depends on whether leaders can actually mobilize members to reward or punish policymakers for particular courses of action.[8]

It is here that the interplay between the strategic options of retrenchment advocates and the mobilizing potential of welfare state constituencies becomes relevant. The constituencies of welfare state organizations must be activated to be politically effective. This is not an automatic process. Interest-group leaders must persuade policymakers that their membership is so concerned about an issue that the wrong decision will have political consequences. The efforts of retrenchment advocates, as I have argued, are directed precisely toward blocking this activation. Under the right circumstances, strategies of obfuscation, division, and compensation can be highly effective. So one must look at other elements in the political system, such as the structures of political institutions and previous policies, to judge the prospects for effective interest-group challenges to retrenchment initiatives.

"NEW INSTITUTIONALISM" AND THE POLITICS OF SOCIAL POLICY

Patterns of governance matter. The "New Institutionalist" resurgence in political science reflects a renewed appreciation of how relatively stable, routinized arrangements structure political behavior.[9] The political institutions of different countries vary along crucial dimensions, such as the rules of electoral competition, the relationship between the legislative and executive branches, the role of the courts, and the place of subnational governments in politics. These institutions establish the rules of the game for political struggles, shaping group identities and their coalitional choices, enhancing the bargaining power of some groups while devaluing that of others. Political institutions also affect the administrative and financial capacities of states. Furthermore, institutions influence the ability of policymakers to achieve the degree of insulation from social pressures that may allow relatively autonomous initiatives, building on (or reacting against) actions of their predecessors.

New Institutionalist research has raised significant questions about the dynamics of welfare state development. New Institutionalists have noted that the power-resources approach has little success in accounting for pre-World War II social-policy developments. The role of Social Democratic parties and union pressure in the formation of early welfare states was limited. New Institutionalists have stressed that political institutions must be considered consequential structures. Power resources, these authors note, are themselves partly the result of institutional variables.

This approach to comparative social policy has been developed primarily by Theda Skocpol and her collaborators.[10] Their research agenda has centered on explaining "American exceptionalism" – the belated and halfhearted development of social-welfare policies in the United States. Just as a focus on Sweden was central to the development of the power-resources model, concentration on the United States has underscored the importance of political institutions.

The American state is distinctive.[11] Its formal institutions create a marked dispersal of political authority (both within the central government and between central and local authorities) that often allows well-placed minorities to veto unwanted policy change. The administrative capacities of the federal government are relatively feeble, impeding the design and implementation of extensive policies. The representation of interests, in significant part because of institutional structures, has not taken the form of strong ideological parties and comprehensive "peak associations." Instead, parties have been weak, operating more as intermittent electoral/patronage machines than as promoters of coherent policy alternatives.[12] Institutional decentralization also encouraged the emergence of highly fragmented interest groups, while the parceling of political authority allowed many of these groups to gain significant access to policymakers. These characteristics of state structure, Skocpol and her colleagues have persuasively

Figure 2.1. *Patterns of institutional design*

		Horizontal integration (concentration of authority within nat'l gov't)	
		Low	High
Vertical integration (concentration of authority at nat'l level)	Low	United States	Canada
	High	Israel	Britain

argued, must be incorporated into an understanding of social-policy development in the United States.

My analysis of retrenchment draws heavily on this school of thought. However, I must stress that we are talking about a family of arguments. Some institutional variables are much more relevant to retrenchment politics than others. The following discussion considers how institutional variables have been linked to patterns of welfare state development, then evaluates their role in retrenchment politics. It is necessary to sort out the possible roles of two factors: the structure of formal institutions and the policy-making capacities of government authorities. A third factor, the role of policy feedback, requires a separate and extended analysis.

Formal institutions

A central feature of New Institutionalism has been a renewed appreciation for the ways in which the structures of formal political institutions influence social processes. Analysts working from a variety of perspectives have argued that institutional structures profoundly influence the viability of alternative political strategies. Institutions steer individual choices in particular directions and thus help to shape political outcomes.

In discussing the impact of formal institutions on welfare state politics, two distinct dimensions of institutional design need to be distinguished. One dimension is horizontal integration: the extent to which power within the national government is concentrated or dispersed (e.g., parliamentary vs. separation-of-powers systems). The second is the level of vertical integration: the degree that power is concentrated nationally or devolved to more local government authorities (e.g., federal vs. centralized systems).

At first glance, one might expect political institutions to account for different policy outcomes in the United States and Great Britain. On both these dimensions, as Figure 2.1 indicates, the United States and Britain represent near-polar extremes. Britain is a highly concentrated system, with only limited powers left to local governments. In the United States (and by way of comparison, in Canada's parliamentary system), subnational political units are often critical political actors. Within the national government, the British system radically concentrates political authority. This is a result not only of its parliamentary system, but of a first-past-the-post, single-member district electoral system, which limits the potential for weak coalition government (Israel's system of proportional representation represents a contrasting case). In the United States that authority is widely dispersed. These differences were in full force during the period under examination. The Thatcher government always had a substantial parliamentary majority. Reagan, on the other hand, operated in a context of "divided government." He had to contend with a Democrat-controlled House of Representatives throughout his two terms; in 1986, Republicans lost control of the Senate as well.

A high degree of vertical integration is often considered a prerequisite for strong government.[13] Many have argued that because the concentration of political authority lowers the number of effective veto points, governments operating in parliamentary systems will have a much greater capacity to pursue radical policy change. So long as the governing party or parties has a majority, legislation can be passed even over heated opposition. By contrast, the American system of checks and balances can lead to deadlock and inaction, especially when a majority of Congress is loyal to a different political party than is the president. Party lines in the legislature are much more fluid in the United States, and even if the president is of the same party as a majority of members of Congress, he may have limited leverage to pass his proposals. There are, moreover, many points in the legislative process at which opponents can effectively block policy changes. Furthermore, legislators are more likely than in a parliamentary system to be held individually accountable for their actions.[14]

Indeed, there is considerable evidence that a low level of horizontal integration probably slows the expansion of social programs.[15] The multiplication of veto points has made it easier for determined minorities to thwart reform. In the United States, for example, even though clear majorities of the electorate have often favored some form of national health insurance, and although Democrats controlled both branches, these political resources were not sufficient to overcome the institutional advantages of determined opponents.[16]

As a basic account of the impact of horizontal integration, this is persuasive. In general, major policy change is likely to be easier to achieve in Britain than in the United States. Whether vertically integrated political institutions facilitate retrenchment, however, is less clear. Although parliamentary systems concentrate authority, they also concentrate accountability; the former tendency facilitates retrenchment, but the latter impedes it.

Recall that retrenchment is generally unpopular. Because governmental power is more centralized in parliamentary systems, accountability is more centralized as well. Governments can act to prevent groups from suffering losses, and the public knows this. Individual legislators in parliamentary systems are not immune from blame for party positions; they are in fact much more susceptible to swings in party electoral support than their counterparts in the United States. This may, in turn, make governments in parliamentary systems even more reluctant to undertake unpopular actions.[17] However, this fear of negative political consequences will be felt not (as in the United States) through open political conflict, but through behind-the-scenes pressure within the governing party.

Furthermore, although the centralization of parliamentary systems increases the government's accountability, it also decreases the accountability of the opposition. Opposition parties in parliamentary systems cannot hope to enact their own policy preferences while out of power; their only hope is to topple the current government by publicizing its misdeeds. Governments in parliamentary systems, anticipating the high political cost of retrenchment actions, may forgo opportunities that concentrated power would have allowed them to undertake.

Thus, the theoretical case for believing that vertically integrated institutions favor retrenchment is weak. We are left with the empirical question of whether concentration-of-power effects outweigh accountability effects. The evidence to be presented demonstrates that the Thatcher government was as reluctant as the Reagan administration to pursue widely unpopular policies. Nevertheless, if concentrated authority does not appear to give an administration an overwhelming advantage in achieving programmatic retrenchment, it does help to structure the choices available to retrenchment advocates. Reagan and Thatcher had to adjust their strategies to fit the contours of different institutional terrains.

For example, different institutional settings led the two administrations to emphasize varying strategies of obfuscation. In the United States, retrenchment advocates often focused on the "traceability" link in voters' causal chains, shifting or obscuring blame for unpopular policies. This was an unrealistic strategy in Britain. Indeed, the government's most prominent attempt to use this technique, the requirement that local governments rely on the highly unpopular "poll tax" to raise revenues, backfired. The concentration of accountability in a parliamentary system meant that blame fell on the Thatcher government rather than on local authorities.

In Britain, those seeking retrenchment used their much greater control over the policy-making process to devise retrenchment strategies that did not raise problems of accountability. In other words, they worked hard to structure reforms in such a way that vocal opposition would not develop. For example, the British Conservatives' solid parliamentary majority allowed them to legislate reform in incremental stages where that tactic would help minimize opposition. In general, the concentration of political authority meant that the Thatcher government was well placed to implement whatever strategies stood to lower opposition. The concentration of accountability, on the other hand, meant that where such strategies were unavailable the government generally had to retreat.

With less complete control over the policy-making process, retrenchment advocates in the United States tried to fashion strategies that minimized the need to force multiple policy changes through the numerous hurdles of the political system. In cases where program structures required positive legislative or administrative action to continue, the Reagan administration was able to turn this institutional feature to its advantage. Retrenchment supporters also exploited the relatively low "accountability effects" of national political institutions to obscure their responsibility for unpopular actions.

When analysis turns from programmatic retrenchment to systemic retrenchment, the impact of horizontal institutional integration remains limited. At first glance, this is puzzling. Many of the policy changes that might further systemic retrenchment are not as unpopular as welfare state cutbacks. When systemic retrenchment could be produced without electoral costs, the much more centralized institutional structure of the British state should have given the Thatcher government a tremendous advantage. That systemic retrenchment did not proceed very far in Britain reflects Thatcher's unwillingness to pursue policy options that the institutional setting probably would have permitted. As I will argue in Chapter 7, this reflects the conflict between pursuing reforms that would constrain the welfare state and other aspects of the Conservative government's agenda.

In the United States, institutional fragmentation generally posed a considerable barrier to systemic retrenchment efforts. Only when that fragmentation could be turned into a political asset – that is, when lowering accountability was important – was systemic retrenchment encouraged. There is, however, one crucial example of this: the Reagan administration's shrewd use of institutional opportunities to enlist high deficits to the cause of constraining social spending. This will be discussed in Chapter 6.

What about the second dimension of institutional design, the degree of vertical integration? The evidence is reasonably clear that federalism constrains welfare state growth.[18] The most important consequence of decentralized institutions is the creation of "fiscal competition" among jurisdictions. Local governments find it difficult to pursue redistributive policies for fear that high taxes will lead business and wealthy individuals to move out while attracting low-income groups who would benefit from generous social programs.[19] Centralized authorities can make such policies uniform throughout a country, limiting the prospects that capital and labor mobility will pose such a dramatic threat to social provision.

This argument probably can be applied equally well to retrenchment politics. All other things being equal, redistributive social policies transferred to local authorities would be vulnerable to a downward cycle of jurisdictional competition. The caveat is that where policy-making authority is shared between local and national officials, the need to produce a common agreement may represent a barrier to change.[20] The Thatcher government responded to this problem by further centralizing authority over social policy. In other words, the government preferred to maximize its control over policy-making rather than exploit the advantages of decentralization.

In the United States, federal institutions created opportunities for certain retrenchment strategies, but also posed occasional obstacles for reform. Pushing authority down to states and localities was likely to put pressure on spending levels, and helped to shift blame away from Washington for program cutbacks.

However, the desire to avoid both of these effects also meant that state and local authorities often mobilized to prevent such changes. The intergovernmental lobby thus became an important source of protection for social programs in the United States. The outcome of these clashes often turned on the structure of particular programs. When reforms threatened key state and local interests, or when Washington was heavily reliant on local officials for implementation, decentralizing reforms were hard to carry through.

If this discussion yields few broad conclusions, it reflects the fact that the role of formal institutions in welfare state politics is complex. Arguments suggesting that one arrangement or another provides sweeping advantages for those seeking expansion or retrenchment are suspect. Particular arrangements are likely to be seen as mixed blessings for policymakers, enhancing certain capabilities while creating problems on other fronts.[21] In both countries, institutional arrangements served to steer policymakers in particular directions because they made some retrenchment strategies appear more attractive than others.

Governmental capacities

Governments vary in the degree to which they possess the resources needed to implement strategies and policies. As Skocpol has argued, beyond "sheer sovereign integrity and . . . control of a given territory" the crucial elements of state capacity, the "universal sinews of state power," are the presence of "loyal and skilled officials and plentiful financial resources."[22] For any given policy, decision makers must consider not only political constraints but administrative and financial ones.

Even if policies can be enacted, they may be impossible to implement. A number of studies have demonstrated how the existence or lack of specific administrative capacities has influenced policy development. In an influential article, Weir and Skocpol argued that previous experience with public-works programs was an important factor in the Swedish government's ability to launch Keynesian policies in the 1930s. Governments without these administrative capacities were likely to turn to more traditional policy options.[23]

Bureaucratic capacities also matter because bureaucrats themselves are politically relevant. Those occupying key positions within government agencies have expertise and command significant institutional resources. They are often given responsibility for devising solutions to pressing problems. Frequently, bureaucrats have the strategic advantage of possessing both a longer time horizon and more focused policy goals than other political actors. Administrators are sometimes energetic policy entrepreneurs, devoting careers to the construction of political coalitions that can further their policy ambitions.[24]

Bureaucratic influence is likely to be especially prominent in laying out alternatives for government action: Those within key agencies can credibly claim to know what the government can and cannot do, what will work and what will not. To the extent that policy evolves through a process of problem solving –

of what Heclo calls "collective puzzlement on society's behalf" – bureaucrats are likely to be important.[25] In his investigation of Swedish and British welfare state development, Heclo placed the autonomous actions of civil servants near the center of the policy-making process.

A focus on administrative capacities might lead one to expect important differences between the process of social-policy change in the United States and in Britain. Britain is generally considered to be a relatively "strong" state, equipped with a well-trained, prestigious, and reasonably autonomous civil service. By contrast, civil servants in the United States have less status. At the higher ranks, movement in and out of public service is common. The administrative capacities of federal agencies, watched suspiciously by Congress as well as by the president, are widely regarded as limited.

Again, however, one must ask whether factors important in determining patterns of welfare state expansion are equally pertinent to patterns of contraction. In fact, there is reason to doubt that administrative structures will be central to the politics of retrenchment "Can we administer it?" is a fundamental question when one is discussing new or greatly expanded public initiatives; but for retrenchment advocates, the primary goal is to dismantle existing efforts rather than create new ones. Closing offices, curtailing services, and cutting benefits do not require formidable administrative capacities. Retrenchment initiatives involving efforts to promote privatization may be more complicated to administer. Even here, however, the reliance on private-sector mechanisms eases the burden on public bureaucracies. The following chapters in fact reveal very little evidence that important retrenchment efforts have been scuttled because governments lacked the administrative capacity to carry them through.

Nor have civil servants been crucial political actors. My examination of the Reagan and Thatcher records suggests that bureaucratic activity has played only a marginal role in the politics of retrenchment. Politicians have been the principal decision makers. Their success has depended on an ability to shape strategies to minimize opposition. Bureaucrats have played some part in identifying these strategies, but the choice of goals and policies, and the factors determining the likelihood that particular strategies will succeed, have all been outside their control. In short, neither governmental administrative capacities nor autonomous bureaucratic activity shaped ultimate outcomes in fundamental ways.

Because governments need money to finance major social programs, a government's revenue-generating capacity is likely to have an impact on the welfare state. Although historical institutionalists have acknowledged this fact, they have not developed systematic arguments about the links between financial capacities and program enactment or expansion. There is, however, significant evidence that the structure of taxation has an impact on how much money governments can raise, and hence on how much is available for social programs. The nature of this link between tax structure and financial capacities fits well with the general approach to policy design advanced in Chapter 1. The less visible the tax system (e.g., high reliance on indirect and payroll taxes rather than on income taxes) the more revenue a government can generate without provoking a taxpayer backlash.[26]

Although administrative capacities become relatively unimportant in retrenchment politics, government financial capacities continue to play an important role. That role needs to be carefully spelled out, however. For retrenchment advocates, the government's revenue-generating capacity is a two-edged sword. As I have already noted, programmatic retrenchment is often facilitated if the government is in a position to compensate at least some of its potential opponents. The healthier the government's financial position, the easier it is to buy one's way out of political troubles. The following chapters provide examples in which the Reagan administration's retrenchment efforts would have benefited from a bit more financial room to maneuver. However, this is likely to be more than offset by the negative consequences for retrenchment of robust financing. Although improving the prospects for programmatic retrenchment, healthy finances impede systemic retrenchment. Increasing the government's revenue-generating capacity makes it harder to create an overall climate of austerity to constrain social provision.

This dual impact of government finances is important because of a major aspect of the two records reviewed in this book: The Reagan and Thatcher governments diverged more radically on tax policy than on any other major domestic issue.[27] Whereas Thatcher increased the British government's revenue-generating capacity, the Reagan administration curtailed that capacity in the United States. This difference in state capacities in turn conditioned retrenchment politics. Financial flexibility allowed the Thatcher government to pursue compensation-based strategies of programmatic retrenchment impractical in the United States. The Reagan administration, however, could use the deficit issue as a powerful tool for constraining overall domestic spending, whereas Thatcher could not.

The argument advanced here is clearly informed by key elements of New Institutionalist theory. However, institutional variables often play a different role in the politics of retrenchment than the one analysts have identified in the politics of welfare state expansion. The changes reflect the distinctive characteristics of retrenchment, such as the new concern with minimizing accountability and blame for unpopular activities. Table 2.1 contrasts the treatment of institutional variables in studies of welfare state expansion with the arguments I have made about the politics of retrenchment. Many of the processes stressed in studies of earlier periods turn out to be relatively unimportant. Whereas the concentration of political authority clearly has a positive affect on social-policy expansion, its impact on retrenchment appears to be more mixed; and although bureaucratic capacity and autonomy influenced welfare state development, they have limited implications for the politics of retrenchment. Financial capacities continue to matter, although in ways that pose dilemmas for retrenchment advocates.

One important component of New Institutionalist analysis remains to be discussed: the policy feedback from previous political choices. I have deferred this

Table 2.1. *Institutional variables and welfare state politics*

	Formal institutions		State capacities	
	Horizontal integration	Vertical integration	Administrative	Financial
Expansion	Positive	Positive	Positive	Positive
Retrenchment	Mixed-P	Mixed/Negative-P	Negligible	Positive-P
	Mixed-S	Negative-S		Negative-S

P = Programmatic
S = Systemic

topic because it is so central to retrenchment politics. One simply cannot make sense of the contemporary politics of the welfare state without considering how the consequences of preexisting policies structure struggles over social-policy reform.

POLICY FEEDBACK AND POLITICAL CHANGE

I have suggested that a major reason for viewing retrenchment politics as a distinctive enterprise is that the political context has changed considerably since the period of welfare state development. Perhaps the most important aspect of this change has been the emergence of extensive patterns of government intervention in social and economic life, that is to say, the emergence of welfare states themselves. In advanced industrial democracies, anywhere from 30 percent to 60 percent of gross national product is filtered through government programs. Large-scale policies are a critical feature of the contemporary political environment. The arrival of big government makes an analysis of policy feedback – again, the ways in which previous policy choices influence present political processes – an integral part of any investigation of social-policy change.[28]

Given the development of these massive public systems of resource extraction and deployment, it is hardly surprising that, as E. E. Schattschneider argued more than a half century ago, "new policies create a new politics."[29] However, political scientists were slow to incorporate Schattschneider's insight into their models of politics. Traditionally, researchers treated policy as the result of political forces (the dependent variable), but rarely as the cause of those forces (the independent variable). In the past decade or so, this has ceased to be true. Scholars working on a range of empirical issues have begun to emphasize that "policies produce politics."

The massive twentieth-century expansion of the public sector has clearly contributed to this new orientation. Increasing government activity made it harder to deny that public policies were not only the result of but important contributors to the political process, often dramatically reshaping social, economic, and political conditions. Intellectual developments have also fostered this shift in research. The "post-behavioralist" emphasis on the structural constraints facing individual actors has led scholars working from a variety of perspectives to begin identifying the ways in which formal and informal rules of the game in political and social life influence political behavior. To date, most analysis has centered on formal governmental institutions and political organizations. However, major public policies also constitute important rules, influencing the allocation of economic and political resources, modifying the costs and benefits associated with alternative political strategies, and consequently altering ensuing political development. An examination of the political consequences of policy structures is a logical extension of New Institutionalist arguments.

Research on policy feedback has stressed two arguments: that policy structures create resources and incentives that influence the formation and activity of social groups, and that policies affect processes of "social learning" among major political actors. In this section I review these claims and suggest two additional kinds of policy feedback. In the following section, I demonstrate the importance of incorporating these arguments into the analysis of welfare state politics.

If interest groups shape policies, policies also shape interest groups. The organizational structure and political goals of groups may change in response to the nature of the programs that they confront and hope to sustain or modify. Policies provide both incentives and resources that may facilitate or inhibit the formation or expansion of particular groups. Such incentives stem primarily from the major social consequences of specific government actions. Public policies often create "spoils" that provide a strong motivation for beneficiaries to mobilize in favor of programmatic maintenance or expansion.[30] Policy designs can also create niches for political entrepreneurs, who may take advantage of these incentives to help "latent groups" overcome collective action problems.[31] The history of the now-formidable American Association of Retired People (AARP) illustrates this feedback process. The inadequacy of health-care benefits for the elderly provided the AARP with a niche for activity. The sale of health insurance prior to the enactment of Medicare, and of "Medigap" policies since then, has provided a strong "selective incentive" for individuals to join AARP, promoting the development of an elderly lobby that is unmatched in other countries.[32]

Not only do public policies create incentives for interest-group activities, they may also provide resources that make such activities easier. The political influence of groups varies dramatically; some are central to the development of policy whereas others are ineffectual, forced to accept gains and losses determined by others. Public policies can clearly feed back into politics in this respect too. Policies can have an effect on the resources of groups, and on the ability of groups to bring those resources to bear on decision makers.

Sometimes government policies create interest-group resources in a straightforward sense, as when legislation gives funding to favored organizations or provides incentives for individuals to join particular groups (e.g., by banning or harassing alternative organizations). In a compelling essay on the development of the Swedish labor movement, Bo Rothstein has demonstrated that policy designs that gave unions authority over unemployment funds provided a crucial impetus to the development of powerful labor confederations.[33] Union administration of these funds gave workers a strong selective incentive to join. Rothstein's analysis indicates that union membership rose rapidly and stabilized at higher levels in countries that adopted such plans.

Policies may also strengthen particular groups by increasing their access to decision makers. Analyses of European corporatism have often stressed the conscious efforts of policymakers to implement reforms that strengthen links between government elites and key interest groups. Students of regulatory "capture" have noted a similar phenomenon.[34] Interventionist government policies often have the paradoxical effect of making the success of particular policies dependent upon group-controlled resources (e.g., information or skilled personnel). This dependence in turn enhances the ability of groups to turn their preferences into government policy.

There is frequently a strong case for standing the pluralist claim that interest groups drive policy on its head. Groups are profoundly influenced by structures of public policy. These structures may give organizations a reason to exist, facilitate or impede efforts to overcome collective-action problems, or provide access to considerable political resources. Feedback effects on interest groups need to be incorporated into our analyses of policy-making.

A second approach to policy feedback starts not from how policies provide resources and incentives for interest groups, but from how policies provide information that helps individuals navigate the social world's complexities. Some scholars have stressed the importance of learning effects in policy-making, concentrating on the efforts of politicians to understand the consequences of their own actions.[35] Political-learning arguments focus on those at or near the center of the policy-making process, and emphasize problems of bounded rationality and uncertainty. Implicitly or explicitly, these analysts build on work in decision making and organizational theory, which emphasizes the variety of techniques used to cope with limited cognitive capacities.[36] Heclo summarized this perspective in an early but still-influential formulation:

Politics finds its sources not only in power but also in uncertainty – men collectively wondering what to do. Finding feasible courses of action includes, but is more than, locating which way the vectors of political pressure are pushing. Governments not only "power" (or whatever the verb form of that approach might be); they also puzzle. Policymaking is a form of collective puzzlement on society's behalf; it entails both deciding and knowing.[37]

The depiction of policy change as a learning process is sometimes presented in sweeping terms. Heclo, for example, talks of both social learning and political learning, and identifies a number of sources of such effects. Prominent among them, however, is the impact of previously adopted public policies, and it is these policy-learning effects that are relevant here. Important political actors may become aware of problems as a result of their experiences with past initiatives. The setting of a new agenda and the design of alternative responses may build on (perceived) past successes or may reflect lessons learned from past mistakes.

Policy learning has emerged as an important line of argument for those interested in how policy feedback affects the cognitive processes of political actors. Heclo's study of the Swedish and British welfare states remains the most sustained effort to develop this idea. "Once implemented," he argues, "a technique such as social insurance has tended to be readopted, to be considered the 'natural' policy response for other types of income risk."[38] Overwhelmed by the complexity of the problems they confront, decision makers lean heavily on preexisting policy frameworks, adjusting only at the margins to accommodate distinctive features of new situations.

Although policy-learning arguments have been applied with considerable force in a variety of settings, their explanatory power and scope of application remain open to question.[39] So far it has proved difficult to demonstrate that policy learning has a significant impact on actors' political behavior other than simply contributing to their *accounts* of their actions. Heavy reliance on case studies has also made it hard to establish how often policy learning is important. If governments both "power" and "puzzle," when should we expect to see one type of process or the other? Learning processes seem likely to be more important when policy-making remains insulated from broader political conflicts. Policy learning is also likely to play a different role at different stages of the policy-making process. Learning effects will be most apparent in the identification of particular policy alternatives, since this is when detailed knowledge is most crucial.[40] It is less clear that policy learning is central to the formation of government agendas or to the final choices between alternative policies.

Despite limitations, these arguments about policy feedback are broadly persuasive. Nevertheless, they miss a level of political consequences that stem from previous policy choices. Policy feedback not only affects the resources of organized interests and the mind-sets of political elites; it also creates incentives and provides information for individual members of the electorate. Indeed, the effects of policies on mass publics are tremendously important. Unless this feedback induces overtly political action, however, it is unlikely to attract the attention of political scientists.

Two feedback processes should be distinguished. First, policies may encourage individuals to adapt in ways that lock in a particular path of policy development. By "lock in" I mean that they bring about the policy-induced emergence of elaborate social and economic networks that greatly increase the cost of adopting once-possible alternatives and inhibit exit from a current policy path. Major policy initiatives have major social consequences. Individuals make important commitments in response to certain types of government action. These commitments, in turn, may vastly increase the disruption caused by new policies, effectively locking in previous decisions.

That this type of policy feedback has not been widely utilized in investigations of policy development is a significant oversight. There is good reason to believe that these lock-in effects can be of considerable significance. To date, economic historians interested in the development of technology have conducted most of the work on such effects. I will begin by summarizing this research and then suggest how it can be extended to the study of policy feedback.[41]

Economic historians using the assumptions of neoclassical economics have recently demonstrated that under certain conditions the development of technology will not proceed toward the most economically efficient alternatives. The QWERTY typewriter keyboard is a classic example. Although more efficient alternatives to the QWERTY key layout existed when it was developed, they were not feasible for use until better machines allowed typists to go faster without jamming keys. However, by the time such machines were introduced, the QWERTY configuration was so well established that alternatives could not gain a foothold in the industry, and the slower standard was effectively locked in.[42] Under what conditions are such outcomes likely? Brian Arthur has identified the following factors:

Large set-up or fixed costs. If initial costs are a high proportion of total expenses, there are likely to be increasing returns to further investment in a given technology, providing individuals with a strong incentive to identify and stick with a single option.

Learning effects. Large learning effects, which may lower product costs or improve their use as prevalence increases, provide an additional source of increasing returns.

Co-ordination effects. In many cases, the advantages an individual derives from a particular activity depend on the action of others. These effects may encourage coordination with others in adopting a single option.

Adaptive expectations. If it is important for individuals to "pick the right horse" – because options that fail to win broad acceptance will have drawbacks later on – individual expectations about usage patterns may become self-fulfilling.[43]

The existence of lock-in effects in the development of technology is now generally accepted, but one can legitimately ask whether this excursion into economic history has any relevance to the current discussion. Douglass North argues persuasively that it does. The factors Arthur identifies as contributing to technological lock-in – increasing returns and high fixed costs, learning effects, coordination effects, and adaptive expectations – are often characteristics of institutions. Consequently, one could anticipate the same kind of historical process, a process of path dependence, in which initial choices of institutional design had long-term implications for economic and political performance.

This argument can easily be applied to public policies as well. North defines institutions broadly as "the rules of the game in a society or, more formally, . . . the humanly devised constraints that shape human interaction."[44] This definition would seem to encompass public policies as well as what we conventionally recognize as institutions, since policies clearly do establish rules and create constraints that shape behavior. The specific example North uses to illustrate his argument about path dependence is instructive. The Northwest Ordinance was a quasi-constitutional initiative, outlining basic rules for "the governance and settlement of the vast area of land in the West and . . . a framework by which the territories would be integrated into the new nation."[45] In this respect, it resembled a formal institution. However, the Northwest Ordinance was also "a specific legislative enactment" – that is, a public policy.

By choosing such a legalistic, foundational initiative – one that created such straightforward rules of the game – North's example obscures the broad application of his argument to policy feedback. Policies may create incentives that encourage the emergence of elaborate social and economic networks, greatly increasing the cost of adopting once-possible alternatives and inhibiting exit from a current policy path. Individuals make important commitments in response to certain types of government action. These commitments, in turn, may vastly increase the disruption caused by new policies, effectively locking in previous decisions.

Like more formal institutions, public policies operating in a context of complex social interdependence will often generate increasing returns and high fixed costs, learning effects, coordination effects, and adaptive expectations. For example, housing and transportation policies in the United States after World War II encouraged massive investments in particular spatial patterns of work, consumption, and residence. Once in place, these patterns sharply constrained the alternatives available to policymakers on issues ranging from energy policy to school desegregation.[46]

Many of the individual commitments that locked in suburbanization were literally cast in concrete, but this need not have been the case, nor need it be in the future. Policies may encourage individuals to develop particular skills, purchase definite varieties of goods, or devote time and money to distinct kinds of organizations. All these decisions generate sunk costs. That is to say, they constitute investments that generate strong commitments. In many contexts, policies may push individual behavior onto paths that are hard to reverse.

Political scientists have been slow to build an examination of lock-in processes into their models of policy development.[47] One reason for this lack of attention is that policy feedback of this kind has a tendency to depoliticize issues. By accelerating the momentum behind one policy path, it renders previously viable alternatives inaccessible. The result is often not conflict over the forgone alternative (which political scientists would generally be quick to identify), but the absence of conflict. In Peter Bachrach and Morton Baratz's terms, lock-in leads to "non-decisions."[48] Another problem is that comparative analysis may be required to study policy lock-ins. An analyst needs a comparative case in which lock-in has not occurred to identify the political effects of policy feedback.

Nevertheless, there is good reason to believe that instances of policy lock-in are widespread. Many public policies create or extend patterns of complex social interdependence in which microeconomic models of isolated, independent individuals smoothly and optimally adapting to new conditions do not apply.[49] The characteristics identified by economic historians, modified to incorporate aspects of social as well as technological complexity, provide an excellent starting point for this research. Lock-in effects are likely to be important when public policies encourage individuals to make significant investments that are not easily reversed, or when individuals face strong incentives to coordinate their activities with other social actors and adopt prevailing or anticipated standards. Policies that involve high levels of interdependence, and in which intervention stretches over long periods, are particularly likely sites for lock-in effects.

Policy feedback may also have a second major effect on large segments of the public. Just as policies provide information that may produce political learning among policymakers, policy-induced cues may influence a private individual's awareness of government activity. In common with policy-learning arguments (which have been applied primarily to bureaucrats), these arguments focus on the signals that policies send to political actors. Policy initiatives may send signals that influence individuals' perceptions of their own interests, of whether their representatives are protecting those interests, of who their allies might be, and of what political strategies are promising.

Besides broadening the range of actors considered, this approach has a significant additional advantage over a focus on policy learning. Not only does it acknowledge that all policy-making takes place in a context of information constraints, but it recognizes that the distribution of this information is often highly unequal. The emphasis of these arguments is on how information asymmetries create space for the strategic manipulation of policy design. Knowledge is indeed power, and the fact that policy structures can influence the role and availability of information makes this an important and contested aspect of policy development. To rephrase Heclo, "powering" and "puzzling" are often part of the same process; power can be utilized to facilitate or impede actors' efforts to understand the consequences of public policies.

Recall Arnold's concept of causal chains, reviewed in Chapter 1. The critical point is that the ability of voters to reconstruct causal chains can vary independently of a policy's actual impact, and that this variation may be a product of policy design. Specific features determine a policy's informational content, influencing these determinants of the electorate's reaction. Policies that distribute benefits widely and intermittently are likely to be less visible than those that distribute benefits to a concentrated group and in a single package. Whether those affected are part of a network (e.g., geographical or occupational) allowing communication with others affected (what Arnold has called "proximity") is another important factor. Homeowners living near the same toxic dump and dairy farmers engaged in a common profession are each likely to be part of networks that facilitate communication and therefore improve the chances that they will become aware of decisions or actions that affect them. Recipients of disability payments who have their benefits cut are unlikely to be similarly linked, since they may be scattered throughout the country and lack organizational linkages.

Because a crucial factor in linking outcomes to policy is the length of the causal chain, the more stages and uncertainties that lie between a policy's enactment and its perceived result, the less likely it is to provoke a popular response. Policymakers have a significant degree of control over this. They may choose interventions that create causal chains of varying lengths. Ideally, they seek to design programs for which the benefits involve short causal chains and the costs involve long ones. Time lags, for example, add greatly to the length and complexity of causal chains, so policymakers favor policy designs that accentuate immediate benefits and delay or camouflage costs.

Traceability – the linking of government action to specific decision makers – may also depend on policy design.[50] Policies can often be structured to heighten or obscure the role of decision makers. As Weaver has argued, indexation mechanisms that put particular policies on "automatic" have proven attractive precisely because they reduce the traceability of outcomes to particular decision makers.[51] To take another recent example, the intricate legislative history surrounding government regulation of the savings-and-loan industry made it practically impossible for even the most incensed taxpayer to know which politicians to hold accountable.

Given significant evidence that the information in policies is important for mass publics, these feedback effects deserve careful attention. Certainly politicians' ability to raise or lower the profile of their actions for different constituencies would seem to give them an important political resource. This potential underscores the point that although policies indeed allocate substantial resources and create powerful material incentives, some of their most important effects may be cognitive. The massive scope of public policies assures that they play a significant role in our efforts to understand and act in an enormously complex political world.

The central claim of policy-feedback arguments is that policies themselves must be seen as politically consequential structures. The rise of active government leaves little room for doubt about this. Nonetheless, that policy-feedback arguments are now widely applied in divergent national contexts and across a variety of issue areas drives home the growing importance of this concept to the study of comparative politics. In a wide range of circumstances and in numerous ways, policies restructure politics. The immediate question, however, is the relevance of these factors for the study of welfare state dynamics.

POLICY FEEDBACK AND WELFARE STATE POLITICS

Arguments about policy feedback are essentially arguments about the consequences of big government. As policy decisions have had increasingly pervasive effects on economic and social life, their impact on political processes has expanded. Given that the welfare state is at the very heart of big government, it should come as no surprise that studies of welfare state development have generated some of the most persuasive arguments about the role of policy feedback.

Heclo's analysis has already been discussed. His investigation of social policy in Britain and Sweden puts great weight on incremental policy-learning processes, in which past policies have provided the intellectual models for policymakers. Skocpol and her colleagues have also stressed policy-learning processes, though with a twist: Orloff and Skocpol's account of the impact of Civil War pensions in the United States emphasizes negative reactions to preexisting policies, and the "learning" took place mainly among social groups rather than among bureaucrats and politicians.[52] Perceived by key middle-class reformers as a scandalous example of patronage politics, Civil War pensions were avoided as a blueprint for incremental extensions of government activity. On the contrary, important political actors drew negative lessons that served as a check on the emergence of significant federal social expenditures in the pre-New Deal era. Negative learning thus had a major effect on the policy agendas and political strategies of prominent middle-class reform groups.

In other essays on welfare state development, New Institutionalists have given weight to the role of policy feedback in shaping interest-group structures. Many observers have suggested that heavy reliance on means-testing in the United States, for example, encouraged a sharp bifurcation between groups interested in middle-class entitlement programs and those concerned about the position of the poor. Esping-Andersen has applied the inverse argument to Sweden and Norway, where universalist policies produced a more solidaristic interest-group politics.[53]

The great expansion of the modern welfare state provides reason to suspect that consequences of previous policy choices will be even more important for the politics of retrenchment. Indeed, I will argue that policy feedback was a crucial determinant of retrenchment results in Great Britain and the United States. In both countries, previous policy choices generated resources and incentives that helped structure the development of relevant interest groups. For example, the fragmentation and underdevelopment of British pension policy contributed to a similarly fragmented and underdeveloped structure of pensioner-interest representation. These groups, in contrast to the powerful elderly lobby in the United States, were easily outmaneuvered by the Thatcher government in the struggle over pension retrenchment.

Lock-in effects have been apparent as well. Where public social provision generates extensive networks of commitments, retrenchment advocates find existing policies hard to reverse. The Social Security system in the United States, to be discussed in Chapter 3, is an excellent example of this kind of policy feedback. Retrenchment advocates in the United States found that their existing commitments sharply circumscribed options for radical reform. Social Security's complex financial arrangements involved a series of implicit promises stretching decades into the future. Huge public expenditures were essentially precommitted. Furthermore, these promises had shaped the retirement strategies of most Americans. The Reagan administration found itself locked in by the dense network of commitments produced by previous policy choices.

Welfare state programs do indeed distribute material resources and generate incentives that help structure retrenchment politics. Just as important, however, is the impact of policy design on political actors' attempts to make sense of the social world. The structures of existing policies may influence the availability of information and hence the prospects for actually mobilizing potential political resources. The information content of existing policy designs becomes crucial in retrenchment politics because of the centrality of obfuscation strategies. As already noted, if policymakers are attempting to pursue unpopular courses of action, they will do their best to camouflage their activities; the options open to them in this respect have already been discussed.

Policy feedback can play a crucial role in formulating retrenchment strategies. Illustrations of this point are discussed in detail in the following chapters. Program structures, which establish eligibility requirements, benefit rules, and patterns of service provision, provide key levers that policymakers will try to manipulate in ways that weaken prospects for mobilized opposition. Whether policy structures produce or inhibit what John Kingdon has termed "focusing events" – dramatic, attention-generating occurrences – can be important for retrenchment politics.[54] In some cases, focusing events may give retrenchment advocates a political advantage by forcing reform onto the agenda despite opposition from program supporters. As I argue in Chapter 3, the specific design of Social Security in the United States has produced intermittent "trust-fund crises." Although lock-in effects prevented radical reform in the United States, these dramatic focusing events helped set the agenda for pension reform, creating opportunities for moderate cutbacks in benefits that might have been politically impossible otherwise. The absence of such events in a particular arena may be important as well, especially when retrenchment advocates are trying to lower the visibility of their efforts. Chapters 4 and 5, which examine housing and income-support policies, show how both governments have identified program features permitting the introduction of automatic retrenchment mechanisms that generate little public attention.

If there is considerable evidence of the role of these various feedback effects in retrenchment politics, policy-learning arguments appear to be less applicable. Whatever relevance policy learning may have in other contexts, its role in the formation of the agendas of retrenchment advocates has been minimal. Reform initiatives did not percolate up from agencies dissatisfied with the workings of current programs. Neither administration pushed reform agendas that responded

Table 2.2. *Policy feedback and welfare state politics*

Feedback type	Expansion	Retrenchment
Interest-group activity	Substantial impact (creation of spoils, niches for entrepreneurs, selective incentives)	Substantial impact
"Lock-in" effects	Negligible during formative period	Substantial impact in specific sectors
Policy learning	Considerable evidence of both positive and negative learning effects	Negligible impact
Information effects	Unknown	Substantial impact (creation of opportunities for retrenchment advocates to pursue obfuscation techniques)

to perceived limitations in specific aspects of the welfare state. Nor were their agendas shaped fundamentally by the ways in which previous policymakers had framed discussions of social policy. Instead, both Reagan and Thatcher offered a virtually complete rejection of all but the most residual social policies. Although both the political strategies adopted and the degree of success achieved varied from program to program – and usually fell well short of such ambitious goals – the reformers' agenda in each case was radical retrenchment. Lessons learned from the specific features of past policies played very little part in the formation of these two governments' programs.

In emphasizing the role of policy feedback, this analysis follows a growing trend among students of policy development. Nevertheless, much dispute remains over how such feedback conditions change. I have suggested that it is possible for policy feedback to influence the prospects for policy change in four ways, summarized in Table 2.2. It bears repeating not only that a wide range of propositions can be placed under the rubric "policy feedback," but that different propositions imply quite distinctive images of the political process. Policy feedback might matter because it determines how policy analysts and bureaucrats learn from and modify past commitments. Feedback might also be important because it influences how social actors organize collectively, and affects their ability to mobilize resources in defense of their interests.

Table 2.2 also indicates which kinds of policy feedback are most important for retrenchment politics. Past research has often emphasized the ways in which reformers – especially bureaucrats – develop new policies in response to the perceived failure of old ones. The current analysis, by contrast, downplays this "policy learning" aspect in favor of other consequences of policy structure.

This shift in emphasis reflects the distinctive qualities of retrenchment politics: widespread public provision, extensive networks of organized supporters, and the unpopularity of cutbacks. In this environment, achieving policy change is likely to be less a matter of learning than one of identifying strategies to weaken or outflank political opponents.

Previous policies matter not because they have transmitted particular lessons to public officials. Welfare state retrenchment is far too controversial and immediate for mass publics to generate such an insulated process of bureaucrat-driven policy change. Instead, previous policies matter because they help shape the distribution of political resources (including information) and provide the raw material from which retrenchment advocates must try to design successful strategies. In this sense, the current analysis tries to bridge some of the gap between New Institutionalist arguments about policy change and those that place greater emphasis on social groups. Social forces are important, because advocates of retrenchment are unlikely to succeed in the face of substantial political opposition. Nevertheless, institutional factors – including the structure of formal institutions, but especially the consequences of previous policy initiatives – are central in determining whether this political opposition actually emerges. As the following chapters explore in detail, retrenchment advocates were able to successfully pursue strategies of obfuscation, division, and compensation only where institutional structures and existing policy designs were favorable.

II
The politics of programmatic retrenchment

3
Retrenchment in a core sector:
old-age pensions

This chapter contrasts the initiatives of the Thatcher government and Reagan administration in a core area of social policy: old-age pensions. As might be expected, attempting to cut these popular social programs was politically dangerous; each government experienced both severe setbacks and occasional success. In the end, however, the Thatcher government implemented far-reaching and probably irreversible reforms in pension provision. This outcome is especially striking because it defies the conventional wisdom that middle-class entitlements are inviolable. Furthermore, it stands in stark contrast to the repeated and politically costly failures of Thatcher's efforts to reform the other pinnacle of British social provision for the middle class, the National Health Service.[1] In the United States, Social Security emerged from the Reagan years essentially intact. Although the Social Security amendments of 1983 produced some significant reductions in future pension benefits, a number of glaring setbacks overshadowed this single and limited political success. In contrast to Britain, reform in the United States modestly scaled back the existing pension program rather than refashioning policy in line with conservative preferences.

A satisfactory account of these events must explain both the marked divergence in final outcomes and the patterns of success and failure in each country. Why did some initiatives fail when others did not? Why did the ultimate form and scope of retrenchment differ substantially in the two cases? My answer to these questions stresses the crucial role of preexisting pension structures – the feedback effects of previous policy choices. In Great Britain, the fragmented nature of state provision left potential opponents of reform divided and weak. Specific features of existing programs, including indexation mechanisms and the strong linkages between public and private pension systems, provided the Thatcher government with opportunities to obscure the extent of public-sector retrenchment. Thatcher did not always get her way, but she controlled the political agenda and ultimately engineered a major transfer of responsibility for retirement provision to the private sector.

In the United States, on the other hand, a single, mature program of public provision dominated the field of old-age security. The system's scope generated a strong and coherent base of political support while creating extensive long-term financial commitments. Both of these conditions diminished prospects for major policy change. Not only did the design of Social Security prohibit radical reform, it also dictated the circumstances under which limited retrenchment would prove possible. Cutbacks occurred only in the wake of financial imbalances in the pension system itself. The scope and structure of Social Security produced trust-fund-driven politics. Despite attempts to seize the initiative, the Reagan administration's role was essentially reactive. Efforts to produce retrenchment outside the context of trust-fund difficulties invariably resulted in politically costly defeats.

The evidence presented here, I will argue, strongly supports the claim that standard explanations for patterns of welfare state development such as national political culture and the power resources of liberal or social democratic opponents cannot account for this important divergence between the experiences of these two conservative administrations. The structure of formal institutions was of greater significance, but made less difference than one might expect. Instead, policy feedback was crucial. Previous pension-policy choices provided the raw material from which retrenchment advocates had to try to design successful strategies. Existing policies influenced the setting of political agendas and the prospects for demobilizing opponents of pension cutbacks. Furthermore, by creating extensive patterns of commitments, existing policies in the United States created lock-in effects that greatly increased the cost of pursuing major reforms.

THE STRUCTURE OF PENSION POLICIES IN BRITAIN AND THE UNITED STATES

The growth of public pensions has been at the heart of the development of the modern welfare state. Like all advanced industrial countries, Britain and the United States greatly expanded state pensions in the past half century. Despite this basic similarity, the two systems differed in crucial respects, including the scope and maturity of public schemes, the role of earnings-related benefits, the treatment of private pensions, and the structure of financing. Surprisingly, it was the United States – generally and with good reason categorized as a "welfare state laggard" – that created the more extensive and resilient public-pension sector.

Indeed, although the United States and Britain are often grouped together as "liberal" welfare states, they represent near opposites in pension development. As John Myles has noted, the postwar period was marked by a gradual convergence of pension systems in advanced industrial societies.[2] Everywhere, governments moved to combine adequate minimum benefits with provisions that partly reflected workers' pre-retirement earnings. Efforts to transform pensions from a safety net into a "retirement wage" required a move toward earnings-related benefits. Significantly, the United States adopted such an approach from the outset, whereas Britain did not successfully incorporate earnings-related benefits into its pension system until 1975.

The Social Security Act of 1935 created a system of earnings-related pensions.[3] Although the system was somewhat more generous to low-income workers, both contributions and benefits were to be tied to previous earnings. Since its inception, middle-class groups have had a strong stake in Social Security. Broad political support helped sustain a long and uncontroversial period of expansion unique in the history of American social-policy development.

By contrast, Britain adopted a system of flat-rate pensions in 1908.[4] The system became contributory in 1925, but serious discussion of adding earnings-related provision did not begin until the late 1950s. Because the scope of any such expansion would have a major impact on the room for private provision, debate between the Conservative and Labour parties was intense. Successive governments proposed legislation implementing earnings-related provision in 1958 (Conservative), 1969 (Labour), and 1972 (Conservative), but each plan was scrapped when the next election brought the opposition party to office.[5] Finally, in 1975 – four decades after the U.S. Congress passed the Social Security Act – a new Labour government was able to forge an all-party consensus on a new plan, the State Earnings-Related Pension Scheme (SERPS).

These distinctive paths of national-policy development yielded quite different public-pension programs by the end of the 1970s. The systems differed in inclusiveness, maturity, treatment of private-sector options, financing, and indexation mechanisms. Although some of these differences might appear to be matters of detail, each was to have important consequences during the struggles over pension reform in the 1980s.

Inclusiveness

For the overwhelming majority of Americans, public retirement provision meant a single program, Social Security.[6] Regardless of age or income (except for those well below the poverty line), Americans expected to turn in their retirement to the same source of public benefits. In Britain, on the other hand, public provision was much more fragmented. The Basic Pension was indeed universal, but its benefits were far lower than those available through Social Security in the United States.[7] As a result, a significantly larger proportion of the elderly were dependent on means-tested support.[8] SERPS added significantly to the confusion. The system was of no relevance to the already retired, who had not had time to build up significant entitlements; it would be of great importance to younger age cohorts, however. These groups were further divided, however, between those directly covered by SERPS provisions and the significant proportion of participants who had opted to "contract out" into a private scheme (see later in this chapter). In short, whereas in the United States virtually everyone perceived a stake in Social Security, the impact of pension reform would vary significantly in Britain, depending on a citizen's age, income, and status in SERPS.

Furthermore, the existence of an extensive and universal pension system in the United States created a highly visible set of government "spoils" that helped spur the mobilization of a strong pensioner lobby.[9] The American Association of Retired Persons (AARP) is one of the most powerful interest groups in Washington. In the much more fragmented British policy environment nothing similar emerged.[10]

Maturity

Although SERPS had been introduced only a few years before, by 1980 Social Security was rapidly approaching "maturity." A mature system is one in which the retired population has paid contributions for an entire working life, and is consequently entitled to full benefits. The transition to maturity takes many years – for SERPS, it was anticipated to occur some time after 2030. What makes maturation important is the "pay-as-you-go" financing common to both the British and American systems. Rather than building up savings as a private plan would, the public sector pays benefits out of the current working population's payroll taxes. Public pensions constitute an intergenerational contract in which each generation relies on the one following to pay its benefits. The maturity of the pay-as-you-go system in the United States means that extensive payroll taxes are already committed to the current generation of retirees. Although this had become true of the smaller Basic Pension scheme in Britain by 1980, it was not yet the case for SERPS.

Treatment of private provision

In the United States, private pensions are designed to supplement the Social Security system. When Social Security was enacted there was some discussion of providing an "opt-out" clause for those with private pensions. However, because private schemes then offered only meager pensions to a tiny fraction of the elderly, the bill's drafters rejected this proposal.[11] In Britain, by the time an earnings-related provision finally reached the political agenda, private pensions were a much more plausible alternative. The first Conservative plan of 1958 introduced the concept of contracting out, meaning that participation in the public earnings-related plan would be compulsory only for those without employer-sponsored private pensions. This arrangement was continued following the complex interparty negotiations over SERPS. The new legislation actually included generous public support for the private option. Thus, whereas in the United States private pensions supplemented public earnings-related benefits, the British arrangement has been aptly described as "a structure of subsidized competition."[12]

Financing

Technically, public-pension systems in both countries possessed separate financial accounts that were supposed to maintain something resembling balance. In practice, however, the financial mechanisms in the two cases operated quite differently. In Britain, the existence of a Treasury contribution insured that the system would be in balance regardless of economic developments. In the United States, however, funding was based completely on payroll taxes. If projected payroll-tax revenues were insufficient to meet scheduled benefits, the Social Security system was said to be out of balance, triggering calls for corrective measures to prevent "insolvency."

Conservatives (including, in this regard, Roosevelt himself at the time of the Social Security Act) had always maintained that a strict reliance on contributions would impose a discipline on the system that general-revenue funding would remove. When poor economic performance caused a trust-fund crisis in the mid-1970s, conservatives clung tenaciously to the principle of exclusive reliance on payroll taxes. Congress rejected a Carter administration proposal that would have solved the imbalance with an injection of general revenues, choosing to rely instead on sizable increases in the payroll tax.[13] Thus, in contrast to the British system, the American pension program continued to be vulnerable to any projected shortfall in payroll-tax revenue.

Indexation

Public-pension schemes usually contain some mechanism of dynamization to insure that benefit levels are adjusted to take into account the significant increases in prices and earnings that occur both in the course of a worker's career and during retirement. Although these key economic variables change slowly, long-term shifts are likely to be dramatic: A pension system that made no adjustments for inflation, for example, would in time play an increasingly marginal role in retirement provision. Both the British and American systems provided for automatic annual adjustments in pension benefits. In Britain, the Basic Pension was adjusted in line with increases in wages or prices, whichever was higher. The provision for wage-based increases was designed to allow pensioners to share in economic growth, maintaining the relative positions of workers and retirees. In the United States, Social Security provided for annual cost-of-living adjustments (COLAs), compensating retirees for inflation.

However, Social Security also possessed a second important dimension of dynamization that the Basic Pension scheme in Britain lacked. Because changes in real earnings over a worker's lifetime are likely to be substantial, some adjustment must be made in benefit calculations or a worker's early years of earnings will dramatically lower his or her pension entitlements. Thus a retiree's initial Social Security benefits are based on lifetime earnings, adjusted for economy-wide earnings growth during his or her working years. The same is true for SERPS. Unlike flat-rate schemes, earnings-related pension systems have a very significant degree of benefit dynamization built into them.

There were, then, differences in the programmatic structures of retirement provision in Britain and the United States. Although many of these may seem matters of technical detail, they proved highly consequential when conservative critics of public social provision were elected. Ronald Reagan inherited a universal, cohesive, and mature public-pension system, financed by employee and employer contributions to an earmarked trust fund, and providing earnings-related benefits that workers could supplement through private arrangements. Margaret Thatcher confronted a system financed by a combination of payroll taxes and general government revenues, with much more limited, flat-rate benefits. A new earnings-related scheme augmented this system but did not yet pay significant pensions, and it competed directly with private alternatives. These different program structures created distinctive opportunities and constraints for those seeking fundamental change in pension provision.

THATCHER, REAGAN, AND PENSION POLICY

Both Thatcher and Reagan were strongly committed to reducing government spending and transferring public-sector activity to the private sector wherever possible. Because pensions account for such a large share of social spending, they became an obvious target for politicians interested in scaling back the welfare state. Nevertheless, if the size of expenditures attracted budget cutters' attention, it also both reflected and enhanced the programs' political strength. Pensions provided large benefits to a population widely regarded as deserving. Perceptions that benefits had been earned by a lifetime of contributions greatly strengthened the general sense that pensions constituted an untouchable entitlement in both Britain and the United States.

Behind the superficial similarity of these two middle-class entitlement programs lay important differences, however. Pension policy in the United States had developed through a long series of largely incremental and consensual steps, and events would demonstrate that Social Security was firmly embedded in American political life. British policy had developed fitfully, and it was not until the mid-1970s that Britain truly embarked toward a mature pension system. This was forty years after the United States, and it would prove to be too late.

The Thatcher government and state pension provision

British pension policy must have seemed a dubious target for reform. Because existing benefits were ungenerous by international standards, cutbacks were hard to justify. Although the new SERPS scheme did promise eventual expansion, it was the product of an agreement for which the Conservatives had repeatedly expressed support. Nonetheless, a government committed to reducing state spending was bound to look for cuts. Despite emerging rather slowly, Conservative efforts to change pension provision eventually produced major reforms. Thatcher's government followed two strategies. Initially, it moved to stop the growth of the basic state pension. The second track of policy, which reached fruition in the Social Security Act of 1986, was an overhaul of earnings-related pension provision.

The Thatcher government's plan for limiting the Basic Pension provides an excellent example of what can be called "implicit privatization." The government sought to freeze the scope of public provision. In a growing economy, this meant that expansion would be channeled into the private sector, leading to a gradual but substantial shift in the balance between the two sectors. The (first) 1980 Social Security Act changed the basis for uprating (indexing) the Basic Pension. From 1973 to 1980, benefits had been uprated in line with higher of prices or earnings, which in practice generally meant earnings. Essentially, this upratings formula meant that pensioners would share in the benefits of economic growth, and the relative role of state pensions would remain stable. The 1980 act, however, provided for upratings only in line with prices.

Though the act generated limited political controversy, it had substantial long-term implications. Because earnings generally grow faster than prices, uprating pensions in line with prices meant that economic growth would gradually diminish the relative role of state pensions. Even in the short run, the real value of pensions has lagged far behind earnings. By 1988, the new upratings formula meant that a married pensioner received £65.90 rather than £79.90 per week, a reduction of almost 20 percent. The change lowered expenditures by 4 billion pounds a year.[14] If this continued, the long-term effect would be dramatic. As the government actuary pointed out, in forty years the Basic Pension for a single pensioner would, assuming 2 percent real annual earnings growth, produce a replacement rate (the pension benefit as a percentage of previous earnings) of roughly half that provided in 1980.[15]

This change substantially reduced expenditure growth at low political cost. Much smaller policy shifts often generated massive public reactions, but for a number of reasons opposition in this case was muted. For opponents, one problem was the difficulty of communicating the argument that earnings-based indexation was the appropriate policy. As long as the Thatcher government could claim that it was maintaining the Basic Pension's real value (and it did so repeatedly), it was difficult for program supporters to portray the new upratings formula as a major assault on state provision. Nevertheless, as Thatcher herself said in a 1986 interview, "If you actually hold [public expenditure] against a background of growth you have got what you want."[16] The decremental nature of the policy change further diminished opposition. There was no highly visible restriction of benefits. Instead, a single reform produced a stream of automatic annual adjustments in benefits. Each adjustment was relatively small, but the cumulative impact was substantial. Finally, the weakness of the pensioner lobby in Britain undermined prospects for forceful opposition. Given the complexity and decremental nature of the reform, a sustained effort to explain its impact and mobilize those who stood to lose was required. The lack of anything equivalent to the AARP meant that in the absence of highly visible cutbacks, a mobilization of the elderly was unlikely.

If the new upratings formula was a major political victory, it nevertheless provided an incomplete solution. The government realized that SERPS promised to substantially increase public spending. Even so, a direct attack on SERPS was politically risky. The program had all the features that were supposed to make it untouchable. Benefits were universal, the link between contributions and entitlements was relatively tight, and the recipients commanded widespread public support. Furthermore, changes in policy would have required an embarrassing public reversal. The Conservatives had publicly backed the enactment of SERPS, and the Thatcher government had repeatedly promised to maintain it. During the prelude to the 1983 general election, the prime minister denied having any "plans to change the earnings-related component of the state pension."[17] If so, then plans must have developed very quickly after the election.

The control of public expenditure was a top priority. Social-security outlays were rising, largely because of Britain's staggering unemployment rate. Nevertheless, the government – and especially the prime minister and the treasury – considered retrenchment within the heartland of the welfare state essential to economic recovery. The new chancellor, Nigel Lawson, released a major report in early 1984 expressing the need for expenditure cuts. The treasury analysis specifically identified pensions as "the major source of future pressures" within the social-security budget. The prime minister, in an interview with the *New York Times* in January of the same year, spoke of the need to confront a "social-security time bomb."[18]

These comments placed a heavy burden on Norman Fowler, secretary of state for social services. Press reports suggested that Fowler had resisted treasury demands for deep cuts in 1983 by agreeing to a review of the entire social-security budget.[19] Fowler asserted that the reviews would "constitute the most substantial examination of the social security system since the Beveridge Report forty years ago."[20] The prominence of pension expenditures ensured that SERPS would receive special attention.

The government accepted submissions from interested parties until the end of July 1984. A special cabinet subcommittee chaired by the prime minister herself reviewed Fowler's preliminary proposals in early 1985.[21] According to a *Financial Times* report, the treasury pushed hard for cuts at these meetings, seeking reductions on the order of £2-4 billion, or between 5 percent and 10 percent of social-security spending.[22]

Expectations that Fowler might offer a "new Beveridge" proved false, but the green paper released in June 1985 contained one undeniable bombshell: the proposal to abolish SERPS.[23] In a bow to political realities, the government called for a lengthy transition period. Nevertheless, the plan was radical. Although those within fifteen years of retirement would stay in SERPS, men under forty and women under thirty-five would lose all SERPS benefits. Those in between would receive partial SERPS benefits because they would have limited time to make new arrangements. In place of SERPS, employees would be re-

quired to make minimum mandatory contributions to either an employer's occupational scheme or to an employee's "personal pension."

These changes met the government's major ambitions for pension policy.
First, SERPS would be eliminated. Admittedly, the process would be slow, given
that the desire to limit political opposition required a long transition. Reductions
in anticipated SERPS expenditures were not expected until 2002. Nevertheless,
by 2033 the plan would save an estimated 75 percent of the enormous projected
SERPS expenditures.[24] Second, and equally important, the introduction of personal pensions was intended to fill many of the gaps in private provision that
previously had led to demands for state pensions.

If the government was pleased with its proposal, however, almost nobody
else was. Despite a commanding majority in Parliament that all but guaranteed
victory, the government was unprepared for the magnitude of public hostility
that the green paper produced. Opposition from the traditional supporters of
social programs was expected. The bold decision to completely abolish SERPS
gave the Labour Party a clear target for criticism. The Trades Union Congress
called the proposals a "colossal breach of faith on the Government's part."[25]
The "poverty lobby" worried about the position of women and the low paid,
arguing that private alternatives would offer far less for them than SERPS. An
analysis by the highly respected Institute for Fiscal Studies (IFS) confirmed this
view. Although a single man of forty could expect transitional SERPS payments
and his private contributions to produce a pension equal to roughly 80 percent
of that SERPS would have provided, a pension including benefits for a spouse
would be reduced to only 70 percent. The IFS added that because private plans
would not duplicate SERPS's generous treatment of shorter work histories,
working women could expect to do significantly worse.[26]

More surprising was the harsh criticism from usually reliable government
supporters: employers and the occupational pension funds. Employers were
alarmed by the cost. In effect, the green paper called for transforming a public
pay-as-you-go scheme into a private funded system. Where SERPS had anticipated that future benefits would be paid from future contributions, the green
paper called for the gradual accumulation of assets to pay retirement benefits.
This produced a "double-payment" problem: Employees (and employers) were
asked to continue making National Insurance contributions to pay for current
retirees while making mandatory contributions to private schemes to fund their
own retirement.

In the green paper the government acknowledged the need for higher contribution rates: "The move to additional funded pension provision will be taking
place while the cost of the pay-as-you-go state system continues unchanged. The
total volume of resources being devoted to pensions will, therefore, increase."[27]
For both employees and employers, the reform meant higher payments for lower
benefits. The *Financial Times* projected the increased annual cost to employers
at roughly £1.5-2 billion.[28]

Not only did the plan require employers and employees to make higher contributions for lower benefits, but in the short run it promised to worsen the government's fiscal position. The state (as an employer) would pay increased contributions for its employees, while the expansion of tax-free private-pension provision would lower government revenues. Concern for these fiscal implications had delayed the release of the green paper, as the treasury argued with Fowler over the budgetary costs of his plans. The social-security review was intended to lower spending, allowing Lawson to offer preelection tax cuts. Instead, the chancellor faced the prospect of higher tax subsidies, which meant lower revenues and less room to cut income taxes.[29]

The insurance companies who ran the occupational schemes saw their "expanded opportunities" as a decidedly mixed blessing. The erratic earnings patterns of many of the private sector's new clients made them expensive to include in plans. Private schemes would also lose some of the generous state subsidization for contracted-out workers that SERPS had provided. Furthermore, insurers feared that if the 4 percent mandatory contributions produced meager pensions, they might face pressure to provide more generous benefits.

Employers and insurers also complained about the administrative headaches the scheme would create, in that for at least fifteen years companies would have to run two schemes in tandem. Finally, pension providers worried that pensions would once again be a "political football." Even before the green paper was released, Labour Party leader Neil Kinnock announced that a Labour government would reverse any major modifications of SERPS.[30] What was the advantage of introducing complex new arrangements if the next government would render them obsolete?

Fowler's "fundamental examination" of pensions had apparently missed some important political ramifications of reform. The government was prepared for complaints from the opposition parties, but probably not for their vehemence. Equally important, the withering criticism from the Confederation of British Industry and from major private insurers caught the government unprepared. Members of the government's own pensions-review team, including Stewart Lyon of Legal and General Assurance (Britain's largest pension fund), were highly critical of the proposals. Lyon argued that the review team had never considered a plan to phase out SERPS.[31]

By the fall of 1985, a rattled Thatcher government was searching for a graceful way out. Faced with heavy opposition from interest groups and rising discomfort among backbench Conservative MPs, Fowler began to backpedal. When the government's legislative proposals finally emerged in December, the pension provisions had been substantially revised.[32] The white-paper proposals, which became the Social Security Act of 1986, reversed the decision to abolish SERPS. Instead, the government substantially lowered benefits while continuing to encourage private alternatives.[33] As with the green-paper proposals, benefits were to be phased in gradually, with the transition affecting those retiring between the years 2000 and 2010.

The white paper reaffirmed the earlier emphasis on expanding private provision through a combination of occupational schemes and personal pensions. Occupational schemes were given increased flexibility. In addition, employees could opt out of occupational plans, setting up personal pensions instead. In this case, employers would be required to make contributions to the personal pension in lieu of contributions to the occupational scheme. As an incentive to contract out, the government said it would add an additional rebate of 2 percent of earnings to the standard rebate for newly contracted-out employees until 1993. These major reforms were enacted in 1986.

Although other aspects of the government's social-security legislation met fierce parliamentary resistance, the pension reforms sailed through with limited dissent. The 1986 reform was generally regarded as a significant retreat for the Thatcher government and further proof of the privileged status of middle-class social benefits.[34] After all, the government had failed to eliminate SERPS. However, this interpretation misses the significance of the government's revised proposals. In combination, the reforms of the Basic Pension and SERPS represent a dramatic change in pension policy. The new arrangements will have significant repercussions for income distribution, the roles of the state and private sector in pension provision, and the evolution of state finances.

The new scheme's distributional impact will depend on how adequately private alternatives substitute for SERPS benefits. The new arrangements will work against those with lower earnings and less stable work histories, since the new formulas will not provide the relatively generous compensation for these factors that SERPS offered. Because women are likely to suffer from both liabilities, they are especially apt to be worse off. The new system will be particularly damaging to middle-aged workers, who will have limited time to build up new entitlements. The government's own statistics suggested that benefits for those staying in SERPS would drop sharply – as much as 40 percent for widows in some age and income groups.[35]

The changes will sharply curtail the state's role in providing earnings-related pensions. Because public pensions have been cut, efforts to achieve higher retirement incomes will be increasingly channeled toward the private sector. Although the public-sector earnings-related system will continue, the new rules are structured to make the private-sector option attractive to anyone with sufficient time to make significant contributions. The extra 2 percent annual rebates, widely derided as a "bribe," will further enhance the private sector's appeal.[36] By the end of 1990 – only eighteen months after personal pensions became available – 4 million people (about 15 percent of the working population) had already contracted out and set them up. That this promises fundamental long-term change is signaled by the fact that three-quarters of those choosing the personal-pension option were in their mid-thirties or younger.[37] In the long run, SERPS expenditures will drop sharply. The changes introduced will make little difference in the short run because of transition arrangements. However, by 2021, SERPS expenditures are projected to drop by well over 50 percent compared with pre-reform estimates, from £16.4 billion to £7.1 billion.[38]

Given the repeated shifts in British pension policy, the crucial question is whether these reforms can be sustained. For example, a future government would not be obligated to limit itself to adjusting Basic Pension benefits for inflation. By adopting price indexation, however, the Thatcher government has assured that the relative position of the Basic Pension will fall in the short run. Future governments are likely to be condemned to a game of perpetual catch-up.

In theory, the government's changes in earnings-related provision could also be reversed, but the Conservatives' 1987 electoral victory sharply increased their chances of institutionalizing a new pension regime. Now that a large number of people have made sizable contributions to private pensions, the "privatization constituency" will be politically powerful. Fowler certainly recognized the importance of quickly cementing his new approach, having offered substantial financial incentives (which have no clear policy justification) to those opting for personal pensions by 1993.

There is some reason, then, to accept the *Economist*'s enthusiastic claim that the shift to personal pensions "could revolutionise personal finance. It could be as important and irreversible as this government's other two privatising innovations, the sale of council houses to their tenants and of nationalised industries to individual investors."[39] In the wake of four consecutive election defeats, pressures on the Labour Party to come to terms with Britain's "new individualism" continued to mount. Efforts to reverse the expansion of personal pensions are unlikely. The Labour Party has come to recognize that its electoral viability depends on maintaining support from precisely those middle-income groups likely to be alienated by promises to restrict investments in personal pensions. Despite significant setbacks, the Thatcher government succeeded in radically reforming British pension policy.

Pension policy in the Reagan years

The Reagan administration's hostility toward Social Security and the system's financial difficulties fueled a number of heated political conflicts over pensions policy in the 1980s. Two results of these struggles are striking. First, the administration's overall ability to achieve pension retrenchment was limited, especially when compared with Thatcher's success. Second, the results of the individual initiatives varied widely. When struggles over Social Security highlighted the administration's desire for cutbacks and involved an effort to enlist Social Security in the battle against the budget deficit, they were inevitably unsuccessful and politically costly. On the other hand, where Social Security's financial imbalances became the issue, there were opportunities for limited structural reform.

In 1981, the simultaneous arrival of a conservative president and a financial crisis made Social Security appear increasingly vulnerable. Despite assurances that reforms adopted in 1977 had left Social Security financially sound, new projections indicated looming deficits. Stagflation was the major source of difficulty. Although the Social Security Administration had predicted 28 percent inflation and 13 percent real-wage growth from 1978 to 1982, the actual experience was 60 percent inflation and 7 percent *negative* real-wage growth.[40] A new rescue package was needed.

During the spring of 1981 there were several small skirmishes over Social Security, but the Reagan administration's efforts centered on cutting taxes and other, politically weaker areas of domestic spending. Growing concern about Social Security finances eventually provoked a presidential response. In the past, Reagan had expressed interest in moving Social Security to a voluntary basis while expanding private alternatives.[41] With other items high on the administration's agenda, however, no long-term reform strategy developed. Instead, Social Security policy was subsumed in the president's confrontation with Congress over the budget.

Social Security's widely publicized troubles seemed to offer the Reagan administration a good opportunity to restructure the program.[42] However, Office of Management and Budget director David Stockman, who took the lead in formulating administration policy, was preoccupied with obtaining immediate budget cuts. One White House aide reported that Stockman hoped for "phenomenal" cuts and saw Social Security as "the best way to get a balanced budget."[43] The OMB director also believed the publicity surrounding Social Security's projected deficits provided a unique opening. The perception of crisis, Stockman thought, might "permit the politicians to make it look like they're doing something *for* the beneficiary population when they're doing something *to* it."[44]

Later events would prove Stockman right: Trust-fund crises did create opportunities for retrenchment. However, Stockman feared that preoccupation with the trust fund would lead to long-term changes that were of little use in his battle to balance the overall federal budget. As Stockman told the *Washington Post*'s William Greider, he had no interest in spending "a lot of political capital solving some other guy's problem in 2010. The Social Security problem is not simply one of satisfying actuaries . . . Its one of satisfying the here-and-now of budget requirements."[45] By focusing on immediate cuts to reduce the budget deficit, however, Stockman redefined the issue and precipitated a major political blunder.

OMB designed a proposal that called for approximately $45 billion in Social Security cuts. The centerpiece was a 25 percent reduction in benefits for those choosing early retirement, scheduled to take effect January 1, 1982. The provision was designed to save $20 billion, but because early retirement had become a frequently used option, it would have sharply reduced benefits for 1.4

million recipients with little advance warning. In addition, Stockman proposed a $4 billion cut in basic benefits and a three-month cost-of-living allowance (COLA) delay.[46]

Reagan's top advisors hoped to keep the president one step removed from the process, insulating him from potential criticism. At Stockman's behest and with Reagan's approval, Health and Human Services secretary Richard Schweiker reluctantly introduced the proposals as his own in May 1981.[47] The administration's recent string of dramatic legislative victories may have made Reagan's aides overconfident. Schweiker's initiative was quickly linked to Reagan, and the Democrats promptly responded. Amid widespread outcry against the proposals, the Senate voted 96-0 to oppose any "unfair" or "precipitous" cuts in Social Security. The Reagan "honeymoon" was over.

The cuts eventually enacted in 1981 were far more modest, less controversial, and clearly inadequate to solve the Social Security system's financial problems. However, neither the president nor congressional Democrats wished to take the lead in proposing painful solutions. President Reagan's advisors had convinced him to propose a COLA delay in a new round of budget cuts announced in September, but this time the White House cautiously floated the proposed cuts in advance. When Republicans in Congress were unenthusiastic, the administration dropped the idea.[48]

Reagan's new reluctance to tamper with Social Security reflected the Democrats' success at portraying the administration as a threat to the elderly. As the trust funds dwindled, the Reagan administration feared that a new initiative would give the Democrats another opportunity to raise the "fairness" issue. Seeking a way out, Reagan announced the appointment of a commission, representing a range of interested parties, to develop a plan for eliminating the projected trust-fund deficits. Conveniently, the commission would not report until after the November 1982 midterm elections.

Such "blue ribbon" commissions can serve an array of purposes, but they very rarely produce policies. Even though the administration may have seen the commission as a useful delaying tactic, House Speaker Tip O'Neill and Senate Majority Leader Howard Baker each appointed members whose support would be essential to any successful bargain.[49] To the surprise of many, key commission members eventually worked out a satisfactory compromise with Reagan's aides.[50] Unlike every other confrontation over Social Security in the 1980s, this struggle actually produced significant program cuts.

Social Security's financial structure played the central role in producing this outcome. As conservatives had long maintained, the existence of a separate "trust fund" that could not be allowed to go "bankrupt" structured the political debate. Faced with the specter of imminent insolvency – probably the only outcome that would cause more political damage than benefit cuts – a wide range of political actors were forced to embrace a compromise solution.

The commission's diverse composition and Social Security's popularity insured that the proposals did not call for a radical restructuring of the program.

The approved changes did, however, include an array of significant revenue and benefit reforms. The biggest short-term source of revenue came from the acceleration of payroll-tax increases. Because these increases were already scheduled to occur in a few years, they did little to reduce the long-term deficit. More significant in the long run was the increase in payroll taxes for the self-employed. The 1983 reforms also continued a well-established practice of raising revenues by expanding coverage to previously uncovered groups – a rather painless approach since the newly covered workers would also be entitled to benefits. All new employees of the federal government and nonprofit institutions would now be included in Social Security.

The 1983 amendments included substantial modifications of benefits. First, a six-month COLA delay contributed significantly to both short- and long-term deficit reduction. This proposal had no effect on nominal benefits; it would take place only incrementally and almost invisibly. A second important change made 50 percent of benefits subject to income tax if adjusted gross income was $25,000 or more for single returns and $32,000 for joint returns. Because these income levels were not indexed, the change would generate large incremental savings. As inflation increased nominal incomes, more and more pensioners would find their benefits subject to tax.[51] Unable to reach an agreement on how to eliminate the remaining shortfall, the commission left to Congress the choice between more reliance on taxes or an increase in the retirement age. Congress voted to raise the retirement age to sixty-seven in a series of small steps beginning in the year 2000. Since most people already retired before sixty-five, few expected the result to be later retirement. Instead, as the Democrats' representatives on the commission pointed out, retirees would receive significantly lower early-retirement benefits because of the reform.

Although the 1983 Social Security amendments were widely seen as a compromise based largely on administration concessions, the result was a sizable cut in long-term benefits. The bulk of the reduction in long-range imbalances came from benefit decreases rather than tax increases.[52] In short, the 1983 act revealed that American political institutions, even at a time of divided government, did not prohibit significant retrenchment. A recent analysis indicated the magnitude of the reductions involved. Between 1985 and 2030, replacement rates (benefits as a percentage of pre-retirement earnings) for a sixty-five-year-old retiree are projected to fall from 63.8 percent to 51 percent for low earners and from 40.9 percent to 35.8 percent for average earners.[53]

Nevertheless, the reform did not alter the fundamental structure of the American pension system, and suggested that the Reagan administration had given up any radical plans for Social Security. Events after the 1984 election confirmed the difficulty of imposing Social Security cuts in the absence of a trust-fund crisis. Conservative desires to limit government spending combined with continued concern over the deficit to keep expenditure cuts on the political agenda. In turn, the recognition that major budget reform was unlikely without a contribution from Social Security led politicians to return repeatedly to the topic of pension cutbacks. In each case, however, Social Security's reputation as the untouchable "third rail" of American politics was confirmed.

Rather than building on the outcome of 1983, struggles over Social Security since 1984 have echoed Stockman's debacle of 1981. Social Security's high profile and massive scope have attracted the attention of budget cutters. These same characteristics, however, meant that serious proposals immediately generated a chorus of dissent, forcing policymakers to retreat. The idea of cutting Social Security to lower the federal deficit reappeared in 1985, although this time the initiative came from Senate Republicans rather than the White House. Having been burned on Social Security before, President Reagan was reluctant to pursue the matter. However, leading Republican senators such as Robert Dole and Pete Domenici worried about both the economic and political consequences of continued high deficits (twenty-two Republican senators were up for reelection in 1986).

Through a long and tortuous process of negotiation, Dole was able to steer a package through the Senate that included a one-year COLA freeze.[54] Hopes that the initiative would produce a bandwagon effect rapidly dissipated. Reagan offered only lukewarm support, and Democrats refused to come on board. The proposed budget passed the Senate 50-49 on an almost straight party-line vote. Nor was the Democratically controlled House more obliging. Despite moments when a complex package that would have included defense and Social Security cuts and tax increases seemed possible, Reagan ultimately deserted the Senate Republican leadership. The president cut a deal with Tip O'Neill preserving Social Security in return for higher defense authorizations. The embittered senators had rediscovered the dangers of tampering with such a popular program.

Though the Reagan administration surely hoped that by now it had heard the last of proposals for Social Security cuts, dramatic events produced a renewed struggle only two years later. On October 19, 1987, world financial markets collapsed, with the Dow Jones losing almost one quarter of its paper value in a single day. With analysts arguing that the budget deficit was partly to blame, political pressures for a governmental response mounted rapidly. Reluctantly accepting the need for a "budget summit," Reagan excluded only one possible target for deficit reduction: Social Security. In a press conference on October 20, he announced that he was "putting everything on the table with the exception of Social Security, with no other preconditions."[55] The carefully worded statement, designed to signal the president's willingness to consider tax increases, provided clear testimony to Social Security's special status.

The mathematics of deficit reduction and the absence of viable alternatives kept pushing Social Security back into the negotiations, however. Given its antipathy to social spending, the Reagan administration probably was not averse to this development – providing that all key participants were willing to share the blame. Early in the second week of discussions, word leaked that COLA limitations were being discussed. Even as the powerful lobbying apparatus of Social Security advocates moved into action, a growing sense that the financial markets were steadying diminished the sense of crisis. In this context, House Republicans signaled their unwillingness to go along with Social Security cuts. Although Senate Republicans continued to push for sweeping reforms, such open opposition within the GOP ruled out any major cutbacks. With Social Security excluded, agreement on broad contributions from tax increases, defense spending, and other domestic programs also proved elusive. The highly touted budget summit ultimately settled for a minimal, face-saving package of new revenues and spending cuts, with Social Security left untouched.

Social Security's recent history is easily summarized. Extensive conservative efforts to erode public-pension provision have resulted in marginal change. Reagan administration attempts to go on the offensive against this extensive system of retirement provision collapsed in the face of massive and unified resistance. Increasingly, the administration found itself on the defensive, forced to respond to a policy agenda not of its own choosing. Although some cutbacks resulted from trust-fund pressures, the Social Security program survived – indeed almost flourished – through a decade of budgetary austerity.

POLICY FEEDBACK AND PENSION REFORM: EXPLAINING OUTCOMES

Despite one limited success, the Reagan administration's effort to restructure state pensions was largely thwarted. The Thatcher government, by contrast, overcame setbacks to introduce fundamental policy reforms. What accounts for the difference? The evidence supports the view that the structure of preexisting pension systems was crucial. Before reviewing the case for this proposition, it is worth considering some alternative hypotheses.

One possible explanation would be the Thatcher government's greater political savvy in executing a politically treacherous undertaking. There is little doubt that Stockman's poorly planned initiative in 1981 put the president on the defensive, aroused opponents, and dampened any enthusiasm Reagan and his advisers might have had for radical reform. Nevertheless, the Thatcher government made mistakes as well – witness the embarrassment when usually reliable allies roundly condemned the green-paper proposals. It was not competence that differentiated the two reform efforts.

Nor is a focus on the two countries' political cultures of much help. Although some scholars have identified elements of public opinion as a source of cross-national differences in policy, political culture is generally used to account for less activist government in the United States.[56] In this case, the United States has developed and sustained a more extensive public sector – exactly the opposite of what an explanation based on political culture would anticipate.

A third approach might emphasize the role of the power resources available to labor movements and their political allies in the two countries. Nevertheless, although the position of the left was weak in both cases during the 1980s, the political outcomes were dramatically different. If anything, a focus on power resources would suggest that reform should have been easier in the United States, where levels of unionization are far lower and there is no true social-democratic party. Whatever the role of labor-movement strength may have been during the era of welfare state expansion, it cannot account for the different outcomes of welfare state retrenchment efforts in these two cases.

Finally and most plausibly, one could stress important differences between the formal institutions of the two political systems. This explanation is at least broadly compatible with the outcomes examined here. It is indeed far easier to legislate reform in Britain's parliamentary system, where the prime minister can usually count on solid majority support, than in the political obstacle course confronted by an American president.[57] Once the Social Security Act was presented to Parliament in January 1986, its eventual adoption was a virtual certainty.

Political institutions clearly did play an important part in the development of pension systems in both countries. An institutional structure that makes continuity an easier course than change facilitated the long, incremental, and relatively consensual expansion of Social Security. Britain's failure to follow the postwar international trend toward earnings-related provision was in large part attributable to highly centralized political institutions that translated frequent alternations of Conservative and Labour governments into equally frequent policy reversals.

Furthermore, the reality of divided government certainly presented significant problems for the Reagan administration. However, there are serious problems with an explanation of retrenchment outcomes based primarily on the structure of formal political institutions. As I argued in Chapter 2, the theoretical case for expecting centralized systems to be more successful is suspect. For a government seeking to implement unpopular policies, the greater centralization of British political institutions was a two-edged sword. Centralized government concentrates power, but it concentrates accountability as well. The Thatcher government's greater institutional control must be weighed against the greater likelihood that it would be blamed for unwanted reforms.

If there are good theoretical reasons for questioning an institutional explanation, the evidence suggests that political institutions provided only a modest advantage to the Thatcher government. Institutional design cannot account for the Reagan administration's single success or the Thatcher government's significant failures. Despite the reality of divided government, under certain conditions the Reagan administration achieved significant cuts in public pensions. Despite its institutional advantages, the British government could not act with impunity: Again, the green paper's demise suggests that Thatcher was hardly insulated from public pressure. Initial proposals had to be recast in a manner to make them acceptable, if not to the Labour Party, then at least to a wide range of interests outside the government. Failure to do so has necessitated retreat, not only in the case of pensions but in other policy arenas such as health care.

The difference between the situations in Britain and the United States was that the British government eventually found it possible to minimize the political costs associated with reform. Ultimately, the explanation for this divergence lies in the policies each government inherited. Five differences between the two pension systems were especially important. First, policy in the United States was built around one dominant, unifying program, whereas the fragmented British system consisted of a number of overlapping components. The greater coherence of Social Security in the United States created broad common interests among recipients, whereas distinct groups of British pensioners relied to different extents on various forms of provision. Not surprisingly, the unifying role of Social Security made it much easier to mobilize the American elderly in opposition to retrenchment proposals.

Second, the preexistence of contracting-out arrangements in the British system facilitated the privatization process by masking the radical nature of the government's proposals. In the United States, allowing people to opt for private provision in return for reduced state entitlements would have constituted radical reform. By contrast, in Britain dramatic change could be implemented quietly. After failing to openly introduce an entirely new system, the Thatcher government adopted a seemingly incremental, modest revision. However, even though the basic alternatives were left in place, the attractiveness of each option was markedly changed. By recasting the rules of competition between the public and private sectors, the government initiated a process that will transform the relative roles of both in the long run.

The third important difference was that Social Security's earnings-related benefit structure offered greater protection against changes in indexation that would produce "implicit privatization." As noted earlier, earnings-related pension systems must compensate for earnings growth over time, or their benefit structures become distorted. This characteristic builds an important element of benefit dynamization directly into the structure of a pension system, providing a crucial protection against the gradual erosion of benefit levels. It is a protection that SERPS shares, but the Basic Pension does not. The relative role of the latter program in retirement provision has dwindled as a result.

The fourth major difference between the two pension systems lies in their financing structures. Social Security politics were trust-fund-driven in the 1980s because the program's design directs attention to the balance between payroll taxes and program outlays. In the early 1980s, trust-fund deficits created an opportunity for significant retrenchment. Thus, programmatic structure also accounts for the one case where pension cutbacks did occur in the United States. However, the logic of the trust-fund issue led not to radical reforms but rather to efforts to "balance" the existing system's finances. In Britain, by contrast, infusions of general revenues have prevented trust-fund balances from becoming an important component of pension politics. The Thatcher government therefore had greater freedom to shape the political agenda.

A final and crucial difference was that the public earnings-related pension system in the United States was "mature," whereas the British one was not.

Once an extensive scheme is developed on a pay-as-you-go basis it is very hard to introduce fundamental alterations. Because private plans must pay benefits from earnings rather than from taxes, privatization means introducing a "funded" system. As mentioned, this presents a double-payment problem: Taxpayers must continue to finance current retirees while saving for their own retirement.

The double-payment problem is likely to create insurmountable political difficulties. The Thatcher government was well aware that the immaturity of SERPS provided a brief window of opportunity for privatization. As then-junior minister John Major noted in the House of Commons debate over pension reform, "The way in which SERPS works means that every year of delay leaves people clocking up expensive rights which must be honoured in the future."[58] In the United States, the double-payment problem was not a future prospect but an immediate reality. The financial resources needed to build a private-sector alternative were already committed, through payroll taxes, to the current generation of elderly. Those advocating steps equivalent to Britain's SERPS reform, like the Cato Institute's Peter Ferrara, remained politically marginal figures.[59]

Thus, differences between the pension systems inherited from the past largely determined the fate of efforts to formulate new policies. Although pensions constituted "middle-class entitlements" in both countries, the programmatic structures in the two cases were quite different. These structures, rather than differences in political culture, the power resources of the left, or the nature of formal institutions, account for the Thatcher government's far greater success.

Past research has often emphasized the influence of policies on administrative capacities and on the way in which reformers – especially bureaucrats – develop new policies in response to the perceived successes and failures of old ones. However, neither of these two feedback processes appear to have been important in this case. By the standards of contemporary governance, the administrative demands of running a pension system are not particularly onerous. In neither country is there any evidence that significant alternatives were ruled out because of the absence of adequate bureaucratic capacities. Nor can a political-learning argument explain the patterns of policy development in the two countries. Reform initiatives were launched by elected officials, not bureaucrats, and were dictated by Reagan and Thatcher's general hostility to public social provision rather than by any lessons learned from previous pension policies. Results differed not because policymakers learned different things from existing policies, but because those policies influenced the political costs associated with reform.

The current analysis stresses three other consequences of policy structures. First, the structures of existing policies influenced the prospects for actually mobilizing potential political resources. Existing policy structures provided opportunities for the Thatcher government to lower the visibility of important initiatives: The change in indexation methods that will gradually diminish the role of the Basic Pension and the new SERPS rules, and which have fueled a shift to private alternatives. The structure of British pensions limited the ability of program supporters to activate their political resources when existing programs were threatened.

Second, in the United States, program structures had a decisive impact on the political agenda for Social Security. Trust-fund crises, which brought attention to the issue, were generated by the specific financing provisions of existing policy. The status of the trust fund not only determined when reform was discussed, but channeled reform efforts in particular directions by determining the definition of a solution.

Finally, policy structures created lock-in effects: elaborate social and economic networks that rendered once-possible alternatives no longer feasible. The lock-in effects in American pension policy were very powerful, as the Reagan administration discovered when confronting dense networks of commitments produced by previous policy choices. Social Security's complex financial arrangements involved a series of implicit promises stretching decades into the future. Furthermore, these promises had shaped the retirement strategies of most Americans. With huge public expenditures essentially precommitted, the Reagan administration found its options extremely limited.

The multiple effects of policy feedback on the prospects for pension retrenchment seem clear. Reagan and Thatcher's efforts to reshape pension systems were strongly constrained by the structure of programs already in place. Originally produced by social pressures, extensive public-pension systems now influence political processes in fundamental ways.

4
Retrenchment in a vulnerable sector: housing policy

The Reagan and Thatcher records suggest that particular features of housing make it a fragile part of the welfare state. At the start of the 1980s, Britain and the United States had radically different housing policies, but both have proven vulnerable to retrenchment. In each case, housing programs benefiting low- and moderate-income families have been cut, targeted more sharply on the very poor, and redesigned to rely more heavily on private markets. Because the public role in housing was far greater at the outset in Britain, changes there have been particularly dramatic.

Housing's vulnerability stemmed partly from the inability of supporters to develop coherent rationales for public programs once absolute shortages of decent housing had been largely overcome. The existence of a highly popular private alternative, owner occupation, makes public programs appear inferior, and, for most of the electorate, irrelevant. Because massive subsidies to owner-occupiers are channeled almost invisibly through the tax system (largely through the mortgage-interest deduction), private housing seems more efficient than public programs financed through on-budget spending. Nevertheless, weaknesses in the rationales for public low-income housing programs cannot provide the whole answer. Indeed, mounting problems of housing affordability and the striking increase in homelessness in both countries during the 1980s could easily have suggested the need for more, rather than less, government intervention.

The distinctive characteristics of housing programs contributed to their political weakness. In both countries, it has proven possible to break up constituencies for low-income housing programs, and to pursue policies that pose limited threats to current benefit recipients yet produce substantial retrenchment over time. What makes housing unique among social programs is that it constitutes a stock of (sometimes literally) concrete assets, requiring very long-term investments. Although housing is a necessity, very few can afford to purchase their shelter outright. Various arrangements have to be made (e.g., renting, mortgages, public construction, provision, and subsidization) to spread the costs of housing over time. This characteristic created tremendous opportunities for retrenchment advocates to buy off potential losers and lower the visibility of cutbacks.

In Britain, the Thatcher government inherited a vast pool of relatively high-quality public housing, which it sold at generous discounts to sitting tenants. Because this massive transfer involved the liquidation of existing assets, it engendered no resentment from the taxpayers who were indirectly footing the bill. The enormously popular council-house sales program served as the cornerstone for a radical redesign of housing policy, providing political cover for a series of steps that on their own would have generated strong opposition. A skillful combination of carrots and sticks, which led council housing's strongest potential supporters to defect to the government's position, isolated the Labour Party's local-government allies. In the span of a decade, there was a fundamental shift in the role of local authorities, who finally presided (with greatly reduced policy autonomy) over a dwindling, increasingly marginalized population.

Change has been less dramatic in the United States, if only because of the already-limited role of government in the provision of low-income housing. Here too, however, cutbacks in public expenditure have been dramatic, and the "capital good" quality of housing has played a critical facilitative role. The main strategy of the administration was to put a "foot on the hose" of public investment, stopping the flow of new public commitments to low-income housing. The consequences of this strategy have emerged slowly, since it takes a long period for these "upstream" decisions to have an effect on housing supply. Nevertheless, this delayed impact greatly lowered the visibility of policy change, permitting cuts of a magnitude unmatched in other areas of American social policy.

THE STRUCTURE OF HOUSING POLICIES IN BRITAIN AND THE UNITED STATES

The housing policies Thatcher and Reagan inherited had significantly different scopes, distributive consequences, and bases of political support. British and American housing policies conform fairly closely to prevailing images of the countries' respective welfare states. The British government has had a major role in the provision of housing, with a strongly articulated (if not consistently practiced) egalitarian impulse. In the United States, extensions of government activity have been hotly contested. Government housing efforts on behalf of the poor have been weak and sporadic, whereas middle-class homeownership has been heavily, but far less openly, subsidized. These distinctive national paths of housing policy have helped shape the options available to the Reagan and Thatcher administrations.

Very early on, British government intervened heavily in the low-income housing market, eventually producing a level of public ownership unrivaled in Western Europe.[1] The imposition of rent controls contributed to a long, slow decline for the private rental market, and public "council" housing emerged to fill the void. By 1938, Britain already had built a million units of public housing – a level of building that the much more populous United States would not reach until the 1970s. Following World War II, alternating Labour and Conservative governments competed to expand the stock of public housing. Between 1945 and 1965, council housing accounted for 60 percent of new construction. Despite some disastrous experimentation with high-rise, inner-city development, much of the housing stock was of high quality and attracted a range of income groups.

The contrast with developments in the United States is striking.[2] Public housing, authorized in the National Housing Act of 1937, has remained marginalized. Then and later, many conservatives opposed public housing's possible competition with the private housing market and the prospect of relocating poor people, especially blacks, to more affluent neighborhoods. These opponents were able to place tight restrictions on public housing. "Equivalent elimination" provisions required the demolition of one unit of dilapidated housing for each unit built. Stringent cost limits were established, and moderate income families were excluded from projects. All these requirements enforced what would remain the dominant pattern for public housing: concentration on the very poor in already-poor central-city areas, with rigid local control over the location of new construction.

Only in the late 1960s did low-income housing initiatives really take hold. Concerns over urban unrest combined with a new strategy to increase the private sector's role in public programs made new, potentially powerful political coalitions possible. Major organizations of builders and bankers backed the Housing and Urban Development Act of 1968. Despite some reverses in the 1970s, low-income housing policy was placed in a more activist stance. By the late 1970s the core programs were public housing, which had continued a slow but steady growth, Section 8 New Construction, which subsidized private construction of low-income housing, and Section 8 Existing, a form of housing allowance. In the second half of the 1970s the total number of subsidized units increased by 50 percent, and the proportion of tenants below the poverty line who received housing subsidies had increased from one-sixth in 1976 to one-fourth by 1981.[3]

Nevertheless, the scope of American efforts to meet the housing needs of the poor remained meager. When Thatcher was elected, fully 30 percent of British households lived in public housing, whereas the figure in the United States was a little greater than 1 percent, with an additional 2–3 percent receiving allowances for privately rented housing.[4] Assistance with housing costs was available to all poor households in Britain. In the United States, that only one-quarter of potentially eligible families received housing assistance reflected the fact that housing had never become an entitlement. In both countries, housing policy included large tax subsidies to middle- and upper-income households. Housing-tax expenditures are steeply regressive. The well-off are much more likely to be homeowners, and to have larger mortgages; and because tax rates rise with income, a given deduction is also worth more to people in this group. Because subsidies to homeowners in Britain coexisted with extensive public housing, per capita expenditures on different classes were roughly comparable.[5] In the United States, tax expenditures dwarfed public spending on the housing costs of the poor. Based on the 1980 census, the National League of Cities provided estimates of the distribution of total housing subsidies, including tax expenditures. Households with incomes of less than $10,000 received an average of $23 per month, compared to $156 for those with incomes greater than $50,000. The 51 percent of American families with incomes below $20,000 received 19.5 percent of all housing subsidies, whereas the 27 percent of families making $30,000 or more received 57.7 percent of them.[6]

Not surprisingly, the American poor shouldered burdensome housing costs. These problems worsened in the late 1970s and early 1980s, as a significant pool of low-income housing was lost either to deterioration or gentrification.[7] At the same time, the number of low-income renters increased significantly. The result was a mounting problem of housing affordability. Though experts generally consider housing costs that exceed 25 percent of income to be excessive, most of America's poor, and many somewhat above the poverty line, spent much more. In 1980, 41 percent of families with annual incomes between $7,000 and $10,000 paid at least 35 percent of their income in rent, and 66 percent of those with incomes between $3,000 and $7,000 did so. Nor did such expenditures guarantee access to decent housing. Among households with less than 50 percent of median income (roughly 125 percent of the poverty line) in 1980, fully 24 percent lived in substandard housing.[8] In Britain, rents for low-income families took a much smaller proportion of income. In 1978–9, average weekly council-housing rents were equal to just 6.6 percent of average adult-male weekly earnings.[9]

These differences in housing provision reflect the different political bases of support for government housing policy in the two countries. In Britain, the massive scale of public housing, extending into the affluent sections of the working class, appeared to provide a secure political base. Nevertheless, the Labour Party had demonstrated increasing ambivalence toward council housing during the 1970s, and the incoming Conservative government's hostility was evident.

America's low-income housing programs have always been politically weak. At a few junctures, low-income housing received increased attention because advocates were able to form broader coalitions, either with middle-class recipients of assistance or with construction and development interests. Thus in the 1930s, late 1960s, and again in the mid-1970s, the United States seemed poised to greatly expand federal housing assistance. In each case, however, broad constituencies proved impossible to sustain, especially as program costs escalated.

REAGAN, THATCHER, AND HOUSING POLICY

Housing has proven to be a vulnerable sector of the welfare state. Although the overall social-policy records of Reagan and Thatcher suggest more continuity than change, both governments were able to implement substantial retrenchment in housing programs. In Britain, where the scope of the public sector made the government's success particularly striking, Thatcher's efforts were aided by the political opportunities that council-house sales created. In both countries, significant delays between cutbacks in spending and the onset of negative repercussions for program beneficiaries greatly facilitated a strategy of obfuscation.

The Thatcher government and housing policy

In housing policy the Thatcher government had a clear sense from the outset of where it wanted to go. Its goals were to limit public provision to a residual role for those who could not afford other accommodations, to expand private home ownership, and to revitalize the private rental market. The centerpiece was the government's "Right to Buy" policy, which promised sitting tenants a chance to purchase their council houses at sizable discounts from market rates. The priority placed on this initiative was indicated by the space devoted to it in the 1979 election manifesto – greater than that allocated to health, education, or social security.[10] The government's single-mindedness stemmed partly from confidence that its ambitions were popular: By 1979, 85 percent of British voters said they favored council-house sales.[11] Following her electoral triumph, Thatcher argued that "thousands of people in council houses . . . came out to support us for the first time because they wanted a chance to buy their own homes."[12]

If the government was eager to provide these benefits to tempt Labour voters, it also saw housing reform as a major opportunity to weaken the Labour Party's political base. By the end of the 1970s, local-authority-run council housing had become an important source of Labour power. In many areas, tight corporatist-style linkages had developed between local governments (usually Labour controlled), labor unions, and council estates.[13] Often the most important local service in budgetary and employment terms, public housing provided opportunities for patronage, and fertile ground for electoral mobilizations. As government policy developed during the 1980s, it became increasingly evident that one of the government's principal goals was the breakup of these Labour-dominated housing empires.

The Thatcher government stressed three initiatives: first, the promotion of owner occupation, primarily through sales of the public-housing stock; second, the restructuring of housing subsidies to encourage the further marginalization of the public sector; and third, attempts to reinvigorate the private rental sector. These policies were mutually supporting. Together, they created a package of incentives and restrictions that spurred rapid change and marginalized the public sector at a negligible political cost. Although the government's efforts were not entirely successful, in combination they have transformed British housing policy.

The "Right to Buy" and the expansion of homeownership. Conservative governments have long favored owner occupation, and the Thatcher government articulated this view with particular clarity. At the heart of efforts to promote the expansion of homeownership has been the sale of council housing to tenants.

Although local authorities had been permitted to sell council housing in the 1970s, sales were relatively low. The Housing Act of 1980 replaced this voluntary sales policy with a "Right to Buy." Tenants who had lived in council housing for at least three years would have the right to purchase their housing at a discount, with the promise of a twenty-four-year mortgage. Discounts would rise to as much as 50 percent of the property's market value for long-term residents. Since 1980, some limited restrictions on the Right to Buy have been removed, and maximum discounts were raised to 60 percent (and later to 70 percent for apartment residents).[14]

The Right to Buy initiative has been astonishingly successful. In the course of a decade, almost 1.5 million dwellings – a fifth of all council housing – were sold. Although the sale rate has peaked, such purchases continue to considerably outpace new council-housing construction. Revenues from these sales reached the staggering sum of £17.5 billion for the period 1979–89, constituting almost half of all receipts from the government's heralded privatization initiatives. The government's other low-cost homeownership programs, which provided "shared ownership" subsidies for those who could not afford to buy outright, and financial incentives for local authorities to renovate unoccupied properties for sale, produced perhaps another fifty thousand new homeowners.[15] Between 1978 and 1988 the rate of owner occupation rose from 54.7 percent to 65.4 percent, whereas the council-tenancy rate dropped from 31.7 percent to 24.9 percent.[16] Roughly three-quarters of the growth of owner occupation during the period of Conservative governance came from council-house sales.[17]

In pursuing the Right to Buy initiative the Thatcher government confronted the welfare state on uniquely favorable terrain. Instead of imposing losses on concentrated groups of voters, the government was providing sizable benefits for a large section of the electorate. Although there has been much dispute over the size of the electoral gains derived from council-house sales – and there is reason to doubt that the consequences were very pronounced – there is no question that the policy was a vote winner.[18]

The Right to Buy constituted a massive transfer to one fortunate generation of council-house tenants. In this case, it was the losses associated with the policy that were uncertain and diffuse. One group of losers was the taxpayers who had, in previous decades, paid for the accumulation of a sizable public housing stock that was now being liquidated at bargain prices. This loss was difficult to identify, however, especially when the sizable capital receipts from sales meant that taxes could be held down during the 1980s. Also among the losers were those not yet in council housing or in marginal residences who might have hoped eventually to move into better dwellings. This "loss," however, was abstract in the extreme. Few of those in the more squalid estates were likely to see council housing as a concept worth defending. Polls showed that even after sales had peaked, remaining council-house tenants – most of whom had little prospect of becoming purchasers – remained strongly in favor of the Right to Buy policy.[19]

In addition to isolating local councils from potential supporters, the government took firm steps to assure that local authorities did not frustrate its intentions. As will be discussed later in this section, changes in subsidies have made local authorities heavily dependent on sales revenues to maintain their remaining stock. Sale receipts funded 70 percent to 80 percent of local-authority capital expenditure in the late 1980s, compared with 25 percent or less a decade earlier.[20] The 1980 act also gave the Department of Environment the power to intervene directly if it believed that a local council was hindering sales. Central government officials could be sent to take control of the administration of the Right to Buy from recalcitrant authorities. The threat – and actual use – of this power undermined local opposition.[21]

As the weakness of its political position became clear, the Labour Party eventually caved in on council-house sales as well. Initially, Labour had taken a hard line, promising in its 1983 manifesto to restore local-council discretion over sales while eliminating discounts. Councils would also be empowered to repurchase homes already sold. This stance was widely seen as an indication of how out of touch with the electorate Labour had become by the early 1980s, and as one of a number of positions contributing to Labour's 1983 electoral debacle. As part of the general move to the center following Kinnock's replacement of Michael Foote as leader of the Labour Party, the policy of opposition to council-house sales was summarily dropped.

Confident of strong backing from council tenants, and with local authorities and the Labour Party on the defensive, the government kept the sales policy moving steadily forward throughout the 1980s. The positive inducements to purchase were evident. Beyond the intrinsic appeals of home ownership were the massive discounts and the opportunity to receive government tax subsidies in the form of mortgage-interest tax relief. With less publicity, however, the government was buttressing these incentives with a harsher prod to action: a radical reform of housing subsidies. Government policies raised the cost of council housing to all but the poorest, further encouraging anyone who could afford to get out of the public sector to do so.

From "bricks and mortar" to people: the reform of housing subsidies. The dramatic success of the Right to Buy initiative has obscured other changes in housing policy that have had profound, if less visible, effects. Indeed, the popularity of sales provided political cover for a series of steps that doubtlessly would have generated fierce opposition under other circumstances. The government made a concerted effort to shift public spending for housing "from bricks and mortar to people." Where traditionally the bulk of expenditures for housing consisted of government subsidies to local authorities to operate and maintain council housing, during the 1980s expenditures were shifted to means-tested housing benefits available to both public- and private-sector renters. These changes were promoted as a way to better target government resources, but they were clearly part of a broader strategy to marginalize council housing. Shifting subsidies from buildings to people had two critical effects: It gradually diminished the scope of local authorities' policy autonomy, and it made council housing less affordable for all but the very poor. If the Right to Buy constituted the carrot in the government's residualization strategy, subsidy reform was the stick.

In 1979, central-government grants covered the bulk of current expenses for local-authority housing, whereas the rest came from rents and local property ("rates") taxation. The government initially focused on restructuring central grants to encourage lower levels of local-authority spending.[22] Although the Thatcher government emphasized its fights with "high spending" (almost always Labour-controlled) local authorities, it was in fact pursuing a more general reduction in central-government subsidies to council housing. There has been a sharp decline in central government grants since 1979. This decline was partly designed to force local authorities to raise rents, and indeed between 1979 and 1984 council-house rents increased by about 40 percent in real terms.[23]

However, this strategy soon produced diminishing returns. As subsidies for most authorities fell to zero, the Thatcher government lost this source of leverage over their policies. Whereas 95 percent of authorities were within the subsidy system in 1981–2, only 25 percent were by 1987–8.[24] With rising council-house rents, declines in central-government grants were partly offset by increasing public expenditures on Housing Benefit (see later in this section). Furthermore, local authorities were often able to replace the lost subsidies with revenues from asset sales and local taxes.

The Thatcher government eventually moved to constrain these revenue sources as well. To encourage council-house sales, authorities had been allowed to plow sale revenues back into investment. Because this permitted continued spending, however, the government gradually reduced the proportion of accumulated assets that could be spent in a given year from 50 percent to 20 percent. Thatcher also pursued a bitter struggle over local taxation. Local authorities relied on domestic and nondomestic rates (property taxes on households and businesses, respectively) to finance spending, including housing expenditures. In a series of highly controversial steps, the government sought to bring local revenue (and hence expenditure) under its central control.[25] The 1984 Rates Bill introduced "rate capping," permitting the central government to set limits on a local authority's total rate levy. In its third term, the government moved further, replacing rates with what it called a "community charge" and its critics termed a "poll tax." The highly unpopular flat-rate tax for local expenditures contributed heavily to Thatcher's eventual ouster, and John Major quickly retreated from it. However, even with the later moderation of policy, the ability of local governments to raise funds for activities like housing has been significantly circumscribed.

With tax reforms restricting local revenues, the government also moved directly to insure that local taxes would not be spent on council housing. The Housing Act of 1988 banned contributions from local taxes to local authorities' housing budgets.[26] Probably more important, the act broadened the definition of central subsidization to include the Department of Social Security's expenditures on Housing Benefit. This redefinition instantly brought local authorities who had long ago lost other forms of subsidy back under the control of central government. The Thatcher government was again in a position to pressure local authorities to increase rents and facilitate sales.

The impact of the redefinition of subsidization reflects the expanded role of Housing Benefit, which was the other major component of subsidization policy in the 1980s. Housing Benefit is a means-tested form of assistance paid to reduce the housing costs of low-income renters. Its dramatic growth was part of the broad Thatcher government strategy of replacing subsidies on buildings with individualized allowances, linked to income and strictly targeted. At first glance, Housing Benefit's track record in the 1980s suggests a flourishing program. Spending on it doubled in real terms between 1978–9 and 1988–9.[27] The reality, however, is one of a program that has been strikingly vulnerable to spending cuts. Rising numbers of beneficiaries and outlays reflect a number of trends, many of them resulting from government policy: mounting unemployment, increasing poverty, a growing pensioner population and higher council-house rents. All of these increased demands on Housing Benefit, which would have grown much more significantly had it not been for repeated government initiatives to curb expenditures.

Cuts have fallen almost entirely on those with incomes above the poverty line, mainly through a sharp tightening of eligibility. The "needs allowance" that limits participation in the program has not been adjusted in line with changes in earnings. More important, the "tapers" that determine how rapidly benefit is withdrawn as income increases have become much less generous. Because of the complexity of the system, the magnitude of the government's cutbacks are difficult to quantify. Hills and Mullings, however, provide the example of a single person older than twenty-five paying a rent of £30 per week. In 1989, this claimant would have lost all benefits at an income of slightly greater than £100 per week; by contrast, in 1982–3 this would not have happened until income reached almost £200. Although the earlier system would have limited housing costs across the range of low incomes to a maximum of about 20 percent of net income, the newer system allowed housing costs to rise to more than 33 percent.[28]

Why has Housing Benefit been so vulnerable to cutbacks? The government justified its cuts by noting the rapid expansion of Housing Benefit payments. With benefits said to be creeping up the income scale, government ministers called the program out of control. In fact, rising outlays resulted from increasing unemployment and poverty combined with explicit shifts in government policy. Benefits to the working population accounted for a very small portion of Housing Benefit expenditures – £140 million in 1982–3.[29] Nonetheless, rising expenditures provided some cover for retrenchment policies. The government has also utilized incremental tactics: Tapers were increased once in 1983 and twice each in 1984, 1985, 1987, and 1988. On a number of occasions, the government attempted to buy off dissent by somewhat scaling back planned reductions. In one case, it assuaged opponents by announcing a commission to review Housing Benefit. Ironically, the result of the review (part of the Fowler initiative discussed in Chapter 3), was a massive additional cut in housing allowances.

These techniques by themselves nevertheless seem insufficient to account for the government's success. As Chapter 5 indicates, no other means-tested program has proven so vulnerable to cutbacks, despite the availability of identical tactics. Similar efforts to cut subsidies to "bricks and mortar," increase council-house rents, and promote the use of means-tested assistance had been introduced by the Heath government in the early 1970s, but were greeted with intense popular resistance.[30] What distinguished the efforts of the 1980s was the ability to combine these unpopular measures with the extremely popular policy of council-house sales. The group that was most adversely affected by subsidy reform – better-off council tenants – was divided. Those who exercised the right to buy had no desire to complain about the government's initiatives. The careful integration of negative and positive incentives in housing policy allowed radical reform without high political costs.

Subsidy reform fueled the residualization of the public housing sector. The combination of declining general subsidies, rising council rents, and mounting reliance on increasingly targeted housing allowances created tremendous pressure for those who could afford to leave council housing to do so. Those above the cutoff for Housing Benefit received declining assistance with their housing costs. Indeed, the 1988 reforms, which limited central-government payments of Housing Benefit if local-authority housing expenditures were considered too high, meant that the rent payments of better-off council-house tenants might be used to subsidize those of their poorer neighbors. Along with the positive in ducements provided by sale discounts and mortgage-tax relief, these negative incentives have generated a steady process of residualization as the more affluent tenants have moved into owner-occupied housing. The Thatcher government's policies generated a "tipping" effect in which the exit of some from the public sector encouraged others to do so.[31] As moderate-income groups with the option left public housing, its image as "welfare" housing grew, furthering the incentives for others to leave. The resulting residualization has been dramatic. Despite the tightening of eligibility rules, the share of council tenants requiring Housing Benefit assistance increased from 40 percent to 65 percent between 1978–9 and 1987–8. Within the bottom income quintile, homeownership dropped from 44 percent in 1979 to 29 percent in 1985, whereas council-house tenancy increased from 43 percent to 57 percent. Among those in the top two quintiles, council-house tenancy dropped from 24.5 percent to 9.5 percent in the same period.[32]

Reviving the private rental sector? Despite tremendous successes, efforts to promote homeownership were losing momentum by the late 1980s. Even with generous discounts, only a limited number of people could afford to buy their council houses. The cost of increasing tax expenditures guaranteed sharp cabinet opposition to further expansions of mortgage-interest relief. Studies of sales confirm that the most affluent tenants had already exercised their right to buy, and the most desirable units had been purchased. Apartment dwellings, for example, made up 30 percent of council-house units, but have accounted for only 3 percent of sales.[33] Even the most ambitious projections for the Right to Buy program suggested that it would leave the majority of council housing untouched.

In short, the government had hit a ceiling on the level of owner occupation achievable without unaffordable levels of subsidization. Furthering the government's goals now required that private renting replace public renting. To achieve this, the government tried to pursue the same two-track strategy used in the pension sector (see Chapter 3): increase the attractiveness and availability of private alternatives while limiting the public sector's ability to provide a quality service. However, unlike the other components of Conservative housing policy, efforts to turn around the private rental market were a disappointment. Despite trying one initiative after another, the private rental market's long slide continued throughout the decade.

The government placed much of the blame for the private sector's erosion on rent control. Although some free-market advocates urged an immediate suspension of rent controls, the government recognized that such a step would be highly unpopular. Wisely, the Conservatives chose an incremental strategy that posed only a limited threat to current tenants. The government agreed to maintain controls on existing rentals while trying to increase the freedom of landlords to raise rents to market levels on new ones. The 1980 Housing Act introduced "assured" and "short-hold" tenancies to encourage such rentals, and the 1988 Housing Act further eased rent restrictions.[34] There is, however, little evidence to suggest that these steps will be successful. The 1980 act had disappointing consequences, as the number of private rentals dropped by an additional 550,000 in the first six years of the Thatcher government.[35] The new legislation's incentives seem insufficient to dramatically alter the situation. A. D. H. Crook has summarized the dilemma facing the private rental market: "Landlords do not get the rents they want. If they did, most tenants could not afford the rent."[36] The private rental market's weakness stems only in part from rent regulation. The structure of subsidies to owner occupiers makes renting an unlikely choice for those who can afford to buy. Those who cannot buy will have difficulty paying profitable rents without public subsidization.

The government's failure to coax new private investment into the rental market also reflects a more fundamental difficulty. Even if subsidies were provided to make renting profitable, fear that a future Labour government would reestablish rent controls makes private investment in rental housing an unattractive prospect. Here, the distinctiveness of housing policy has been a stumbling block for conservative reformers. The "capital good" quality of housing, with its requirements for long-term investment, has facilitated certain reforms, especially the crucial innovation of council-house sales. However, that same quality acts as a deterrent for private rental investment, particularly in Britain's highly centralized political system, in which a Labour government could easily reimpose rent controls. The government's latest effort to substantial tax subsidies to investors as part of the 1988 Housing Act was only one more in a long series of failed government efforts to turn things around.

Somewhat more promising were the government's efforts to expand the role of housing associations, nonprofit providers of rental housing that represent a middle ground between council housing and the private market. From the government's perspective, housing associations had significant advantages – the most important being that they were not run by local authorities and were less implicated in the old local corporatist networks. Their small size also made them heavily dependent on central government subsidization for support. During the 1980s, the government steered its remaining support for new construction increasingly toward housing associations. The housing-association share of public construction increased from roughly one-sixth in 1979 to more than one-third in 1988, though this was more the result of the precipitous decline of council-house construction than of any boom in housing-association building plans.[37] However, housing associations faced many of the same limitations as the private market: Deep subsidies would be required to allow them to remain financially viable while offering apartments for rent. Despite the government's efforts, housing associations are still dwarfed by both the council-housing and private-rental sectors.

Having failed to establish positive inducements to reinvigorate renting outside of council housing, the government has increasingly sought to erode council housing's role directly as a way of generating demand for its favored alternatives. As William Waldegrave, minister of housing, announced in 1987, "I can see no argument for generalised new build[ing] by councils, now or in the future. ... The next great push after the right to buy should be to get rid of the state as a big landlord and bring housing back to the community."[38] The government's white paper for the 1988 Housing Act argued that council housing was rife with bureaucratic inefficiencies, and inhibited consumer choice. It suggested the need to turn local authorities' role into a "strategic one, identifying housing needs and demands, encouraging innovative methods of provision by other bodies to meet such needs, maximising the use of private finance, and encouraging the new interest in the revival of the independent rented sector."[39]

Comments by government ministers were less subtle. Waldegrave, in a well-publicized address at the annual conference of the Institute of Housing, spoke of the need "to get people off the most deadly of all social drugs, the drug of dependence – on the state, or bureaucracy, or whoever. ... It is essential to introduce a much greater element of choice into the rented sector."[40]

The government's goal seemed to be nothing less than the breakup of local-authority housing empires. Part of the plan involved the subsidy reforms already outlined, which were designed to further the residualization process. The government also hoped to repeat its Right to Buy success by transferring huge blocks of council housing to the private and nonprofit sectors. The Housing Act of 1988 allowed council tenants to replace the local authority with a private landlord, and encouraged local authorities to voluntarily spin off their housing programs as new housing associations. In addition, the legislation created Housing Action Trusts (HATs) – government-sponsored agencies with the power to assume ownership and management of the most run-down inner-city council estates.

Much of this seemed a heavy-handed but potentially powerful assault on remaining council housing. The proposal's administrative complexities were widely criticized, as were provisions that biased the procedures against local authorities. For example, tenants who did not vote in referenda were to be counted as votes in favor of a change to private management. Observers suggested the possibility of another million residences being removed from the public sector.[41] Little of this came about; the government seemed to have been carried away by its own rhetoric about the horrors of council housing. In fact, tenants had little incentive to opt for the private sector and good reason to fear that the result would be higher rents. An extensive advertising campaign for "tenants' choice" fell on deaf ears. In one London case, a highly touted private company received the support of only 4 out of 217 tenants. By early 1990 only 11 of 455 district councils had carried out ballots that resulted in a yes vote, generating a net transfer of only 50,000 units out of council housing.[42]

Thus, the establishment of an affordable alternative to low-income public housing in Britain remains the unfulfilled aspiration of Conservative housing policy. Nevertheless, alongside this setback stand some remarkable successes. Although council housing remains in place, it has been thoroughly residualized, and the government has significantly expanded the scope of homeownership. These changes will be difficult to reverse. As the discussion of pensions in Chapter 3 indicated, privatization can be self-reinforcing. The movement of households from the public to the private sector strengthens the constituency for private-sector subsidies. If tax expenditures for homeowners proved a difficult target for the 1974–9 Labour government, these subsidies will be even less vulnerable now that a significantly greater share of moderate-income families have become owner occupiers. Any such reform would be damaging to a part of the electorate that Labour can scarcely afford to alienate if it hopes to achieve a parliamentary majority.[43]

If the Conservatives have succeeded in weakening public housing, there are nevertheless serious problems with its overall privatization strategy. Most critical has been the failure to reinvigorate the private-rented sector. Owner occupation cannot easily be expanded further, and with the public sector's ability to meet existing needs strictly limited, the shortcomings of current housing policy are becoming more visible. Homelessness has risen rapidly in the past few years. The number of households accepted by local authorities as homeless – a conservative estimate of the problem's seriousness – increased from 60,000 in 1978 to about 130,000 in 1987. At the same time, the public sector's ability to meet these pressing demands has been reduced. The government revealed its determination to limit public housing regardless of the social costs. It chose to house homeless families in squalid and expensive Bed and Breakfast hotels – an option that is both inferior to and more costly than new council housing.[44]

It is difficult to predict how this impasse will be resolved. Unlike the case of pensions, where the Conservatives created a credible private substitute for public earnings-related pensions, the lack of private-sector options has hindered housing reforms. As in most social-policy domains, John Major's treatment of housing issues has revealed a degree of moderation. He acknowledged that "for the foreseeable future, council housing will remain the tenure for many people," and promised to preserve its quality.[45] However, even though a beleaguered council-housing sector is likely to remain, it will have a greatly impaired capacity to supply inexpensive, relatively high quality housing with limited stigma. The Conservatives' housing policy represents a striking example of retrenchment success.

The Reagan administration's housing policy

In 1981, low-income housing programs in the United States had just completed a period of significant growth. President Carter had increased Housing and Urban Development (HUD) outlays and shifted federal activity toward new construction. The last Carter budget reduced these efforts somewhat and diminished the emphasis on new construction, but program activity was higher than at any time except the early 1970s. By 1981, the long-term federal budget obligation (money authorized but not yet spent) was $250 billion, compared with less than $90 billion in 1975.[46]

Believing that this commitment was excessive, Reagan advanced a number of initiatives to cut back federal housing efforts: a virtual halt to new construction, a restructured, voucher-centered system of housing subsidies, and finally (in a conscious imitation of the Thatcher government), a plan to privatize much of the public housing stock. All of these reforms were clearly signaled in the report of the President's Commission on Housing, released in 1982. Unlike the Social Security Commission (see Chapter 3), the housing commission was dominated by those who shared the administration's outlook.[47] Beyond emphasizing the need to reduce federal involvement in housing, the commission's main proposal was to make housing vouchers the primary instrument of low-income housing assistance.[48] The Reagan administration suggested that direct subsidies to low-income households were far more efficient than government construction programs.

Reagan's radical plans provoked broad-based opposition that nevertheless ultimately proved weak.[49] Political and economic events of the early 1980s demolished the traditional subgovernment relations between interest groups, HUD, and the relevant congressional committees. Among interest groups, sustained opposition to retrenchment came from those with a core attachment to low-income housing, such as the National Association of Housing and Redevelopment Officials (NAHRO) and the Low-Income Housing Coalition. Although not negligible, the resources of these groups were limited. Traditionally, they had drawn support from other groups with a more marginal commitment to housing for the poor, including powerful housing interests (realtors, developers, and bankers) and local and state governments. Indeed, the basis of the flurry of federal activity in the late 1960s and 1970s had been the design of policies to enhance the limited interest of these powerful groups in low-income housing. This strategy proved difficult to sustain in a climate of austerity. The private housing market was in the midst of its worst downturn since the depression, and a range of public programs crucial to state and local governments were under attack from the Reagan administration.[50] With many of their more central concerns in jeopardy, former allies were at best likely to see low-income housing as a low priority for which they could spare little attention. At worst, they came to see low-income housing as a rival in a struggle for dwindling resources.

At the same time, HUD ceased to be a source of support for low-income housing advocates. By all accounts, policy-making authority over the agency remained in the hands of the Office of Management and Budget and the White House. HUD secretary Samuel Pierce was a weak figure, disinclined to fight for more funding in any case. The administration used its control over personnel policy to cut staff and concentrate authority in the hands of political appointees in Washington. From 1980 to 1986, permanent, full-time staff in HUD was reduced by 21 percent, including a 38 percent cutback in the Washington office.[51] Those out of step with the new policy outlook were transferred or cut out of decision making, while top positions were given to individuals with no background in housing. Numerous reports suggested that longtime staff members were demoralized by the agency leadership's commitment to scaling back federal housing efforts.[52]

The final components of the housing subgovernment, the relevant congressional committees, were also in a somewhat weakened position. Traditionally strong support in the House, based on a long-standing tradition of committee partisanship and the continuation of urban Democrats in leadership positions, remained.[53] However, Republican control of the Senate meant that (especially before 1986) Congress itself was divided. Although less hostile than the Reagan administration, the Senate majority was open to many of the criticisms of existing policy. Even more important, the institutional position of House Democrats was weaker in housing than in other arenas. Unlike most of the components of the American welfare state, housing was not an entitlement. Entitlement programs must be funded at established levels unless new legislation reduces benefits or tightens eligibility rules. In this context, a key committee can often play an important blocking role. In housing policy, however, it was insufficient to simply deflect proposed reforms. Positive majorities had to be fashioned to provide continuing authorizations for housing. Given Senate skepticism and the ever-looming prospect of a Reagan veto, the nonentitlement status of housing gave retrenchment advocates a significant institutional advantage.

The dismantling of supply-side programs. The administration was most successful in limiting new construction. Congress proved to be relatively sympathetic to Reagan's concern with the rising costs of Section 8 New Construction. Building new units required roughly twice the budget authority needed to subsidize an existing unit, and budgetary strain made this consideration compelling.[54] Although the president's proposals met some congressional opposition, especially in the House, advocates of new construction were clearly fighting a rearguard action. Construction programs were in a highly unfavorable position in the early 1980s. As in Britain, that these programs required enormous up-front expenditures while their benefits were delayed created significant opportunities for retrenchment. Cutbacks would have no effect on the low-income housing stock for many years. The desertion of low-income housing's intermittent but powerful allies in the for-profit sector made matters worse. Skyrocketing interest rates and a deepening recession were decimating the entire housing industry. In this context, realtors, construction interests, and banks had neither the time nor inclination to come to the aid of housing for the poor. Forced to choose between a range of unpalatable cuts, it is not surprising that Congress found construction reductions the least distasteful.

After 1981, Congress generally provided more funds than Reagan requested, but reductions in construction were dramatic. By 1983, the Section 8 New Construction program was eliminated, and public-housing starts had been drastically reduced. Because many projects were already authorized and "in the pipeline," it took some time before Reagan administration policies began to affect the actual number of subsidized housing starts. By 1986, however, starts had fallen more than 80 percent from the 1982 level.

The reform of demand-side subsidies. As in Britain, cutbacks in construction were part of an overall shift from subsidizing "bricks and mortar" to subsidizing people. At the same time, conservatives sought to reform subsidies to households by cutting back on the level of assistance, targeting assistance on only the poorest households, and restructuring allowances to more closely conform to market mechanisms. In all these respects, the administration's efforts met with considerable success, although cutbacks were much less severe than they were for construction programs.

The Reagan administration sought to reduce subsidies for assisted households. In 1981, Congress agreed to raise the tenant's share of rent payments from 25 percent to 30 percent of income. Besides lowering the level of subsidization, this made assisted housing less attractive for those with higher incomes. The policy, along with legislation to limit to 10 percent the proportion of beneficiaries with incomes above half of the local median income, met the administration's goal of targeting housing benefits on the very poor.

Reagan requested further subsidy reductions in his 1983 budget, which proposed the inclusion of food stamps in income calculations and a reduction in the fair market rent (the rent estimate used to calculate government subsidies).

Combined with the increased tenant payments passed in 1981, the proposals would have reduced average subsidies per household by 44 percent. An average participating household with two parents and two children would have seen its annual benefit cut from $2,804 to $1,459. Although Congress rejected these sharp reductions, the 1981 changes alone represented a cut of 14 percent.[55]

A major component of the administration's subsidy reform was a concerted push to introduce housing vouchers. The voucher proposals resembled Section 8 Existing allowances, but contained a number of important changes. Under the administration's plan, the government would pay the difference between 30 percent of a tenant's income and a payment standard equal to 40 percent of average area rents. Unlike Section 8 Existing, which required tenants to find apartments meeting a specified rent level, the voucher scheme would allow tenants to rent any apartment meeting minimum quality standards. If rents were less than the payment standard, a tenant would pocket the savings; if rents exceeded the standard, the tenant would have to pay the difference. The administration in 1983 proposed that 120,000 families already receiving assistance be transferred to the voucher system and that 45,000 new families be added to the program.

The Reagan administration's arguments echoed those that housing analysts had used in the 1970s to advocate aid for housing consumption rather than production. Vouchers would be less expensive than new construction, and would allow recipients greater latitude in choosing housing and in trading off housing needs against other possible uses of their limited income. Given that many analysts shared the conviction that the housing problems of the poor derived more from lack of affordability than from unavailability, the administration seemed to have a strong case.

Vouchers were touted as a new way of meeting the need for affordable housing, but a significant part of their appeal to the administration was clearly related to their low cost and relatively restricted intervention in the market economy. It is at least possible that the administration also saw vouchers as a transition toward a complete retreat from low-income housing initiatives. As HUD secretary Pierce pointed out in a 1981 interview, "We hope that by 1984 or '85, that we will have interest rates down enough that it will stimulate housing so that we don't have to use the voucher system. We hope that maybe we'll even get out of that." He acknowledged that one advantage of the short contract terms of vouchers was that they could be ended quickly.[56]

The administration's proposals met significant congressional resistance. Opponents suggested that there were a number of flaws in the voucher strategy. Despite evidence from voucher experiments, for example, housing advocates worried that vouchers would simply drive up the cost of rental housing, leaving tenants no better off. Since vouchers carried no ceiling in tenant payments, in theory all the cost of vouchers could simply be passed on to landlords in the form of higher rents. In cities with very tight rental markets, as many as half of all voucher participants were unable to locate apartments that they could afford even with the subsidy.

Nevertheless, the primary objections to vouchers were political. Skepticism regarding the administration's intentions tempered sympathy for the voucher concept. The Reagan proposals were widely viewed as part of a strategy aimed at cutting the federal role in low-income housing. The short term of voucher authorizations (five years compared to fifteen for Section 8 Existing) and the relative ease of changing the payment standards on which vouchers were based could make the program susceptible to cuts. By focusing housing policy on direct payments to the very poor, vouchers could strip low-income housing of the broader political base needed to maintain its long-term position. Relatively small groups of producers with a high stake in a program are generally far easier to organize than consumers.[57]

In light of these concerns, Congress moved very slowly to embrace the voucher concept. Initially, only 15,000 vouchers were authorized as part of a demonstration project. Over time, however, there were signs that the voucher system was becoming more firmly established. Congress provided permanent authorization for vouchers in the Housing and Community Development Act of 1987, and since then the program has grown considerably. In many respects, however, the debate over vouchers masked the administration's substantial success in reorienting government spending on low-income housing. The differences between Section 8 Existing certificates and vouchers are far less significant than their common reliance on assistance targeted toward renters rather than toward the expansion or upgrading of the low-income housing stock. The struggle between construction support and housing allowances was resolved largely on the administration's terms.

Privatizing public housing? Although vouchers were the administration's main innovation, the president's housing commission also advocated steps to sell off much of the public-housing stock. This third Reagan initiative to restructure low-income housing policy was less significant and less successful, but it highlighted an interesting contrast between housing policy in the United States and in Britain, and it indicated again the importance of preexisting policies. The plan to encourage the sale of American public housing to tenants was a conscious imitation of Thatcher's initiatives. Homeownership initiatives for the poor were a staple of conservative rhetoric throughout the eighties. With the administration's backing, Republican congressman Jack Kemp introduced legislation to encourage such sales, with units offered at 25 percent of market value. Meanwhile, HUD begun an experimental program of tenant purchases.[58] When Kemp became secretary of HUD following Bush's 1988 election, his aspirations expanded considerably, floating the possibility of a million public-housing tenants becoming homeowners.[59]

Given the nature of American public housing, the idea that expanding homeownership to existing tenants could be a major component of public policy was extraordinary. A quick glance at American public housing suggests the implausibility of duplicating the Thatcher government's privatization program. American low-income housing policy has generally excluded all but the very poor, a practice that Reagan's policies reinforced. According to estimates from the National Association of Housing and Redevelopment Officials, the average public-housing resident had a household income of $6,539 in 1988, or about 25 percent of the national mean.[60] Even at Kemp's very generous terms, few of these tenants could afford such a purchase. In addition, the elderly, for whom purchase is unlikely to be attractive, make up almost half of public-housing residents. Finally, whereas much of Britain's public housing consists of detached residences, the American stock is mostly apartment buildings, which are much harder to sell to residents. Warren Lundquist, assistant HUD secretary for public and Indian housing, estimated that only 20,000 to 30,000 of the nation's 1.2 million public housing units could be sold to tenants.[61]

Another privatization option was the development of tenant-management schemes, which the Reagan administration hoped could be based on a combination of public and private investment. At Kemp's urging, these initiatives later became a major component of Bush's housing proposals. Again, however, conservative rhetoric far exceeded realistic prospects for tenant-management schemes. The development of the Kenilworth project in Washington, D.C., is instructive. Kenilworth became a showcase for the potential of tenant-management initiatives, and meetings with its charismatic director, Kimi Gray, were a mandatory photo opportunity for conservative housing reformers. Creating Kenilworth's public image, however, required massive renovation subsidies that made it one of the most expensive housing projects in American history. Similar renovations for the rest of the public-housing stock would require outlays of $70 billion.[62]

Proposals for privatization were not realistic bases for a low-income housing policy, but they provided conservatives with a positive program to counter the negative image associated with budget cuts. In a climate in which living testament to the crisis of housing affordability was visible on the streets of every American city, the ability to proclaim a new agenda was politically useful. Unlike in Britain, however, privatization plans could do little to offer tangible, positive inducements to potential members of a retrenchment coalition. For a brief period, however, the Reagan administration was able to achieve a form of "retrenchment patronage" from the innocently named Moderate Rehabilitation program, which represented a small part of HUD's shrinking budget.

Retrenchment as patronage: conservatives and the HUD scandals. After almost a decade of quiet but extremely effective retrenchment, the Reagan administration's housing policies suddenly attracted intense scrutiny in 1989 following a string of revelations about influence peddling and fraud in HUD. The "HUD scandals" included a range of activities such as widespread defaults in some loan-guarantee programs, embezzlement, and kickbacks from developers. Losses to taxpayers from the agency's actions were estimated as high as $6 billion.[63] Politically most significant, however, were indications that even as HUD was overseeing the drastic curtailment of federal-housing activity, it managed to create a powerful Republican patronage machine. Having managed to centralize decision making over the Moderate Rehabilitation program, which offered generous subsidies to private developers undertaking rehabilitation projects, political appointees within the department steered project grants to influential Republicans acting as developers or consultants. In one notorious case, a developer paid former secretary of the interior James Watt, who had no experience in housing policy, several hundred thousand dollars for a few phone calls to Pierce. Senate Majority leader George Mitchell decried the use of HUD as "a political slush fund." Deborah Gore Dean, the assistant to Sam Pierce who found herself at the heart of the controversy, acknowledged that the Moderate Rehabilitation program "was set up as a political program" and "run in a political manner."[64]

There was a close connection between the Reagan administration's overall retrenchment strategy for housing and the HUD scandals. Retrenchment contributed to the scandal's development in a very direct way. Until 1983, Moderate Rehabilitation funds had been allocated to each state by formula. As the number of funded units fell from 20,000 a year to roughly 6,600, HUD argued that a broad formula would spread limited resources too thinly. The agency asked for, and received, discretion in the selection of projects. Ironically, the very reduction in the size of the program was turned into a mechanism for expanding the scope of patronage efforts.

The scandal also demonstrates the heightened opportunities retrenchment advocates possess when program structures enhance the capacity for autonomous agency activity. Checks on HUD's politicization during the 1980s were minimal. As already noted, HUD was overhauled in the 1980s, with power concentrated in the hands of strong critics of government activism. As two close observers commented:

The Reagan HUD political appointees in leadership positions were . . . ideologically hostile to the very programs they were responsible for managing. Over eight years, the hostility to policy and program of top management in Washington penetrated to many career appointments in program and field office staffs. Such appointments were made in openings created by systematic attempts to remove from office many career professionals who were experienced and dedicated to the programs they were managing . . . Politically ideological appointments, deliberately induced career staff turnover (transfers, RIFs) and new career hires re-populated the HUD management structure from top to bottom.[65]

At the same time, retrenchment pressures put the squeeze on developers, heightening competition for scarce subsidies and probably fueling resort to back-channel strategies. Finally, retrenchment also left congressional defenders of housing in an all-consuming effort to protect housing outlays, diverting attention from careful oversight of specific programs.

The consequences of delayed cutbacks: retrenchment and the preservation crisis. While discussions of influence peddling produced headlines, a second issue competed for the attention of housing policymakers during the late 1980s: the crisis of preserving units of publicly subsidized low-income housing. Two different categories of housing were affected. The first consisted of privately owned units that had received public subsidization in return for a promise to keep them available to low-income households for a specified time. These units were reaching the point where developers would be eligible to prepay their mortgages and convert them to more profitable use. The second category included many units run by nonprofit organizations that faced the expiration of operating subsidies. Many developments were expected to go bankrupt in the absence of renewed funding.

The size of these twin problems was staggering.[66] In essence, the federal government now confronted the consequences of lagged cutbacks. The extended time commitments involved in housing obligations meant that the consequences of low investment in the early 1980s were delayed, but required massive outlays when the bill finally began to come due. The nature of housing policy made it possible to create a "creeping crisis." Increasingly, policymakers would find themselves running hard to stay in place.

The dire warnings of some housing activists that the crisis would precipitate a full-scale federal retreat from low-income housing have not materialized. Although it took several years to work out an accommodation on details, the Bush administration accepted that funding needed to be provided to preserve these low-income units. Nonetheless, the implications for housing policy are substantial. Funds to prevent the loss of existing stock compete with outlays for new initiatives. In combination with pressure generated by the budget deficit, these fiscal realities have helped lock in the Reagan administration's radical reforms. A number of developments in the late 1980s had given housing activists cause for hope – the rise of homelessness as an issue, the arrival of a somewhat more moderate administration, and Jack Kemp's high-profile promises to return HUD to a more activist stance. However, intense competition for scarce financial resources has made it difficult to translate more activist rhetoric into substantial policy initiatives.

U.S. housing policy after a decade of retrenchment. During the 1980s, the president and Congress argued over the size and shape of low-income housing policy. The House vigorously opposed Reagan's initiatives, although the Senate was somewhat more sympathetic. The substantial gaps between the positions of all three institutional actors prevented the formation of any coherent policy. Indeed, after 1980, Congress repeatedly failed to provide authorization for housing expenditures through normal channels.

Policy gradually drifted toward the administration's position. Outlays stabilized while budget authority, which provides a much better indicator of policy, plummeted. Congress consistently allocated far more money to low-income housing than the president requested, but there was nonetheless a drastic curtailment of initiatives. Changes in the structure of assistance were as significant as the budget reductions. New construction was virtually eliminated, with budget authority targeted on rehabilitation, housing allowances, or the new voucher program. The number of new units assisted has dropped steadily. Budget authority declined far more rapidly because the most expensive programs – those involving new construction – were most sharply scaled back.

By the end of 1986, new housing legislation finally became possible. After several years in which the Senate Banking Committee had refused to proceed with legislation, the Senate and House appeared ready to compromise. The 1986 Senate elections, which produced a Democratic majority, meant that low-income housing would get a more sympathetic hearing. Indeed, as the Senate finally passed a housing-authorization bill in March 1987, Senator Chris Dodd announced "the end of a seven-year assault on federal housing policy by the Reagan administration" and "the start of a new era."[67]

Nevertheless, this bill provided evidence of how much had changed. It called for a cut in real HUD authorizations of more than 10 percent during the next two years, on top of the sharp reductions made in previous years. The bill authorized almost no new construction. New initiatives included a small plan to encourage homeownership among moderate-income groups, the possible sale of public-housing units to tenants, and the permanent authorization of housing vouchers (formerly a demonstration project). All of these proposals operated within the Reagan administration's preferred framework for housing policy. Even so, conservatives attacked the bill as a "budget buster," and Reagan threatened a veto unless further changes were made. The compromise bill finally agreed upon in December 1987 produced even more extensive retrenchment in federal housing programs.[68] The bill, and a somewhat more generous piece of legislation passed in 1990, demonstrate that even though the limits of retrenchment may have been reached, the new status quo stabilized federal low-income housing policy at an even more minimal level.

EXPLAINING THE SUCCESS OF RETRENCHMENT IN HOUSING POLICY

Housing programs have experienced sharp cutbacks in both Britain and the United States. Why has housing proven to be such a vulnerable sector of the welfare state? Economic change produced particularly severe pressures on housing policies, while the structure of programs limited the capacity of supporters to resist cutbacks. High inflation and interest rates in the late 1970s and early 1980s drove up the costs of both housing and government programs. Thus, housing programs felt an acute version of the squeeze that has affected the entire welfare state.

A number of features of low-income programs undermined efforts to fend off advocates of retrenchment. First, in part because existing programs lacked a clearly defined role, they enjoyed limited credibility in the eyes of policymakers and the public. When the problem was defined as one of housing availability,

as it was (especially in Britain) after World War II, public-construction or producer subsidies were seen as rational responses. By the 1970s, when policymakers began to identify affordability as the problem, supply-oriented programs
began to look increasingly questionable. In moving toward subsidies for housing
consumption rather than for construction, the Thatcher and Reagan administrations were part of a general trend.[69] What distinguished their efforts was the
thoroughness with which public-sector production cuts were pursued, and the
successful containment of subsidies for consumers other than owner occupiers.

The Thatcher and Reagan records demonstrate why many housing advocates
continued to favor production subsidies over consumption-based ones: The latter
approach was politically vulnerable.[70] Although labeled ''housing allowances,''
consumption-based programs increased recipients' incomes but did little to increase housing consumption. Functionally, they were little more than thinly dis-
guised income-support programs.[71] As such, they appealed to a relatively narrow
constituency and were attacked as an unnecessary and inefficient duplication of
actual income-support programs. Both Reagan and Thatcher were successful in
significantly reducing the generosity of housing allowances.

Nevertheless, to argue that conservative policies just reflected the temper of
the times would be overly simplistic. Other programs with equally confused
rationales, such as tax subsidies to homeowners that increase in inverse relation
to need, have proven more durable. If housing programs were in disarray, the
rise of homelessness in both countries and the acute problem of unaffordable
rents in the United States should have indicated the continuing need for a public
response. Although a loss of direction among housing advocates weakened low-
income programs, retrenchment also depended on program features that limited
their political clout.

In both countries, existing housing policies contributed to their own problems. Experiments with high-rise, inner-city public housing – designed, ironically, to keep costs down – had been expensive failures. More important, they
provided powerful images, like the demolition of the Pruitt-Igoe project in St.
Louis, that stigmatized the entire public sector. Even so, the public sector's
reputation for inefficiency was also intimately connected to the structure of housing subsidies in each country. The high visibility of government expenditures
made public provision seem far more expensive and inefficient than the indirectly subsidized private sector. The pattern of retrenchment in housing policy
revealed the profound political implications of channeling middle-class subsidies
through the tax system. Both governments were able to cut programs for the
nearly poor on the rationale that they were not going to the ''truly needy,''
while tax-based subsidies benefiting the affluent remained sacrosanct.

The political weakness of housing programs also stemmed from the large
percentage of housing expenditures devoted to capital spending. Although capital spending had provided a basis for political coalitions between the poor and
producer interests, the alliance proved to be vulnerable in a period of economic
and budgetary stress. Both governments pursued monetary policies that gener-

ated high interest rates and unemployment, severely weakening the political position of housing producers. As public and private construction declined and unions floundered, the traditional public-housing constituencies lost influence over policy. Forced to establish priorities, producer interests emphasized support for private home construction rather than public-sector housing programs.[72]

The lag time between producer and consumer benefits further fragmented the low-income housing constituency. Cuts in capital expenditures did not directly affect current recipients, and the impact on potential recipients was diffuse and hence nearly invisible. Although the latter might eventually have a harder time finding affordable housing, such effects would occur years after the political decisions were made. In both the United States and Britain, cuts in new construction proceeded more rapidly than reductions in subsidies to current tenants.

Distinctive features of each country's housing policy also facilitated retrenchment. In the United States, low-income housing assistance's nonentitlement status narrowed the program's constituency and made expenditure cuts easier. Because housing programs depended on annual authorizations, expenditures were open to direct congressional control rather than being driven by changes in demand. Nonentitlement status left housing assistance particularly vulnerable to cuts because of a major consequence of Reagan's policies: the much tighter expenditure climate generated by high deficits. As Chapter 6 explores in more detail, the politics of social expenditure in recent years has become increasingly "zero sum," with protection of some programs coming at the expense of others. Housing assistance has generally fared poorly in this context, and only the least-costly housing programs have escaped drastic cuts. The gradual expansion of Reagan's voucher plan owed a great deal to this changing budgetary climate, which made the minimal budgetary authority required by vouchers a major selling point.

Accounting for the Thatcher government's success is more challenging. At first glance, British low-income housing policy seemed an unlikely candidate for retrenchment. The public-housing stock was enormous, and although it primarily served working-class families, explicit means-testing was limited. Council housing's scope and its obvious importance to tenants suggested that cuts would be hard to achieve.

A number of features, however, made dramatic change possible. The role of capital spending in weakening resistance to cuts has already been mentioned. Ironically, the prominent role of local authorities (usually Labour controlled) in housing policy also strengthened the Thatcher government's position. Subsidies for council housing came from central government, but local authorities set rents. With reduced subsidies, local authorities were left with a range of unpalatable options: raise rents, increase local taxes, or run a deficit that could land officials in jail or leave them personally liable.[73] The Thatcher government remained one step removed from the pain inflicted on tenants and relatively insulated from the discontent caused by rising rents.

The Thatcher government also successfully shifted debate from its dramatic spending cuts to its struggle with "high spending" councils controlled by the "loony left." The government broke decisively with the quasi-corporatist networks, involving local authorities and construction interests, that had dominated British housing policy until the late 1970s.[74] These networks were in disrepute after the 1974–9 Labour government's collapse, and the recession that began in 1980 further diminished the political strength of the local council-housing-construction alliance. The Thatcher government was well placed to exploit these opportunities.

Although structural features of British housing expenditure helped to dissipate potential opposition, the crucial factor was probably the opportunity provided by the option of selling assets. Normally, those receiving public-sector benefits would be the strongest opponents of cuts. In this case, however, a significant fraction of the group facing cuts became advocates of the government's policy. Public housing's most affluent and well-organized recipients were offered the opportunity to become owners of their own homes at rates well below market value. As a result, opposition to the change in policy was limited; the option of an attractive "exit" discouraged the exercise of "voice."[75]

Interestingly, the sale of public assets to particular individuals at large discounts has also been popular with the general public. In part, this reflects the fact that the costs are diffuse and long-term, whereas taxpayers benefit immediately from the lower taxes that asset sales make possible. The popularity of sales also stems, however, from what Ulf Torgerson has called the "institutional peculiarity" of socially provided or subsidized housing.[76] Most social expenditures produce a visible flow of payments or services. Public housing provides a largely "once-and-for-all" transfer that yields long-term disposition of a residence with considerable (and gradually increasing) market value. Once provided, that housing is hard to withdraw, and the occupant is likely to develop a feeling of quasi-ownership. The sense that council houses already "belonged" to their occupants explains why the sales proved to be one of Thatcher's most popular domestic reforms.

The existence of tangible assets – in this case, houses for sale at cut-rate prices – was a critical ingredient in the Thatcher government's success. The sales fragmented political opposition to council housing's residualization. More important, they allowed the government to showcase its fulfillment of citizens' desires for "choice" and ownership. This success has overshadowed the fact that these policies have also meant rising housing costs for the poor, the imposition of extensive means-testing, greater class segregation in housing, and a fall in low-cost housing construction that is related to a sharp rise in homelessness.

The overall experience of housing policies in both countries underscores the importance of disaggregating the welfare state into individual program areas when analyzing retrenchment. Housing has proven to be unusually open to reform because of its unique characteristics. As a single, very expensive product rather than a flow of benefits, it has been subject to particularly severe economic dislocations that have generated pressures for reform. These same characteristics have made it relatively easy for those seeking retrenchment to divide producers from consumers, current from future tenants, and those who can buy from those who cannot. The consequences have been dramatic.

5
Retrenchment in a residualized sector: income-support policy

No area of the welfare state has provoked such persistent controversy as have programs providing income support for the able-bodied poor.[1] The controversy stems largely from these programs' interference with what is both a strong cultural expectation and a fundamental aspect of market-oriented economies: that whenever possible, potential workers should support themselves by earning a wage. Disputes over income-maintenance programs are usually regarded as highly partisan. Conservatives, given their preferences for minimizing government intervention and their sensitivity to employers' interests, have criticized income-maintenance initiatives. Liberals, with union support, have been less reluctant to weaken the dependence of the able-bodied on a steady job to avoid impoverishment.

Given these partisan differences, and the vigorous rhetorical attacks of British and American conservatives on existing income-support policies, the Reagan and Thatcher administrations were expected to produce radical reforms. Early analyses often argued that they were succeeding.[2] Indeed, the 1980s turned out to be a brutal decade for the poor. High unemployment and mounting international competition weakened the labor market for those with limited skills. In Britain, the number of households living on less than half the average income (a common international measure of poverty) more than doubled between 1979 and 1987, rising from 9 percent to 19 percent. In the United States, the poverty rate was 13 percent in 1980 and 13.5 percent in 1990, but was substantially higher for most of the decade, peaking at 15.2 percent in 1983.[3] Although the position of the poor worsened both as a consequence of economic change and government policy, retrenchment in income-maintenance programs made only a limited contribution to this. Some cuts in benefit levels occurred, but there was not a radical restructuring of income-support policies. The basic explanation for this outcome is that in both countries, most income-support policies for the able-bodied poor already operated within a residualist framework. These programs closely adhered to the conservative model of minimal benefits, maintained an ever-vigilant watch for fraud, and targeted only the poorest. Squeezing significant cutbacks from these programs was no easy task.

There have been only a few possibilities for major retrenchment, and these often occurred in programs that do not just serve the poor, such as unemployment insurance (UI) and (in Britain) family allowances. The varied fate of income-maintenance programs also reveals how the interaction of political institutions with program structures influences retrenchment politics.

It is in this area of the welfare state that the institutional differences between the United States and Britain have had the greatest influence on prospects for programmatic retrenchment. Distinct institutional structures facilitated different retrenchment strategies. Retrenchment was successful when program structures permitted the implementation of strategies appropriate to each country's institutional setting. In the United States, programs with shared federal and state responsibilities proved most vulnerable. Where policy was already decentralized or could be further decentralized (UI and, among targeted programs, AFDC), the Reagan administration was able to harness burden-shifting techniques and interstate competition in the service of retrenchment. In Britain, where this decentralization option was not available, centralization often facilitated the Thatcher government's efforts to craft low-visibility initiatives. For both Child Benefit and Unemployment Benefit, retrenchment took the form of "death by a thousand cuts." An endless series of incremental adjustments added up to sizable reform without generating the kind of public outcry that a single large package of cutbacks would have produced.

The complexity of retrenchment outcomes confounds the standard expectation that the broader electoral appeal of nontargeted programs makes them politically stable, whereas means-tested programs can easily be whittled away.[4] The weakness of means-tested programs is in fact already reflected in their size, and it is not obvious that the targeted status will explain changes in that size. In both countries, some means-tested programs have been vulnerable; others have not. The same has been true for universal programs. The durability of programs turns on more than whether or not they are targeted to the poor.

The lack of a straightforward relationship between targeting and political vulnerability has a number of explanations. There are indeed factors that make means-tested programs vulnerable. For one, those advocating retrenchment in means-tested programs are unlikely to be deterred by the political activities of program beneficiaries. The poor are rarely well organized, their turnout at elections is low, and they would be unlikely to support conservatives in any case. The organizational weakness of program supporters, then, does make cutback initiatives less politically dangerous. Furthermore, because of their emphasis on work incentives, conservatives may aggressively seek to undercut all sources of income for the able-bodied poor.

However, there are offsetting factors as well. For example, one must consider the compelling reasons for retrenchment advocates to look closely at universal programs. An ideologically committed and consistent conservative government would object most strongly to governmental provision for the middle class. It is universal rather than targeted programs that compete with viable private-sector alternatives. If conservatives could design their ideal welfare state, it would consist of nothing but means-tested programs. Furthermore, conservatives are very concerned with reducing spending, and it is hard to squeeze much spending out of marginal, means-tested programs. The largest potential targets are bound to be those that include the middle class; budget cutters will find their attention drawn to universal programs.

In addition, there are vexing problems with a direct attack on means-tested programs. Beyond a certain point, cutting such programs tends to produce significant policy problems, increasing bureaucratization and worsening work incentives. Means-testing is a rigid structure, inherently operating within narrow bounds. Both the Reagan and Thatcher administrations discovered that a more thoroughgoing residualism produced substantial irrationalities. Heightened use of means testing and stricter requirements increased the problems of bureaucracy, work disincentives, and dependency that conservatives had promised to eradicate. Finally, conservatives have had to worry about the "fairness issue." Because the programs provide direct assistance to the very poor, opportunities to obscure cutbacks by substituting private alternatives or pursuing indirect strategies were limited. Direct cuts created political difficulties, not because of the modest influence of beneficiaries but because of the symbolic importance of these programs for administrations already vulnerable to accusations of mean spiritedness.

In combination, these restrictions limited most efforts to obtain substantial cutbacks in means-tested programs. Although the complex federal arrangements governing AFDC allowed the Reagan administration to oversee the continuation of a long downward trend in state-level benefits, Reagan and Thatcher more often found that their initiatives had changed little, but had been politically costly. Although clearly not reluctant to increase inequality, these administrations generally preferred to do so in ways less visible than large program cuts targeted on the poor.

The two administrations found universal programs of income support – unemployment insurance and, in Britain, child allowances – somewhat more malleable. In times of austerity, the argument that universal income-support benefits are poorly targeted has proven persuasive, and supporters of social programs have often felt a need to protect the poorest first. The Thatcher government, for instance, emphasized that cuts in Child Benefit made it possible to increase targeted assistance (although only a small share of the government's savings found its way into the social-assistance budget).

The universal, insurance-based status of unemployment benefits also provided limited protection. Unlike other social-insurance benefits, unemployment benefits go to individuals expected to be available for work. The argument that payments to the able-bodied must be cut so they will seek jobs, which has traditionally constricted means-tested programs, has been applied more forcefully to comparatively generous unemployment-insurance benefits. Despite the universality of unemployment benefits, mobilizing political support against such cuts has been difficult. Unlike health or pension benefits, few are likely to realize their stake in unemployment programs until they are unemployed, at which point they are less likely to devote much energy to political action. In this context, the presence of some durable organizational base for political support becomes crucial. Here is one place where the power-resources perspective continues to be relevant to an analysis of social-policy development. Whereas other social programs have developed new constituencies to supplement or supplant the role of organized labor, unemployment insurance has not; and although the weakening of unions has had a limited impact on most other programs, it has effectively removed the one enduring source of political support for unemployment insurance.

If the biggest programmatic losers in the 1980s were often universal programs, the biggest winners were in fact targeted ones: Family Credit in Britain and the Earned Income Tax Credit in the United States. These programs, which both expanded dramatically in scope and generosity during the 1980s, were strikingly similar. Each was targeted on working-poor families, and was designed to lower work disincentives and bring higher incomes to these hard-pressed households. Because there could be little argument about the worthiness and need of these families, and because the programs provided a relatively simple mechanism for improving work incentives, these credit schemes appealed to many conservatives and to some of their opponents as well. Nevertheless, their expansion was a setback for those who wanted to restrict the public-sector role in income maintenance to all but the very poorest. Opposition to wage supplements for the poor in the United States, for example, was strongest within the Republican Party and indeed, among Reagan's top aides. The success of these programs in spite of such powerful opposition within conservative circles indicates the limited room that existed for further constriction of means-tested provision in both countries.

THE STRUCTURE OF INCOME-MAINTENANCE POLICIES IN BRITAIN AND THE UNITED STATES

The constraints that means-testing places on income-support systems have been evident in the development of policy in both Britain and the United States. When contrasted with most European welfare states, both countries are distinguished by their heavy reliance on means-tested assistance for the poor. In the United States, this dominance was never seriously questioned, and debate centered on how generous these programs could be without undermining work incentives. In Britain, the residualist model gradually asserted itself after a lengthy political struggle.[6]

The structure of British and American income-support policies differed in three major respects: the scope of provision, the extent of reliance on means-testing, and the degree of centralized authority over income-support policies. The scope of provision was considerably more extensive in Britain. Although far less affluent than the United States, Britain's system of social provision basically acknowledged rights to a minimum level of economic well-being.

There were few restrictions on eligibility for the basic welfare program, Supplementary Benefit. The system was designed to provide what was considered a poverty-threshold income, and it was indexed to changes in prices. Britain also had a small program, Family Income Supplement (FIS), targeted on working-poor families.

In the United States, the core welfare program of Aid to Families with Dependent Children (AFDC) was restricted to families with children, and often to single-parent families. The incomes provided were generally well below the poverty line, and the program was not indexed. The other major federal expenditure program, food stamps, was available at somewhat higher income levels, for a wider range of households, and was indexed. Even in combination, however, these programs left the American "safety net" far more threadbare than its British counterpart. The addition of a small program similar to FIS for the working poor, the Earned Income Tax Credit, in 1975, did little to change that. The British system also made greater use of non-means-tested benefits in providing income support for the able-bodied poor. Although both countries had unemployment-insurance systems, the British plan provided more complete coverage of the work force and offered longer-lasting benefits. In addition, in 1977 the British government introduced an indexed system of non-means-tested flat-rate family allowances, called Child Benefit, to replace the previous system of tax allowances. This program, long advocated by poverty groups, was designed to provide assistance to families with children in a way that would not create work disincentives.

Finally, the two systems differed considerably in the degree of program centralization. Whereas British income-support policy was firmly under the control of the national government, the United States had never fully nationalized income-maintenance policy.[7] Even though AFDC and unemployment insurance were part of the Social Security Act, both maintained prominent state-government roles from the start. AFDC was a joint state-federal program, with national authorities providing roughly half the financing and setting basic policy parameters, but with states continuing to exercise considerable discretion over both benefits and eligibility. Unemployment insurance was also structured to maintain considerable state discretion and control over funding.[8] Each state operated a separate trust fund. Central constraints on benefit and eligibility rules were left relatively loose. The duration of benefits was kept short, with the federal government having to vote on an ad hoc basis to authorize extended benefits in times of high unemployment. In a system that already provided comparatively meager assistance to the able-bodied poor, this decentralized programmatic structure turned out to be Reagan's one promising lever for reform.

REAGAN, THATCHER, AND INCOME-SUPPORT POLICY

Reagan and Thatcher shared a common critique of existing income-maintenance policies. Although affirming the need to help those who truly could not help themselves, they argued that existing arrangements extended far beyond those bounds. Both leaders repeated a list of familiar complaints: Existing programs were expensive, intrusive, bureaucratic, fraud-ridden, and discouraged individual initiative. Both administrations promised radical reform, making a series of energetic attempts to clean up what American critics have termed the "welfare mess." The story of these efforts is complex, but the basic result is clear: Although repeated assaults have made means tests more restrictive and further eroded universal programs, dramatic reforms have proven elusive.

Like their predecessors, Reagan and Thatcher found themselves squeezed within the tight parameters of a residualist approach to welfare. The side effects of income testing meant that tightening these programs generated new, embarrassing irrationalities. Furthermore, although programs for the poor were unpopular, efforts to reduce those programs threatened to increase each government's vulnerability to accusations of unfairness and heartlessness. In this context, neither administration found radical retrenchment attainable.

The Thatcher government and income maintenance

The Thatcher government, harshly critical of existing income-maintenance programs, stressed four goals in formulating reforms: (1) more specific targeting; (2) lower expenditures; (3) stronger work incentives; and (4) greater simplicity. The government discovered, however, that these goals were mutually incompatible. Steps to reduce expenditures and improve targeting meant expanding reliance on means tests, but this increased work disincentives and administrative complexity. The government made repeated but futile attempts to reconcile the irreconcilable. Ultimately, it gave priority to expenditure cuts and increased reliance on means-testing. By doing so, it pushed British income-maintenance policy toward a more thoroughgoing residualism.

The politics of decrementalism: non-targeted income-maintenance programs. The Thatcher government's income-support policies must be viewed in the context of Britain's staggering economic difficulties of the early 1980s. The economy moved into recession in 1980, and unemployment rates rose sharply, from 5 percent to 12.5 percent between 1979 and 1983.[9] Higher unemployment contributed heavily to steep increases in social-security expenditures. As unemployment and government spending rose, the Thatcher government's ministers looked skeptically at universal benefits. In a budget deemed to be out of control, poorly targeted programs seemed a particularly promising source of cutbacks. In the case of unemployment benefits, concern about the "unemployment trap" reinforced this inclination. Government ministers claimed that high unemployment benefits produced a "why work?" question. In fact, there was little evidence to suggest that unemployment benefits were generous enough to contribute much to unemployment rates.[10] If income differentials between those working and those out of work were in fact inadequate, a variety of techniques could have addressed the problem. The attractiveness of low-paying jobs could have been increased by cutting taxes on low-paid workers, or by introducing a minimum wage or a wage subsidy. Furthermore, concern about the unemployment trap would seem to justify an increased reliance on non-means-tested benefits such as Child Benefit.

The Thatcher government, however, opted to cut unemployment-insurance benefits. Despite the program's universal status, a number of factors made it possible to introduce substantial retrenchment without generating a significant political outcry. The plausibility of arguments about the impact of unemployment benefits on work incentives strengthened the government's position. The insurance element of Unemployment Benefit provided limited ideological protection when it seemed to allow the able-bodied to avoid work.

More important, although unemployment insurance was "universal" in the sense that covered workers were eligible regardless of their income level, the program had little immediacy for most people. The electorate was divided into two groups: The unemployed were in little position to exert political influence, whereas the employed were unlikely to see much immediate stake in preservation of the program. The development of a dual labor market in Britain, with growing numbers of people either highly marginalized or in relatively secure employment, made the benefit less salient for a sizable share of the electorate. Even with the mounting unemployment of the 1980s, public opinion suggested that spending on unemployed was a low priority. Revealingly, in contrast to the case for universal programs like health care and pensions, opinion polls indicated a considerable gap between the lowest and top income groups in support for unemployment benefits.[11]

With little popular support and a constituency that was transient and difficult to organize, the burden of defending unemployment benefits fell on the beleaguered labor movement, which was caught between the twin pressures of mounting unemployment and a vigorous government attack on union power. Close political ties and the government's commitment to an income policy had given organized labor significant political leverage over the Labour governments of the 1970s, but Thatcher's willingness to use unemployment to hold wages and inflation down limited union bargaining power. Possessing declining resources and under pressure to fight on a wide number of fronts, organized labor failed to mount a spirited defense of unemployment benefits.

In this political climate, the Thatcher government succeeded in introducing substantial retrenchment initiatives. Under terms of the Social Security Act (No. 2) of 1980, earnings-related supplements to Unemployment Benefit were phased out beginning in January 1982. Even the minister introducing the bill in Parliament had to admit that it was "one of the most uncomfortable and unpalatable Bills that any Minister has had to bring before the House of Commons in a long time." Nevertheless, political opposition was surprisingly limited.[12] As the Child Poverty Action Group (CPAG) lamented, "Clearly we have failed so far in our efforts to get across the damage that this legislation will do to millions of claim-

Table 5.1. *Major changes in unemployment benefits in Britain, 1979–88*

Reform (and year enacted)	Impact
End of earnings-related supplement (1980)	Savings of £95 million in 1978–9
Taxation of unemployment benefits (1980)	Tax yield on National Insurance and supplementary benefit payments to the unemployed of £375 million in 1986–7
Abolition of lower-rate benefits (1986)	Savings of £27 million estimated in 1986–7
Abatement for occupational pensions (1981, 1988)	Savings to National Insurance Fund of £65 million in 1989–90
Extension of disqualification period (1986)	Savings of £25–30 million estimated in 1988
Tightening of contribution conditions, other changes (1988)	Savings to National Insurance Fund of £380 million in 1990–1

Source: Tony Atkinson and John Micklewright, "Turning the Screw: Benefits for the Unemployed, 1979–1988," in Andrew Dilnot and Alan Walker, eds., *The Economics of Social Security* (Oxford University Press, 1989), p. 21.

ants."[13] This pattern was to continue, as the Thatcher government used its administrative discretion and large parliamentary majority to repeatedly chip away at unemployment benefits.

A careful study by Anthony Atkinson and John Micklewright has charted these reforms.[14] By 1988, the government had adopted at least seventeen significant changes in Unemployment Benefit, most of which were clearly unfavorable to recipients. As Atkinson and Micklewright conclude, "Little by little the system has undergone major changes of principle without any widespread public recognition."[15] Taken in isolation, each of these reforms had a fairly modest impact. Together, they resulted in a substantial residualization of policy for the unemployed. The overall impact of the reforms is difficult to measure, but one can contrast the cost of just those revisions in Table 5.1 with total expenditures on Unemployment Benefit in 1987-8 of £1.5 billion. These changes greatly lowered replacement rates (benefits as a percentage of previous earnings) for the unemployed.[16] The restrictions on Unemployment Benefit and the spread of long-term unemployment also sharply increased the reliance of the unemployed on the means-tested Supplementary Benefit. Whereas in 1980-1 only 52 percent of the unemployed had been dependent on Supplementary Benefit, by 1986-7 that figure had grown to 74 percent. In short, there was both a sizable cut in the generosity of Unemployment Benefit and a substantial shift away from universal, insurance-based provision for the unemployed toward means-tested social assistance.

The other universal benefit of interest to the able-bodied poor, Child Benefit, also received the Thatcher government's attention. Although CPAG and the Labour Party regarded universal child allowances as the cornerstone of antipoverty policy, the Conservatives remained unconvinced. This universal benefit was seen as "wasteful" because much of it went to those above the poverty line. Because its universal status made Child Benefit expensive, it also attracted the attention of treasury officials eager for substantial budget cuts. Without expressing outright hostility to Child Benefit, a succession of ministers indicated their preference for more sharply targeted benefits. In a well-publicized speech, Secretary of State John Moore argued in September 1987 for improved targeting: "The indiscriminate handing out of benefits not only spreads limited resources too thinly, it can also undermine the will to self-help and build up pools of resentment among taxpayers who are footing the bill . . . " He followed this in Parliament the following month by emphasizing the high cost of Child Benefit and describing it as "ill-targeted."[17]

On numerous occasions Child Benefit was rumored to be in danger of elimination or radical reform – either by the introduction of means testing or by taxation of benefits. The government's think-tank report of 1982 suggested its abolition; press reports claimed continuing discussions throughout the 1980s.[18] The reviews directed by Secretary of State for Social Services Norman Fowler in 1984-5 (see Chapter 3), are instructive. Child Benefit looked vulnerable to radical reform. Throughout the review, Conservatives stressed the program's inefficiency, asking why the wealthy should receive government handouts. Public sympathy for Child Benefit was also more limited than it was for other benefits, and the prime minister was known to view the program with suspicion.[19] CPAG's representatives noted that the team reviewing benefits for children and young people seemed eager to establish "the alleviation of poverty" as social security's sole priority. In such a framework, Child Benefit was likely to appear inferior to means-tested alternatives.[20]

Changes in Child Benefit were therefore widely anticipated. The *Financial Times* reported that Fowler and Lawson initially agreed to abolish or tax the program, but could not agree on how to spend the savings. However, the massive publicity such a dramatic change would have generated undermined the case for radical reform. When the cabinet subcommittee reviewing the Fowler proposals turned to the issue, according to Robin Pauley, Thatcher simply "could not stomach" the anticipated reaction from the middle class and backbench MPs.[21] CPAG's vigorous campaign to maintain Child Benefit, joined by a number of women's groups and targeted on moderate Conservatives, proved successful.[22]

Even as Child Benefit survived frontal assaults, however, low-visibility efforts to let inflation and economic growth curb its role were quite successful. As with many other programs, even a maintenance of real benefits meant a shrinking role in an expanding economy. The government, moreover, acted on a number of occasions to uprate Child Benefit in line with price increases only partially, or to freeze it entirely. Indexation was partial in 1985, and benefits were frozen in 1988, 1989, and 1990. These more incremental reforms, although widely decried by the poverty lobby, generated limited public response. Their combined impact was nevertheless substantial. The contrast with personal-tax allowances for adults is striking: These increased 25 percent between 1979 and 1989, whereas the real value of Child Benefit fell by nearly 14 percent.[23] Ironically, the Callaghan government's decision to change child-tax allowances into the more effective antipoverty device of universal child benefits increased the program's political vulnerability. Budgetary practices made the "wasteful" universal benefits highly visible to treasury and cabinet officials eager for reductions in the social-security budget. Personal allowances, which were far less effective antipoverty instruments, received little scrutiny.

In the past few years, the tide seems to have turned back in favor of Child Benefit. Conservative MPs became increasingly vigorous in criticizing the continuing freeze.[24] A number of prominent Tories, including former Social Security ministers Keith Joseph, Patrick Jenkin, and Norman Fowler, issued strong statements in favor of Child Benefit. Conservative policy analysts, such as David Willetts, the well-respected head of the Center for Policy Studies, increasingly acknowledged that some form of family allowance should be an important part of government policy.[25] The replacement of John Moore at Social Security indicated that even before Thatcher's resignation the government was backtracking somewhat from an aggressive stance on income-maintenance issues. Nonetheless, since 1979 the real value of benefits has fallen considerably. Like Unemployment Benefit, it found its universal status a source of limited protection, especially against a centralized administration that could chip away at benefits time and again, always being sure to keep the changes below the threshold that would generate significant political opposition.

Reforming targeted programs: the fruitless search for a "New Beveridge." Although the government's decisions on universal programs demonstrated clear hostility to them, it was ambivalent toward means-tested programs of income maintenance. Demands for expenditure constraint meant continued budgetary pressure on means-tested programs. However, increasing means testing's role required time, effort, and possibly money, to make such programs work reasonably effectively. The government initially followed its predecessors in implementing various incremental adjustments to cope with the administrative problems that inevitably cropped up in programs requiring intense scrutiny of beneficiaries. Seeking a more radical approach, the Thatcher government eventually turned to a review of the entire system of means-tested benefits.

Far from representing a radical departure, the government's initial action on Supplementary Benefit essentially implemented the outgoing Callaghan government's proposals. The reforms contained in the Social Security Act (No. 2) passed in November 1980 resulted from a lengthy review initiated in 1975. The review team's stated goal had been to adapt Supplementary Benefit to the reality of its "mass role."[26] Because the reforms were designed to streamline the program without increasing costs, they were acceptable to the Thatcher government.

The limited nature of the review also assured that the reforms would be modest.[27] Because "winners" had to be offset by "losers," and because losers tend to be more conscious of policy changes, redistribution was limited to a slight shift of benefits from elderly claimants to families with children. The legislation also attempted to reduce the role discretionary supplements, known as "single payments," played in the system. The case for reducing discretion, with its heavy administrative requirements and inherently intrusive qualities, was strong. Still, the changes adopted contributed little to the Thatcher government's main goals. Instead, the government relied on Supplementary Benefit to ameliorate the consequences of cuts in Unemployment Benefit and rising unemployment. The Supplementary Benefit rolls grew rapidly after 1979, as did the proportion of recipients who were unemployed.

Like that of Supplementary Benefit, the transformation of Family Income Supplement (FIS) stemmed as much from the increasing number of low-paid families as from changes in the program itself. Between 1979 and 1983 the number of low-income families (those with a net income no higher than 140 percent of the Supplementary Benefit line) almost doubled. The number of FIS recipients grew even more rapidly, increasing from 80,000 to 200,000.[28] FIS did not grow faster than the low-income population because of an increase in the rate of participation among the eligible population. This take-up rate continued to be about 50 percent. Instead, the extra increase in beneficiaries reflected the liberalization of benefits and eligibility rules between 1979 and 1983, even as most other social-security benefits were struggling to maintain their real value.[29] This generous treatment reflected the distinctive position of FIS within the Conservatives' emerging income-support policy. Specifically designed to supplement the incomes of the working poor, FIS also contributed to maintaining work incentives. Increases in FIS could also be used to deflect criticisms of the government's attacks on Child Benefit. The government claimed that the need for better targeting justified an emphasis on FIS, although only a small proportion of Child Benefit savings actually found their way into the FIS budget.

Bolstered by the 1983 election results, the second Thatcher government turned with renewed vigor to the goal of producing retrenchment in the social-security system. Of the four review teams working in 1984-5 to produce Fowler's green paper detailing reforms, two focused largely on the system of income support for the non-aged poor. Given this indication of the government's priorities and the massive publicity surrounding the reviews, large-scale changes were anticipated. Fowler himself claimed that the review was intended to offer a radical redesign of social-security programs. Nevertheless, even though the long-awaited green paper contained dramatic proposals for pension reform, the plans for the working-age poor were far more incremental. As Michael Prowse of the *Financial Times* observed, the Fowler proposals were "conservative with a small 'c,' " in essence "a spruced up version of the existing compromise."[30] Before describing the changes introduced, it is worth considering why more ambitious alternatives were rejected.

The major option for radical reform was an integration of tax and benefit schemes. In 1984 a group of analysts at the respected Institute for Fiscal Studies had published *The Reform of Social Security*, a sweeping and elegant analysis of the system's failures combined with a plan of reform.[31] The authors argued that a modified "negative income tax" could greatly simplify the system, improve work incentives, and provide more for those in need while nevertheless producing significant savings. Achievement of these impressive results would require the application of means tests to all social-security benefits. The authors defined social security's purpose as the alleviation of poverty (rather than, for example, as protection against sharp drops in income). Those not "truly in need" would receive no benefits. Thus the proposal's aspirations dovetailed nicely with the government's publicly expressed concerns. That fact, combined with the IFS publication's timing and impressive quality, guaranteed wide discussion for the integrated tax/benefit proposal.

Nevertheless, the government rejected the idea.[32] Fowler's green paper argued that tax/benefit integration was technically impossible at the time, though Fowler conceded that computerization might eventually change that.[33] The treasury's separate green paper on taxation, finally published in March 1986, stressed the public's support for a distinct system of national-insurance contributions and benefits.[34] Given past Conservative positions on income-support policy, neither of these justifications was entirely persuasive. Conservatives, after all, had pushed a tax-credit scheme themselves in the 1960s and early 1970s, and had expressed no strong attachment to national insurance.[35] For a government conscious of the dynamics of retrenchment politics, however, the IFS scheme looked far better on paper than in practice.

Two consequences of tax-benefit integration were particularly unpalatable to a government dependent on middle-class support and preoccupied with the rate of personal income taxation. First, the scheme would openly and rapidly remove substantial benefits for middle-class constituencies. Making an IFS-type scheme work required the elimination of benefits for those well above the poverty line, and any such change was politically unacceptable. The necessary reform of taxation would also have had little appeal. As the treasury green paper acknowledged, shifting from National Insurance contributions to the more progressive personal income-tax structure would also redistribute net income away from the government's core constituencies.[36] To make matters worse, an integrated plan could look like a sharp tax hike. Even though actual tax bills might be reduced, payroll taxes are less visible and more popular than income taxes. An integrated scheme would have raised the basic income tax rate from 30 percent to around 40 percent.[37] Given the government's preoccupation with bringing that rate down, this alone probably doomed the proposal.

Failing to produce a far-reaching reform, Fowler's team proposed a series of more limited alterations to the major means-tested programs. The focus was on increasing coordination between the three major means-tested schemes: Supplementary Benefit, FIS, and Housing Benefit. In the process, the government tried to shake out some significant savings. Even harsh critics of the government, while fighting the proposals, acknowledged that the changes were far from radical. As Ruth Lister, head of the Child Poverty Action Group at the time, later commented, "the Green Paper betrayed a faltering of purpose."[38]

The green paper proposed to streamline Supplementary Benefit, which was to be renamed "Income Support." It suggested a "Social Fund" to replace the existing scheme of discretionary supplements, which included "additional requirement payments" and "single payments" for one-time needs. The Social Fund, ostensibly introduced to simplify the system, was clearly designed to cut costs as well. Entitlements were reduced; loans largely replaced grants. The fund was to be cash-limited, meaning that once budgeted funds ran out there would be no additional payments that year. Ironically, the resulting savings would most harshly affect those whom the government claimed to be most concerned about. Families with children received fully two-thirds of single payments, an average of £4.15 per week in 1985–6.[39]

Unlike Supplementary Benefit, FIS (renamed "Family Credit") was to be significantly expanded, with broader eligibility rules and higher benefits. Spending was expected to rise (in 1986 pounds) from £170 million to £440 million.[40] The government also proposed to pay Family Credit through the wage packet (usually to the father) rather than, as FIS had been, by an order book cashable at the post office (usually by the mother). Fowler argued that this would improve the take-up of benefits among those eligible and highlight the link between wages and benefits. It would also represent a significant, if limited, step toward the integration of taxes and benefits, since for at least one group of workers the employer would administer both.[41] This proposal proved to be a recipe for political controversy.

As explained in Chapter 4, the major target for spending cuts within the means-tested programs was Housing Benefit. The government again sharpened the tapers (which determined the speed with which benefits were removed as income rose), this time from 29 percent to 33 percent. By 1988–9 this change cut £450 million from the Housing Benefit budget.[42] Since Family Credit's expansion largely offset the reductions in Supplementary Benefit, the sharper taper represented the green paper's major proposal for savings within the means-tested budget.

Fowler's plan also increased integration between the major means-tested programs. The proposed rates for Family Credit were aligned with the rates of child premiums in the Income Support (Supplementary Benefit) program. Housing Benefit was to be paid on the same basis for those in and out of work. To reduce the poverty trap, benefit calculation would be based on net income and calculated sequentially: Family Credit would be based on income after the deduction of income tax and National Insurance. Housing Benefit would be based on income after tax, National Insurance, and Family Credit payments. As a result, marginal tax rates in excess of 100 percent – the worst examples of poverty traps – would be eliminated.[43]

The government's proposals generated opposition, but nothing like the reaction to its plans for pensions (see Chapter 3).[44] The poverty lobby's attention centered on three features: the Social Fund (especially the lack of an independent review for claimants); the decision to pay Family Credit through the wage packet; and the sharp cuts in Housing Benefit. Although these reforms were all significant to recipients, none could be considered a radical change. These concerns reflected a general recognition that the government's proposals were surprisingly moderate.

Bowing to backbench pressures in the House of Commons, the government agreed to reevaluate the right to independent review and the method of payment of Family Credit. These same matters proved contentious in the House of Lords. The government finally gave in to the peculiar coalition of employers (who did not want the administrative responsibility) and women's groups, and agreed that Family Credit would be paid directly to the primary caretaker. This represented a major setback for those who had seen Family Credit as a first step toward an IFS-type scheme. The Lords also amended the Social Security Act to exclude the requirement that Income Support recipients pay at least 20 percent of their local tax bills, and to provide an independent right of appeal on the Social Fund. Embarrassed by these defeats in a supposedly Conservative-dominated chamber, the government restored the original provisions when the bill returned to the Commons.

With the exception of the change in Family Credit payment, the legislation finally enacted in July 1986 was strikingly similar to what had been proposed a year before. Nevertheless, if the government was pleased that it had pushed its proposals past the poverty lobby, it could hardly claim to have achieved radical reform. The government had sought to improve targeting, strengthen work incentives, simplify the system, and cut costs. Fowler argued that the new system achieved all four goals; but any improvement was, in reality, marginal. Targeting was improved by reducing housing benefits for the least poor. When the scheme was introduced in the spring of 1988, five million recipients were to receive lower benefits, and a million (mostly at the upper end of the income limits) were to lose entitlement completely. Despite government claims to the contrary, however, those who lost benefits had quite low incomes. More than 97 percent of housing-benefit payments went to nonworking families.[45] Many of the poorest families were also worse off. The green paper had stressed that families with children were now the poorest of the poor. Among this group, as DHSS studies confirmed, the unemployed were especially hard-pressed. Even so, improvements in benefits went to working families (those receiving Family Credit) rather than to the unemployed. Many families among the nonworking poor actually lost benefits with the introduction of the Social Fund. When the benefit levels for the new Family Credit and Income Support schemes were finally announced in October 1987, it was clear that real reductions in benefit had taken place even without considering the loss of single payments.[46]

This failure to direct help to the neediest resulted from a fundamental tension between the government's concern with targeting, its desire to improve work incentives, and its insistence on cutting spending. Raising benefits for the unemployed without increasing the overall budget would have had the unacceptable effect of decreasing work incentives. Nor would the government relax the budget constraint, which would have permitted more generous treatment of the unemployed without affecting work incentives. Raising benefits to unemployed families would have required higher Family Credit benefits to maintain differentials between working and nonworking households. This, however, would have meant much higher costs and, more important, swept the very large cohort of families just above the Family Credit income cutoff into the means-tested net. This in turn might have necessitated an increase in Child Benefit to float this large group off of Family Credit. The government's impasse vindicated CPAG's strong defense of Child Benefit. As Richard Berthoud of the Policy Studies Institute put it, "It is necessary to increase the net income of *all* families with children in order to improve the lot of the poorest without closing up the already narrow differentials within the group."[47] Unwilling to pay that cost, the government repudiated its professed goal of helping the poorest families.

Despite worsening the position of many of the very poorest, the government made at best trivial progress on the issue of work incentives. The government proudly claimed that the reform eliminated the poverty and unemployment traps, but this was a dubious assertion. Although the reforms ended marginal tax rates greater than 100 percent, they actually increased the number of people facing marginal rates in excess of 80 percent. Extending Family Credit's scope expanded the reach of benefits subject to rapid withdrawal as income increased. A family of four doubling its wages from £75 to £150 a week could see its net income rise by less than £5.[48] Within a no-cost budget constraint, work incentives proved just as hard to improve as the position of the neediest.

The government was on firmer ground in claiming to have simplified social security. Each of the three programs was more straightforward, and the interactions among the three had been streamlined and rationalized. Nevertheless, the experience of previous reforms suggested that implementation might produce unexpected snags. Even before the reforms were introduced in 1988, DHSS officials convinced the new team of social-security ministers brought in after the 1987 election that the Social Fund was unworkable. Their efforts to scrap that particular reform were beaten back (in part by an indignant Norman Fowler), but the attempt suggested the possible gap between planners' blueprints and smoothly operating programs.[49] Certainly the reforms did not create a very simple system. Despite the elimination of some of the most glaring tangles, social security remained highly bureaucratic and confusing to claimants. Indeed, if revamping the means-tested programs without touching the simpler insurance programs and universal benefits eventually leads to greater reliance on the former, the reforms will *increase* complexity.

The 1986 act did reduce expenditures, although the government's reluctance to issue useful figures has made it difficult to determine the extent of cutbacks.

Reductions in Housing Benefit amounted to around £450 million. Introduction of the Social Fund saved about £300 million more, in addition to perhaps £200 million from the insufficient uprating of Income Support scale rates. Weighed against this is the expansion of Family Credit, costing roughly £250 million. All told, the government probably reduced annual social-security expenditures by about £700 million. This is a substantial sum, and it will come almost entirely from those living near or below the poverty line. Nevertheless, given the government's initial aspirations (and the fears of its opponents), it hardly constitutes a radical cut. The combined budget of Supplementary Allowance (that is, supplementary benefits excluding pensioners), FIS, and Housing Benefit in 1987-8 was £12.3 billion. In other words, means-tested programs were cut by less than 6 percent, and the cuts represented less than 2 percent of total social-security expenditures. As a *Financial Times* editorial concluded, "Historians are likely to regard the 'Fowler' social security reforms as little more than a penny-pinching stopgap."[50]

These cuts nonetheless produced an outcry when they took effect in the spring of 1988. The government's timing contributed to the problem: The cuts were introduced at almost the same time as the announcement of the "champagne" budget of 1988, which introduced sizable tax cuts overwhelmingly targeted on the well-off. In response to public criticism, the act's proposed cuts in Housing Benefit were slightly reduced. Furthermore, the government was forced to add more significant transitional protections for those negatively affected by the changes.

Despite repeated assaults, then, the main structure of income maintenance remained intact after a decade of Thatcherism. The major change was a gradual erosion of the universal systems of unemployment insurance and child allowances. Britain's highly centralized political system made it possible for the Thatcher government to implement carefully designed incremental cutbacks that eventually weakened these programs considerably. On the other hand, every effort at radical reform of the means-tested programs ran into major obstacles. The government had to be careful about introducing sharp, visible cuts in programs for the poor. The tendency of greater residualization to create major problems of work disincentives also limited room for reform.

Income-support policy under Reagan

The Reagan administration advanced three major retrenchment strategies for income-support policies. The first aimed for direct cuts through lower benefits and tighter eligibility rules. Despite some initial successes, most of these efforts ran out of steam by the end of 1982 after producing only marginal changes. Only in the case of programs in which states and the federal government shared responsibility – AFDC and unemployment insurance – did more significant cutbacks occur. Particular weaknesses of each program contributed to their vulnerability, but the ability to implement decentralizing, burden-shifting strategies was critical in each case. The second approach sought to build on these partial successes by transferring full responsibility for food stamps and AFDC to state governments. The New Federalism proposals were radical, but after generating limited enthusiasm from state governments and outright hostility from Congress, they went nowhere. Finally, the administration tried to redesign welfare by introducing work requirements, popularly termed "workfare." Whatever limited retrenchment potential this strategy offered remained unrealized as a skeptical Congress first refused to approve Reagan's plans and then appropriated workfare rhetoric to put program expansion back on the political agenda.

The assault on income-maintenance spending. The administration's first major effort was a direct attack on spending for income-support programs. Discussions of Reagan's domestic-policy initiatives have understandably stressed the unprecedented cutbacks achieved in the budget rounds of 1981 and 1982. AFDC and food stamps, the major income-support programs for the able-bodied poor, were among the programs hit hardest by the administration's actions. However, the magnitude of these cuts should not be exaggerated; the early reforms trimmed means-tested programs considerably, but left their basic structures intact. Furthermore, the administration was unable to follow up on these successes after 1982; despite conservative resistance, political momentum swung modestly back toward program expansion.

Accounts of the administration's 1981 domestic-spending cuts have often focused on David Stockman's skillful use of the reconciliation process to force through an otherwise unattainable program.[51] Rather than being broken into separate pieces, the administration's budget was offered as a unified package. By presenting a single "up or down" vote on the administration's budget-cutting proposals, the matter could be presented as a referendum on economic policy. More important, Congress was freed from the pressure of having to vote on individual cutbacks. A series of votes would have increased the traceability of cutbacks to individual politicians, and the House leadership tried to force such a procedure. However, they were defeated by the Republican-Southern Democrat coalition on a key test vote.

A number of other factors contributed significantly to the administration's early successes. If reconciliation tactics permitted sweeping congressional approval of the 1981 cutbacks, such approval also stemmed from fairly widespread public support for the administration's requests. The 1980 election substantially shifted the balance of power within Congress. Republicans now had a Senate majority, leaving harsh welfare critics well positioned to reform major programs. Jesse Helms, the new chairman of the Senate Agriculture Committee, called food stamps "a fiscal monster" and promised to go after the "parasites who have infested the . . . program."[52] Though he confronted a supporter of food stamps in new Nutrition subcommittee chairman Robert Dole, Helms's prominence was one clear indication of the Senate's rightward shift. In the House, Democrats still outnumbered Republicans, but this partisan majority was not matched by an ideological one. Republicans picked up thirty-three seats in 1980, greatly enhancing the position of conservative, mainly Southern, Democrats, who were willing to vote with Republicans on a range of issues. The Reagan administration initially proved quite effective at mobilizing this support.

The shifting composition of Congress reinforced perceptions that Reagan had a mandate to reduce social expenditures. The reality of such a mandate has been hotly disputed, but the perception – not least within the Democratic leadership in the House – was evident.[53] The shock of Reagan's victory, combined with Democratic setbacks in Congress, other signs of a middle-class backlash against government spending (such as California's tax-limiting Proposition 13) and disillusionment with the Democrats' traditional economic recipes, all undermined congressional willingness to obstruct Reagan's initiatives.

There were some challenges to the president's 1981 budget proposals. Dole was able to significantly reduce food stamp cuts, and the Senate Finance Committee, which he chaired, scrapped the president's mandatory workfare proposals. In the House, the Ways and Means Committee adopted only two-thirds of the administration's AFDC cuts, but this effort was overturned when the full House accepted the Republican ("Gramm-Latta") reconciliation bill. The administration came very close to getting all its requested income-support cuts during 1981.

Reagan's attempts to extend these cutbacks subsequently were far less successful. The president's 1982 proposals were severe, asking for $1.2 billion in AFDC cuts and $2.3 billion in food stamp cuts. The requests repeated proposals such as mandatory workfare that had been rejected in 1981, attempted to reduce spending by counting other government programs as income in making benefit and eligibility calculations, and imposed penalties on states for errors.[54]

Very little of this became law. The steep recession that began in late 1981 greatly accelerated the usual loss of momentum presidents experience after their "honeymoon" period. The economic downturn simultaneously reduced faith in Reagan's economic program, allowed marginal members of Reagan's coalition (especially Northern "gypsy moth" Republicans) to act more independently, and heightened concern for the poor. In this changed political context, Congress adopted cuts in AFDC designed to save about $100 million annually by FY1985. Most of these involved penalties to states rather than actual benefit reductions. The House actually tried to restore some of the 1981 cuts, but the Senate rejected these proposals.[55] By 1983, the direct budget-cutting strategy had run its course. The November 1982 elections considerably strengthened the Democrats' position in the House, and the deep recession generated growing political resistance to attacks on poverty programs. Although Reagan continued to request sizable cuts, Congress did not take these proposals seriously.[56] In 1984, Congress actually passed legislation that very slightly expanded AFDC, and the Gramm-Rudman structure of automatic cuts exempted both AFDC and food stamps.

Estimating the impact of the Reagan administration's strategy of direct cuts is difficult, because it requires speculation on how individuals respond to changing program rules. What is clear is that the fate of individual programs diverged. Over the course of Reagan's two terms, food stamps fared relatively well. That this program was purely federal and protected by indexation was critical. Under the Omnibus Budget Reconciliation Act (OBRA), reductions in food-stamp spending were substantial, roughly $1.5 billion in FY1982. This was $1 billion more in cutbacks than Carter had proposed in his outgoing 1981 budget. Close to a million of the 20 million food-stamp recipients were expected to lose all benefits.[57] Cuts in 1982 amounted to about $500 million annually for the next three years. All told, the Congressional Budget Office (CBO) estimated that expenditures on food stamps from 1982–5 were reduced by 13 percent from what pre-1981 policy would have produced.[58]

Nevertheless, many of the cuts in food stamps were designed to produce good budget numbers while minimizing real change. The largest savings came from a temporary reduction of the Thrifty Food Plan (which determined benefit levels).[59] This was precisely the opposite of a decremental cut, producing large immediate savings that would not be sustained. The tactic depended heavily, however, on the peculiar nature of food-stamp benefit calculations, where the "base" was a basket of goods, unaltered by delays in indexing.[60] With growing public resistance to cutbacks, policy became more liberal after 1982. The original base for indexation was restored in 1984 and liberalizations of benefits and/ or eligibility were enacted every year between 1985 and 1990.[61] Some of these changes were quite significant. By 1990, average monthly benefits were more than 10 percent higher in real terms than they had been a decade before. Coverage of the poor population, which had fallen from 65 percent in 1980 to less than 59 percent in 1988, was starting to expand again.[62]

Among means-tested programs, AFDC turned out to be the most vulnerable in the 1980s. The direct assault of 1981–2 had some significant consequences. Congressional Budget Office estimates suggest that the AFDC changes enacted in the 1981 OBRA legislation reduced federal spending by about $680 million per year from FY1984 onward. Up to 500,000 AFDC families may have been removed from the program as a result of the changes, although an unexpected rise in the rolls suggested that many removed may have found their way back on.[63] After 1982, there were a few marginal liberalizations in federal policy, and some significant ones in the Family Support Act of 1988, to be discussed later in this section.

Far and away the most significant retrenchment in AFDC occurred at the state level, where individual benefits are determined.[64] A number of factors left these state programs vulnerable. Advocates for the poor were even less well organized at the state level than in national politics. Benefits were not indexed, which made it easy for states to let inflation erode their real value. The interaction of AFDC benefits and food stamps gave state governments limited incentive to increase welfare payments, because higher AFDC benefits lower an individual's entitlement to the federally financed food stamp program. Probably most important, concerns about interstate economic competition (both the need to keep taxes low and fear of becoming a "welfare magnet") served as an effective brake on state generosity.[65] It is important to stress that the Reagan administration had little to do with this continued erosion of AFDC benefits. Benefits had been falling steadily since the early 1970s. Indeed, the rate of decline slowed in the 1980s, largely because less-rapid inflation dampened the impact of benefit freezes. Ironically, in this very narrow sense, the administration's commitment to bringing inflation down provided some badly needed breathing room for AFDC.

Unemployment insurance (UI) also fared poorly in the 1980s. Despite its social-insurance design and universal status, unemployment insurance's decentralized structure created opportunities for significant retrenchment. Unemployment insurance had a complicated three-tier system of benefits: regular benefits (usually of twenty-six weeks); extended benefits triggered by high unemployment rates (thirteen additional weeks with costs shared by states and the federal government); and additional supplemental compensation that had been legislated in recessions during the 1970s but was not required by law. OBRA introduced a number of restrictions, the most important of which was the tightening of criteria for the extended-benefit program. These changes reduced benefits dramatically during the deep recession of the early 1980s, saving an estimated \$4.6 billion in 1983 alone.[66]

Reagan's position was greatly strengthened by the fact that UI had traditionally relied upon ad hoc adjustments to the system during times of high unemployment. The need for positive action maximized the president's veto leverage. Reagan had the luxury of simply opposing the imposition of the discretionary benefit expansions and trust-fund bailouts that had taken place in past recessions. Thus, a program of federal supplemental compensation benefits was not enacted until late 1982 – just in time for the midterm elections, but later in the recession (and on less generous terms) than had been the case in the 1970s. Despite a much higher level of unemployment, real benefits for the long-term unemployed were roughly one-third lower in the early 1980s than during the recession of 1975–7.[67] In addition, the extra assistance was funded by taxing the benefits of better-off recipients of unemployment insurance, which was itself a kind of benefit cut. All UI benefits were made subject to tax in the 1986 Tax Reform Act; full taxation essentially resulted in a reduction of about 16 percent in the value of UI benefits.[68]

Much of the retrenchment in unemployment insurance, however, occurred at the state level in response to trust-fund difficulties. As with Social Security, the design of programs to include a trust fund offered retrenchment opportunities when the solvency of the fund was in question. Many of the state trust funds had long been on precarious financial footing. Economic difficulties of the late 1970s had led many states to turn to the federal government for loans, which left them ill-prepared for the sharp rise in unemployment that began in 1981. Although the federal government had previously been responsive to state requests for aid, states received a far less sympathetic hearing in the 1980s. One of the major changes introduced in OBRA and extended in 1982 was the tightening of federal-state lending arrangements, putting heavy pressure on state unemployment-insurance systems to tighten their belts.[69]

States responded by altering their programs, and given concern about economic competitiveness, many changes took the form of benefit and eligibility restrictions. The combined impact of these policy changes is unknown, and it is impossible to estimate how much would have occurred without changes in federal rules. What is known is that the strength of the UI safety net weakened considerably in the 1980s. The proportion of the unemployed receiving UI benefits dropped from 50 percent in 1980 to a low of 32 percent in 1988 before recovering somewhat, to 37 percent, in 1990. A report by Mathematica Policy Research for the Department of Labor attributed 22–39 percent of the decline to state policy changes, and 11–16 percent to the new federal taxation of unemployment benefits. Although the magnitude of the impact these findings suggest has been disputed, states clearly responded to severe fiscal pressures by tightening their programs.[70]

With the exception of unemployment insurance, national efforts to directly challenge income-maintenance programs had limited success. Where federal institutions were important, however, important opportunities for significant cutbacks emerged. Although the Reagan administration failed to exploit these opportunities fully in its first initiatives, it did not take long before it made a systematic effort to utilize the decentralized political institutions of the United States for further retrenchment.

Income-support policy and the New Federalism proposals. The only administration initiative that really contained the potential for radical reform of targeted programs was the New Federalism scheme announced in Reagan's State of the Union address in February 1982. Reagan's domestic advisors had been exploring the possibility of shifting major income-support programs to the states for some time. In 1981 aides considered including a proposal to transform AFDC into a block grant in the president's budget, but rejected the idea as politically impractical.[71]

Nevertheless, with the 1981 budget battles behind them, and needing to divert attention from economic problems, administration officials latched onto the plan for a federalism initiative. The administration proposed a swap of responsibilities, in which the states would take charge of AFDC, food stamps, and about forty smaller programs (including several important to the poor, such as the Women, Infants and Children nutrition program [WIC] and Low-Income Energy Assistance). In return, the federal government would take full responsibility for Medicaid. It would also transfer revenue to the states, initially through a trust fund and then by ending excise and windfall oil taxes that the states could choose to pick up if they so desired. The administration claimed the proposal would be revenue neutral, with states neither winning nor losing from the changes.

The New Federalism initiative provides an excellent example of the administration's efforts to use the structure of American political institutions to rein in the welfare state. As a strategy for producing retrenchment, the proposal had much to recommend it. Reagan's proposal would have strongly reinforced the decentralized structure that has traditionally held down American income-support spending, reversing the nationalizing trend of the previous five decades.[72] Income-support programs are highly vulnerable to fiscal competition between states; local jurisdictions are reluctant to raise benefits, fearing that this will produce an influx of the impoverished and an exit by businesses seeking lower tax rates.[73] It was easy to demonstrate that once funds were not earmarked specifically for AFDC and food stamps, states were likely to cut spending. As a report of the Center for Social and Budget Priorities noted: "If AFDC and Food Stamps are 100 percent state funded, and each state dollar brings in no additional funds, then the pressure to shift substantial sums to other state functions with more powerful constituencies will be overwhelming."[74]

From the outset, however, the politics of the proposed swap were precarious. By 1982, Reagan's ability to control the legislative agenda had diminished significantly, and Congress was certain to be skeptical of plans to relinquish its authority. To succeed, Reagan needed to build a political coalition strong enough to force congressional approval. The administration recognized that support from the states would be crucial, but the governors looked to be improbable allies. Ever since the New Deal, the largest state governments had pushed the federal government to assume more of the burden for income-support programs. Getting the states to reverse course would require powerful incentives. Administration strategists identified federal assumption of the Medicaid program as one such incentive. Medicaid was imposing a heavy and rapidly escalating fiscal burden on the states. Reagan's aides hoped that the federal government would have a better chance of bringing these costs under control, since its growing share of health expenditures would increase federal leverage over health-care providers.

The scheme's financing arrangements, however, could not withstand close scrutiny. The revenue sources to be turned over to the states consisted largely of excise taxes – a tax source that would grow very slowly – and the windfall-oil-profits tax, which after the trust fund expired would be available only to the handful of oil-producing states. Even accepting the administration's revenue estimates, it was doubtful that the swap was financially equitable. Claims that costs would balance were based on the assumption that Congress would accept all the administration's severe AFDC and food stamp cuts. State officials were also skeptical of the administration's cost projections for the income-support programs.

Nonetheless, negotiations between the administration and the National Governors' Association continued through the spring of 1982. Fiscal pressures on the states were mounting as the economy faltered, and the governors clearly hoped that a compromise could be fashioned that would offer them fiscal relief. This strain might have allowed the administration to obtain an agreement not normally acceptable to the states. In the end, however, the search for a compromise collapsed and the New Federalism proposals vanished without even being introduced in Congress.

The roots of the impasse were financial. State officials had no interest in a swap unless it promised real help with their budgetary problems. This required the federal government to either accept a larger programmatic burden or transfer more revenues to the states. Neither option was ultimately acceptable to the administration, because each would have worsened the federal government's already embarrassing budget deficit. In short, there was a conflict between Reagan's desire for radical reform and his need for immediate budget savings. The position of OMB is instructive. Stockman's initial interest in the initiative stemmed from his hope that it would provide an avenue for deficit reduction. As negotiations dragged on and it became clear that the Governors' Association would not accept structural reform if it was merely a cover for cutbacks, OMB's position gradually shifted to indifference and finally outright obstruction.[75]

As Timothy Conlan has noted, "There is little doubt that Reagan could have achieved an agreement with the governors on a common federalism plan if he had been willing to devote additional federal resources to their concerns, just as Nixon had done before him."[76] In this respect, the New Federalism proposals were hardly unique. They indicate the mixed consequences of large deficits for programmatic retrenchment. Although the federal deficit had increased pressure for expenditure restraint in social programs, it had made it almost impossible to free up the kinds of resources that might have allowed compensation strategies to ease the path to difficult structural changes. If retrenchment requires the minimization of pain, one of the best ways to accomplish that is to pay for it – that is, to buy off the "losers." The budget deficits made the cost of doing this prohibitive, and in that sense hindered the search for radical programmatic reforms.

Workfare as a retrenchment strategy. If the administration's New Federalism proposals vanished without a trace, its third approach, which sought to introduce "workfare" requirements for welfare recipients, was transformed by Congress into a vehicle for modest program expansion. Again, the president was to find that reform would cost money rather than save it. Congress was receptive to the idea of increasing efforts to move welfare recipients back into the labor market, but resisted efforts to do so in a punitive way. Instead, it suggested a significant expansion of training and support services as well as transitional protections for those leaving AFDC. The reform process remained stuck between congressional unwillingness to make AFDC harsher and Reagan's refusal to countenance significantly higher spending. Despite the claims made at the time of its enactment, the Family Support Act of 1988 (like Britain's reforms of 1986) was in most respects a modest compromise that reflected the tight political parameters constraining reform of means-tested programs.

The idea that welfare recipients should be made to work for their benefits had been a Reagan staple since the early 1970s. The plans advanced in 1981 were modeled on the legislation Reagan introduced in California in 1972, which created the Community Work Experience Program (CWEP).[77] CWEP had in fact been extremely ineffective. Promising to produce thirty thousand jobs, the program at its peak managed barely a thousand, many on state payrolls.[78] Nevertheless, Reagan remained firmly wedded to the workfare approach, and included proposals for mandatory state workfare programs in his 1981 economic program.

Congress gave these proposals short shrift, though it allowed the states the option of implementing workfare programs. In fact, this was the only significant part of Reagan's initial plan for AFDC that Congress rejected. Even so, the experimental option set in place a classic process of policy feedback that eventually produced the Family Support Act of 1988.[79] With a number of states enacting a range of work-oriented experiments that showed promising if modest results, the 1981 legislation gradually led state governors to press for further federal legislation to extend these reforms. Lobbying efforts by the National Governors' Association, and particularly by Arkansas governor Bill Clinton, played a critical role in the passage of legislation in 1988.

Seeking to accelerate movements toward workfare, Reagan proposed a new welfare-reform initiative in his 1986 State of the Union Address. Reagan's announcement produced a flurry of welfare-reform reports with seemingly similar themes. There had in fact been a good deal of attention to workfare proposals in the intervening years, fueled in part by state-level experimentation. Concerns about welfare "dependency" had surfaced among liberals as well as conservatives. Many speculated that a "new consensus" might provide the basis for a new approach to income-support programs, based on a "contract" between recipients and government with work requirements at its core.[80] A number of analysts have also argued that the Family Support Act represented a "policy learning" process, in which new research on state-level programs provided a clear guide to congressional action. However, even though the areas of bipartisan and academic consensus had some impact on the specific design of the legislation, broader political constraints tightly circumscribed the scope and thrust of the act.[81]

Large gaps remained between the liberal vision of "rehabilitative" workfare and conservative conceptions of "deterrent" workfare. Liberals argued that strategies to link welfare benefits to work should lead potential workers back into the labor force; this implied a heavy investment in training and counseling, along with efforts to make jobs available and attractive. Ironically, such approaches refocused attention on the huge barriers to work created by America's sharply targeted income-support system, and generated new liberal demands for program expansion. "Making work pay" required that day care and health care be available to the working poor. It also meant that wages needed to produce incomes at least near the poverty line, which would require a higher minimum wage and/or some kind of wage subsidy.[82] The new programs in California and

Massachusetts contained some of these features. As a result, although analyses suggested that these workfare plans might well be cost-effective in the long run, they increased short-term expenses.

The Reagan administration never intended workfare to cost money. The goal was to deter potential welfare recipients rather than to provide more resources for them. This helps to explain why administration officials worried so little about the way that the 1981 budget cuts had worsened work incentives within AFDC. Workfare would generate work incentives by making AFDC less appealing, without requiring the budget outlays that less punitive approaches (such as allowing welfare recipients to keep some of their earnings from work) required.[83] Nevertheless, this deterrent vision of welfare had limited political appeal, either with Congress or among the states. Although public opinion (and apparently, most welfare recipients) looked quite favorably on the idea of expecting some kind of reciprocity in return for benefits, this fell short of accepting punitive programs that offered participants no real opportunities.

The initiative on welfare reform shifted to Congress almost immediately after the president's speech. Perhaps because of the recognition that even a workfare-based reform was bound to cost money, the administration's domestic-policy group called only for further encouragement of state experimentation in its long-awaited report.[84] After a series of false starts, the administration backed a bill sponsored by some House Republicans, but the legislation came nowhere near approval.

The flexibility of workfare as an abstraction allowed liberals and conservatives alike to use rhetoric that sounded as if an agreement had been reached. However, a broad policy consensus remained elusive. Where conservatives saw an opportunity to expand the use of "sticks," liberals searched for new "carrots." Democrats in both houses were able to agree on a basic reform strategy. New legislation would include a work or training requirement for recipients except those with very young children. Child-support rules would also be strengthened to try to increase fathers' responsibility for children and cut welfare costs. At the same time, resources for education, child care, and job training would be expanded, benefits would be made more generous (including a requirement that states make AFDC available to two-parent households) and work incentives would be restored and strengthened by expanding transitional health benefits. Because the House version's benefits were significantly more liberal, its costs were higher: $5.7 billion over five years, compared to $2.3 billion for the Senate bill.[85]

However, the scope of these initiatives suggested the limited range of politically practical options. Even the more expensive House bill would have increased AFDC spending by only about 5 percent a year over the five-year period. Reagan's veto power left him in a strong position, and Southern Democrats were also skeptical of significant increases in spending. The most progressive parts of the House legislation, such as proposals to establish a national minimum welfare standard, were dropped early on. Following the passage of House and

Senate versions, the old "conservative coalition" of Southerners and Republicans resurfaced in a key test vote in the House, instructing House conferees to accept the Senate's spending limits.

These developments caused an erosion of liberal support for the Family Support Act. Many income-maintenance advocates complained that Reagan's pressure and deficit fears had stripped the reform of its liberal features, leaving only those provisions designed to attract conservative support. Nevertheless, the legislation that finally passed contained a number of new entitlements: AFDC for poor two-parent families was extended to all states; and training, childcare, and transitional benefits for working recipients were expanded.[86] As Michael Wiseman summed up the meaning of the Family Support Act, "President Reagan may have begun the decade with the intention of reducing Washington's role in public assistance, but in the end it grew."[87]

At the same time, the significance of this legislation for AFDC has often been vastly exaggerated. Once the areas where there was no consensus and no willingness to compromise were stripped out, not much was left. The act's most important provisions are probably those strengthening state child-support enforcement, which will have only a peripheral impact on AFDC. Most analysts doubt that the limited fiscal resources provided under the legislation will be sufficient to fund adequate training and educational programs, and even the success of well-funded state programs has been modest. According to Judith Gueron, a leading expert on job training, replicating such programs on a national level would require expenditures on training and support services of approximately $4.5 billion a year, rather than the roughly $1 billion currently being spent. Even then, such programs might reduce the welfare rolls by only 10 percent.[88]

As always, the limited fiscal capacities of state governments will be a major constraint. Twenty-four of the thirty-three states that implemented new training programs mandated under the Family Support Act before October 1990 were unable to claim their full federal allocation because they could not come up with the required matching funds, and in 1991 only $600 million of the federal government's $1 billion authorization could be used, for the same reason.[89] Like the Fowler reforms in Britain, the Family Support Act clearly indicated the constraints on structural reform within means-tested programs, especially when the government had little money to spend.

Flourishing despite austerity: the earned-income tax credit. The outcome of struggles over AFDC stands in striking contrast to the experience of the means-tested income-maintenance program that underwent the greatest change in the 1980s, the earned-income tax credit (EITC). The changes in the EITC, however, were dramatically expansionary rather than illustrative of successful retrenchment. Indeed, the EITC stands out as the great political success of the retrenchment era.[90] The refundable tax credit for working-poor families was indexed and considerably expanded in the Tax Reform Act of 1986. Another sizable increase came as part of the budget agreement of 1990. From 1980 to 1990, the number of families receiving the EITC grew from 7 million to 11.3 million, while expenditures rose from $2 billion to $7 billion, and were projected to rise to $9 billion by 1992.[91]

A number of considerations made the EITC an attractive vehicle for expanded income support. Because it went only to working families, the recipients were clearly deserving, and the program served to improve work incentives. In a period in which government intervention was viewed with some skepticism, the market-orientation and simplicity of a tax-credit scheme had wide appeal. That much of the spending involved was off-budget made the program easier to sell in a time of fiscal stress. Furthermore, the program was ambiguous and flexible enough that it could be attached as a solution to a variety of problems: regressive taxation, low wages, and the affordability of child care.[92] The EITC could potentially attract broad bipartisan support.

Although these aspects of program structure explain why the EITC was the preferred vehicle for expanded income support, they do not explain why expansion was considered in the first place. The Reagan administration had earlier expressed hostility to the idea of providing benefits to the working poor. As David Stockman put it in defending the removal of working families from AFDC in 1981, "We just don't accept the assumption that the Federal Government has a responsibility to supplement the income of the working poor."[93] Between 1975 and 1985, the real value of the EITC declined. It was only with the reversal of political momentum after the early 1980s that expansion became a possibility. Democrats sought a variety of ways to increase spending on income-support policies. Following public reaction to the cutbacks of 1981 and the emergence of the fairness issue, Republicans showed increasing concern that their policies not be seen as overly regressive. In both 1986 and 1990, EITC expansion was added to broad policy packages to improve the progressivity of the overall legislation.[94] The growth of EITC, which by the early 1990s involved expenditures almost as great as the federal government's share of AFDC expenses, provided considerable evidence that the impetus behind retrenchment in income support had dissipated.

EXPLAINING OUTCOMES

Income-support programs have been consistent targets for conservative rhetoric, but not for radical reform. In each country, the structure of income support remains fundamentally similar to that found by conservative governments when they took office. In the case of means-tested programs, both the strategies adopted and the outcomes were remarkably similar in the two countries. Both Thatcher and Reagan had harshly criticized the major means-tested programs and promised important changes. Instead, they produced some marginal tightening of benefits and eligibility, but no fundamental reform. This stemmed largely from the already-residualist nature of the major means-tested programs.

Although Thatcher and Reagan had criticized the inefficiency and work disincentives of existing programs, these were inherent features of residualist approaches to income support. Both administrations found that the only viable ways to make these programs markedly more efficient and supportive of work required greater expenditures and broader eligibility. This was signaled clearly by the glaring failure of each administration's highly publicized review teams to produce a blueprint for radical reform. Fowler settled for some streamlining of the existing system, while the White House's staff ended up calling only for further state experimentation.

Forced to fall back on straightforward spending cuts, both administrations quickly found that this effort to make means tests meaner ran into serious political difficulties. Means testing generally does make for weak programs, but this proposition needs to be placed in perspective. There are a number of factors that at least partially offset the political weakness of the poor. First, means-tested income-support programs offered few opportunities for retrenchment strategies that minimized visible pain. As previous chapters have indicated, cutbacks are facilitated when governments can somehow reduce their salience. Successful strategies include efforts to buy off opposition by substituting private alternatives for some recipients, shifting of the responsibility for cuts to local jurisdictions, or decremental approaches that spread the impact of reductions over time. In this case, however, such opportunities were limited: There are no private substitutes for income support, and the explicitness of direct transfers makes any cutback highly visible. Thus, although constituents supportive of the existing programs were politically weak, Reagan and Thatcher were unable to fully capitalize on that because assaults on income-support programs were so open.

High visibility combined with a second factor to limit opportunities for cutbacks: the vulnerability of both administrations to the "fairness" issue. Despite Reagan and Thatcher's electoral success, polls consistently indicated that each was perceived to treat the poor unfairly. Popular hostility to programs for the poor, which had helped to elect Reagan and Thatcher, dissipated rapidly. The recognition that equity concerns posed a potential threat to their political support forced both leaders into a series of retreats from efforts to directly cut programs benefiting the poor. Furthermore, over time both administrations found themselves considerably expanding the most palatable targeted program – supplements for working families with low incomes.

This is not to suggest that the fairness issue has prevented either government from pursuing sharply inegalitarian policies. In particular, the labor-market position of low-income workers has been seriously undermined, through antiunion actions and (in the United States) efforts to reduce the real value of the minimum wage. Income distribution has become significantly more unequal in the 1980s in both countries, and especially in Britain. Even so, the means-tested programs are highly visible symbols of a government's attitude toward the poor. Both Reagan and Thatcher learned that cutting these programs risked tarnishing their images on an important issue.

Perhaps surprisingly, universal benefits have been somewhat more subject to change. In part, this simply reflects the fact that the relative generosity of these programs gave conservative governments more room to maneuver. Nevertheless, universal programs, especially unemployment insurance, also possessed certain political weaknesses. In both Britain and the United States, unemployment-insurance programs have proven to be the most vulnerable sectors of income-support systems. The weak political position of the labor movement, which provided the only enduring support for unemployment benefits, helped to leave these programs unprotected. Another critical source of weakness has been the prominence of work-incentive issues. Austerity has made what British conservatives termed the "why work?" question a compelling concern. Unemployment-insurance programs offered opportunities to combine lower spending and stronger work incentives. In both countries, benefit reductions have fallen on the best-off recipients, as cutbacks have taken the form of taxation of benefits and, in Britain, an end to earnings-related supplements.

In the United States, two peculiar features of the UI program also facilitated retrenchment. First, for once the administration occupied the institutional high ground. The unemployment-insurance program had always been expanded during recessions in an ad hoc manner that required positive federal action. To diminish UI's role, Reagan needed only to prevent the traditional policy response. Second, the program's decentralized structure allowed Reagan to shift much of the burden for austerity to the states. By restricting federal support for state trust funds, the administration was able to pressure states to curtail their UI systems.

The other universal program covered in this chapter, Child Benefit, has proven to be slightly more durable. As a universal benefit unrelated to work effort, Child Benefit is not vulnerable to the work-incentive arguments that weakened unemployment insurance. Despite its critical contribution to alleviating the poverty trap, however, it is widely regarded as poorly targeted and is probably the least popular of Britain's universal benefits. This political weakness did not allow a vigorous, straightforward assault on the program, but did permit the Thatcher government to pursue a strategy of decremental cutbacks. Carefully timed low upratings eroded Child Benefit's real value somewhat, and its relative role substantially.

The limited success of efforts to cut programs for the able-bodied poor should not be taken as evidence of the political appeal of these programs. Rather, their endurance reflects that policy in this area has rarely ventured far from the residualist model. That, combined with the contradictions inevitably associated with expanded means tests and the difficulty of designing retrenchment strategies to dissipate potential opposition, largely accounts for the relatively small impact of Reagan and Thatcher on these programs.

III
The embattled welfare state

6
The impact of conservative governments

How successful were Reagan and Thatcher's efforts to achieve retrenchment? Answering that question requires a return to the distinction drawn in Chapter 1 between programmatic and systemic retrenchment. Programmatic retrenchment modifies individual sectors of the welfare state; systemic retrenchment modifies the context for future struggles over programs. This distinction illuminates the divergent experiences of Britain and the United States. Different policy areas have offered quite different political opportunities for programmatic retrenchment. There is more variation in the outcomes among particular programs than there is between the overall records of the two countries. In neither country has there been a marked curtailment of social expenditure or a radical shift toward residualization. Nonetheless, programmatic retrenchment generally progressed further in Britain.

If the British Conservatives had only modest success in pursuing programmatic retrenchment, their record in achieving systemic retrenchment was if anything less impressive. Several changes in the political context in Britain have probably weakened the prospects for radical change in the welfare state. Shifts in public opinion, modifications of political institutions, and the restructuring of government finances have all tended to diminish rather than enhance prospects for further retrenchment. The Thatcher government did have some success in reducing the political influence of welfare state supporters – and of unions in particular – but its overall record could not be regarded as one of notable systemic retrenchment. In most respects this was also true in the United States. However, there is a major exception: The Reagan administration's success in curtailing the federal government's long-term capacity to fund social programs. The emergence of a "politics of deficits" in the United States will impose a substantial constraint on the American welfare state for the foreseeable future.

This chapter provides evidence to support these assertions. The first section offers brief examinations of major programs not covered in the last three chapters. The second section joins this discussion to the evidence presented on pensions, housing, and income support, to evaluate the overall success of programmatic-retrenchment efforts. The third section turns to the broader environment, where change might foster systemic retrenchment, to round out an assessment of retrenchment outcomes in the two countries.

PROGRAMMATIC RETRENCHMENT IN HEALTH CARE, AND DISABILITY AND SICKNESS PROGRAMS

An evaluation of the outcome of programmatic-retrenchment efforts requires consideration of program areas other than those examined in the preceding three chapters. This section extends the analysis to two additional sectors: health care, and sickness and disability benefits. These cases indicate again the widely disparate fates of different welfare state programs. While providing further evidence of how features of institutional and programmatic-design influence the prospects for retrenchment, they confirm the profound difficulties confronting Reagan and Thatcher. With limited exceptions, the record in these policy domains was generally one of painful setbacks and minimal progress toward fulfilling the conservative social-policy agenda.

Health care

Health care is a key sector of the welfare state. Involving matters of life and death, it is often the site of heated controversy; and because it is also an area of extensive economic activity, a staggering array of powerful interests compete over policy reform. More than in other social-policy domains, retrenchment advocates had to be cognizant of these constraints. As advocates of market processes, the administrations were further circumscribed in health care by the economic and political realities surrounding private alternatives to public provision. Although the subject of continued debate, the evidence suggests that private health-care systems have great difficulties controlling costs – at least without resorting to politically unpalatable techniques. Hemmed in by popular sensitivities, powerful interests, and economic realities, both governments generally found health care to be a cause of political headaches rather than a target for successful retrenchment.

This was especially true for the Thatcher government. The National Health Service (NHS) is the "Jewel in the Crown" of the British welfare state. Offering a comprehensive, state-owned and managed health-care system for all citizens – with minimal charges – it is the most striking British example of an institutional welfare state program.[1] As such, it became an object of scorn for the most ideologically committed retrenchment advocates within the Thatcher government. Nevertheless, the NHS has proven to be remarkably resilient. Early searches for radical reform proved impractical, and the government's cost-containment efforts were politically damaging.

The Thatcher government simultaneously investigated prospects for explicit privatization and decremental cutbacks. The ultimate goal of both strategies was to substitute private health insurance for public provision. Proponents of privatization advocated a program of mandated private insurance to replace the NHS. Advocates of decrementalism hoped that a slow erosion of the quality of the NHS would gradually enhance the private sector's appeal. Such a process, they believed, might eventually result in a two-tier system of health care, and generate the kind of "tipping effects" that fostered radical retrenchment in housing policy.

The surge in private insurance coverage after Thatcher's election gave encouragement to proponents of retrenchment. Thatcher's first Social Services secretary, Patrick Jenkin, set up a working party to evaluate the NHS. The team eventually suggested a system of mandatory private insurance. This proposal was followed by the Central Policy Review Staff (CPRS) report, leaked in the fall of 1982, which considered a similar approach.[2]

The proposals nevertheless proved unattractive for a number of reasons.[3] First, the popularity of the NHS ensured widespread opposition to any scheme jeopardizing universal provision. The structure of the NHS, which provided a wide range of services with no charge at point of delivery, insured that any cutbacks would generate an immediate reaction. Second, and probably just as important for the Thatcher government, privatization appeared likely to be expensive. However unattractive to conservative ideology, the concentration of control over health-care provision had proven to be a powerful cost-containment technique.

The expansion of private insurance confirmed the incompatibility of privatization and cost containment. Coverage expanded rapidly from 1979 to 1981, and proponents hoped that a fifth of the population might be covered by the mid-1980s. With growth, however, came a cost explosion. Although the retail price index rose 14 percent from 1981 to 1983, the average premium cost rose 61 percent. As a result, the expansion of private insurance had slowed considerably by 1982.[4] Norman Fowler, Jenkin's successor, publicly rejected mandated insurance schemes in 1982, signaling the government's clear recognition of the likely costs of such a plan to employers, if not directly to the public sector.

If the high cost of private insurance forced the rejection of radical reform proposals, it also hindered the government's more incremental strategy. The first Thatcher government took a number of steps to increase the attractiveness of private provision. Contributions to health plans for workers making less than £8,500 were made tax deductible, and restrictions on private practice by NHS doctors were loosened. The Labour government's decision to phase out "pay beds" for private care in NHS hospitals was also reversed. Even so, the escalating costs of private insurance undermined these efforts by the end of 1981.

The government's efforts to restrain NHS expenditures to increase the relative appeal of private care were also unsuccessful. The popularity of the NHS and the strength of its political supporters have made cutbacks politically damaging. The government's initially ambiguous view of the NHS gave way to Thatcher's assurance that "the National Health Service is safe with us." Demands for austerity were supplanted by announcements of the government's sizable improvements in the NHS. The government increased expenditures far faster than inflation, although demographic and technological pressures meant that increases in real provision were small.

The demise of privatization prospects for the NHS was confirmed in 1988. A cabinet committee established to consider comprehensive reforms and chaired by the prime minister began with a range of radical options including compulsory private insurance and contracting-out schemes like the one adopted in pension policy.[5] The same circumstances that had blocked privatization efforts in the early 1980s quickly came into play again. Proposals for dramatic changes were rejected, and the government fell back on alterations within the structure of the NHS. The promise to increase "competition" within the public sector by creating an internal market offered the government a chance to put a free-market gloss on its decision. In words that echoed the claims made for the Fowler review of social security, the internal market was touted as "the most radical reform of health care in forty years." In truth, however, the outcome was in broad terms a ratification of the status quo.[6]

As with every NHS reform, there have been those who warn that the "internal market" is the first step down a road to privatization. Nevertheless, the repeated rejection of more dramatic alternatives even when the Conservative government was at the height of its political power suggests otherwise. A number of features of health-care policy made serious cutbacks or privatization unlikely, and led Thatcher to reluctantly accept the continuation of Britain's most universal social program. First, privatization would cost a fortune. Even a limited expansion of private insurance had demonstrated its vulnerability to cost explosions, which would be expensive to employers, voters, and (if tax expenditures were used to promote private care) the government. Second, privatization, especially if pursued by initially driving down the quality of the NHS, was certain to be overwhelmingly unpopular. The privatization of housing and pensions was facilitated by the way government policy focused popular attention on new private benefits while delaying the onset of public-sector limitations. In the case of housing, private benefits (the right to buy council housing) took place immediately, whereas public-sector costs (a more limited, residualized public-housing stock) appeared problematic only in the long run. In the case of pensions, the onset of both private benefits and public costs was delayed, since those near retirement age were left unaffected. For health care, however, the privatization strategy required an erosion of the care available through the NHS to encourage people to use private alternatives. This approach maximized the government's exposure, heightened opposition from providers and consumers, and forced Thatcher to repeatedly expand the resources made available to the public sector.

No issue was more consistently vexing to the Conservatives in the 1980s than health care. Government supporters as well as opponents identified it as Thatcherism's Achilles' heel.[7] Even a hint of privatization efforts caused a powerful backlash, and the government frequently found itself pressured to put more resources into the NHS. Finding that the issue was probably its most potent weapon, the Labour Party repeatedly moved to mobilize the electorate in favor of public health care for all, free at the point of delivery.[8] By the end of the decade, despite riding high on her third electoral triumph, Margaret Thatcher found herself carefully penning a foreword to the white paper on the internal market reforms, presenting herself as a defender of the central principles of the NHS.

If British Conservatives struggled unsuccessfully to strengthen the private sector's limited role in health care, the Reagan administration had to wrestle with the deeply troubling legacy of a long-standing American commitment to a predominantly private system. Alone among major industrial nations, the United States has failed to develop a system of national health insurance. The impasse between liberals seeking a larger role for public provision, and conservatives (backed by health-care providers) seeking to maintain a market-oriented approach, has yielded a hybrid system. Extensive private health-care provision coexists with two major public programs: Medicare, which provides support to the elderly and disabled who are eligible under Social Security, and Medicaid, a means-tested program restricted largely to those eligible for AFDC and Supplemental Security Income (SSI).[9] By the time Reagan entered office, this hybrid system faced a cost explosion.

Demographic and technological pressures increased health-care costs, but there is little question that the specific design of the American system greatly exacerbated those pressures. Public-health programs injected significant spending into the system, but without the controls that might restrain costs. The reliance on a diffuse group of "third parties" to pay medical expenses after the fact provided powerful incentives for cost escalation.[10] By the early 1980s, the situation was clearly out of control. Total health expenditures had increased from 6.1 percent of GNP in 1965 to 9.4 percent in 1980 and continued to rise. Public expenditure for Medicaid and Medicare increased (in constant 1986 dollars) from $23.9 billion in 1970 to $67.4 billion in 1981.[11]

The crisis of this hybrid health-care system has dominated the evolution of policy in this arena. The Reagan administration did find that this complex, fragmented arrangement offered room for some retrenchment strategies, but a push toward market mechanisms did nothing to alleviate the cost crunch and may have exacerbated the problem. Policy change revealed the paradox of sizable cutbacks in benefits provided by public programs, especially in Medicare, with a continuation of escalating costs. The failure of these efforts meant that by the late 1980s, the political momentum shifted, raising the prospect of a renewed effort to expand governmental control over health care.[12]

At first, the Reagan administration sensed little tension between its concern with expenditure constraint and its desire to expand the role of private markets in health care. The cost explosion was attributed to a too-intrusive public sector; health-care inflation reflected the invisibility of costs to consumers. Along with congressional allies, the administration began to design a set of "procompetitive'' reforms to foster competition among providers and a heightened awareness of the costs of health care among consumers.[13] Regulatory impediments to a fully functioning health-care market were to be stripped away, while the role of third-party payment was to be diminished. Vouchers for Medicare would lead to a new cost consciousness, as would a cap on tax subsidies to employer-provided health care.

These proposals generated both technical and political difficulties. Few in Congress shared the administration's confidence that a reduced federal role would solve the cost-containment problem. The strategy's reliance on increasing the financial burdens facing health-care consumers was a major political weakness. ''Making the market work'' required that consumers pay more of the cost of their care, but this entailed imposing obvious costs onto a large constituency, an approach to policy that Congress loathed. As the administration became more preoccupied with immediate budgetary savings after 1981, broad market-oriented reforms increasingly gave way to cost-shifting to consumers, which promised a more immediate contribution to deficit reduction. This shift in emphasis, however, was precisely the kind that was sure to block congressional support for the Reagan initiatives.[14]

Nevertheless, the pressure to do something was intensifying. Health-care costs continued to rise far faster than inflation in the early 1980s. In 1982 alone, such costs rose 11 percent, whereas the overall inflation rate was less than 4 percent.[15] Like Social Security, the Medicare system faced an impending trust-fund crisis. As budget pressures forced Congress to cut popular programs, escalating health-care costs became intolerable; in this context, Congress acted. In less than a year, it managed to introduce the most radical reform of Medicare since the program's enactment in 1965: a new system of prospective payments.

Prospective payment required the institution of centralized price controls on particular medical procedures eligible for Medicare reimbursement. The establishment of elaborate price scales for diagnosis-related groups (DRGs) was designed to impose greater pressures for cost containment. It also represented the kind of governmental regulation of the health-care industry that conservatives and medical interests have traditionally fought to avoid. That DRGs nonetheless became law provides a striking indication of the difficult choices the health-care cost explosion had created.

Requirements for tougher cost controls were first floated in the deficit-reducing Tax Equity and Fiscal Responsibility Act (TEFRA) of 1982. TEFRA called for strict controls to be introduced if a system of prospective payment was not implemented within a short period. The imposition of this deadline led the Reagan administration and the hospitals (though not the health-insurance industry) to back DRGs as the lesser evil. As a result, the legislation flew through Congress, aided by its attachment to the essential Social Security legislation of 1983.[16]

In addition to this important piece of cost-containment legislation, public-health programs have been repeated sources of expenditure constraint since

1981. Although the trend toward cutbacks has slowed or even reversed in other areas of social policy, in health care the pressure for austerity has remained high. Again, this pressure reflects the severity of the financial crisis in this field. Indeed, it is difficult to know how to portray these efforts. Exploding costs meant that real spending grew rapidly even as benefits diminished. Because policy changes have been heavily restrictive, it is probably appropriate to use the term retrenchment; however, it is important to recognize that expenditures have continued to rise.

Surprisingly, the universal Medicare program has been at least as prominent a target as means-tested Medicaid. In 1981 Medicaid faced larger cutbacks – primarily because eligibility was reduced by changes enacted in AFDC. In all, OBRA removed roughly 500,000 families from the Medicaid rolls.[17] However, Reagan failed in his effort to transform the program into a block grant with a cap on federal expenditures; many of the reductions introduced were designed to be temporary, and were allowed to expire in 1985. From 1984 on, Congress moved in a series of incremental steps to expand Medicaid coverage. Legislative changes were introduced in every year between 1984 and 1990.[18] Furthermore, Medicaid was excluded from the automatic cutback provisions of Gramm-Rudman, whereas Medicare was not.

Despite being a "middle-class entitlement," Medicare has faced sustained budgetary pressure. Virtually every budget round since 1981 has involved some significant effort to reduce Medicare expenditures. Medicare contributed heavily to the spending cuts agreed to in the "budget summit" of November 1987, and fully one-third of the outlay cuts made in 1988.[19] The 1990 budget negotiations tested the limits of political tolerance for Medicare retrenchment. The initial bipartisan agreement called for $60 billion in Medicare cuts over five years – almost half of the total projected domestic-spending cutbacks. This proposal was widely regarded as so extreme (and so weighted toward direct cuts on beneficiaries) that Congress rejected the entire package, eventually agreeing to $43 billion in cuts falling primarily on providers.[20] The 1990 budget agreement nevertheless indicated Medicare's precarious position. After a strong public outcry major cuts were still introduced, although only after they were redesigned to reduce the visible impact on voters. Social Security, by contrast, remained "off the table" throughout the negotiations.

It is extremely difficult to estimate the total size of cutbacks in health-care programs. Projections of costs in the absence of reform are inexact, and it is hard to distinguish among "gimmick" cuts that meet budgetary-spending targets but do not actually reduce spending, cuts that produce efficiency gains without reducing services, and cuts that reduce services or shift costs to consumers.[21] An Urban Institute analysis suggested that cuts enacted in the first three Reagan budget rounds reduced spending on Medicare by 6.8 percent and on Medicaid by 2.8 percent.[22] Subsequent cutbacks have added significantly to this total. Estimated Medicare expenditures in 1993 are projected to be 27 percent lower than they would have been without reforms – a savings of $61.5 billion per year, although there is good reason to believe that these congressional estimates substantially overstate the true savings.[23] More than 80 percent of these cuts initially fell on providers, with an unknown amount being passed on to consumers. Medicare's protection of the elderly from the financial risks associated with health care has clearly deteriorated. Between 1980 and 1988, out-of-pocket health-care expenses for the elderly rose from 12.8 percent of total income to more than 18.2 percent. Put another way, whereas in 1980 it took the equivalent of 2.8 Social Security checks to cover health-care expenses, in 1988 the average recipient needed to spend 4.5 checks.[24]

This leaves two critical questions: Why has health care proven relatively vulnerable to retrenchment, and why has this been more true in the case of universal Medicare than means-tested Medicaid? Two major factors appear to account for the health-care sector's vulnerability. First, the existence of a clear financial crisis within the sector forced drastic action. Second, in contrast to arrangements in Britain, the structure of the American health-care system offered opportunities to shield consumers from the direct impact of cutbacks.

The health-care crisis occurred both inside and outside of public programs.[25] General medical-cost inflation pushed up prices while threatening the Medicare trust fund with insolvency. Both aspects of the problem made Medicare vulnerable. Cutbacks were easier to justify when something was so clearly wrong, and when it could be noted that real spending was actually increasing in spite of retrenchment. The need to balance the trust fund provided a sense of urgency that, as with Social Security, facilitated a rapid response.[26] That the trust-fund crisis played a major role is indicated by the focus of cutbacks on the Part A hospital-insurance part of the Medicare program, where trust-fund imbalances loomed, rather than Part B physician reimbursement, which faced no immediate crisis.

The structure of health-care programs, which allowed politicians to impose retrenchment on health-care providers rather than on the massive constituency of Medicare and Medicaid consumers, also facilitated cutbacks by allowing individual groups to be isolated and then hit with losses. More important, the split between producers and consumers allowed a strategy of obfuscation. Rather than imposing cutbacks directly on consumers, promoters of retrenchment could act indirectly, encouraging providers to pass on cost increases to their patients.

Congress has repeatedly rejected sharp increases in consumers' contributions to health-care costs in favor of reductions in reimbursements to hospitals and physicians. Although many of these cutbacks may have been passed on to consumers in one form or another, their impact has clearly been less visible and therefore less politically damaging. The fragmented nature of the health-care system made this tactic possible. In Britain, it was impossible to pass on costs to consumers without introducing an overwhelmingly unpopular new feature into the system. In the United States, as Allen Schick has noted, "Uncle Sam had a weak voice in determining how health care was to be delivered. In the cutback era . . . Congress has turned this weakness to political advantage. Because it only pays the bills, the federal government need not dictate where the cuts are to be distributed. It can leave this task to providers and states.''[27]

The relative resiliency of Medicaid appeared to stem from a number of factors. Unlike Medicare, Medicaid faced no trust-fund problem. Medicaid was also a widely accepted part of the social safety net, and with Medicaid eligibility already (like AFDC) eroded by the inflation of the 1970s, future cutbacks were hard to justify. Because the states feared they would have to make up reductions in federal spending on the jointly funded program, they constituted a powerful lobby against reductions in the Medicaid program in the early 1980s (although rising costs have also made them reluctant to accede to the expansions of the past few years).[28] Perhaps the most surprising allies for Medicaid have come from the private sector. A wide range of provider groups and employer interests, concerned that the growing ranks of uninsured among the working poor were fueling pressure for much more serious health-care reform, have rallied to support expansions of Medicaid.[29]

The unusual sight of private sector actors rushing to shore up and even expand public social programs indicates how retrenchment prospects have been constrained by the limitations of private health-care systems. In both countries, cost-containment issues made strategies of compensation in which private care would be substituted for public programs an unpalatable alternative. Publicly financed, publicly provided care remains the norm in Britain. In the United States, although there have been some significant examples of retrenchment in public programs, the Reagan-Bush era ended with the federal government poised to extend its role in the health-care system.

Sickness and disability

Few groups are as likely to be considered more deserving of public support than the sick and disabled, and thus it might be expected that efforts to achieve retrenchment in this arena would be difficult. In fact, both governments failed to achieve dramatic reforms. Initially radical cutbacks introduced in the United States failed to be sustained; the Thatcher government, for its part, managed to institute reforms that were superficially striking but largely devoid of real content.

Britain has fully developed public programs for sickness pay and disability insurance. The Thatcher government had moderate success in curbing disability expenditures. Although the reform of sickness pay was touted as an important example of privatization, the changes were largely cosmetic. Instead, the evolution of government policy on sickness pay demonstrates the limitations of compensation strategies and provides a glaring illustration of how preoccupation with public-expenditure cuts can overrule coherent social-policy objectives.

Disability expenditures grew significantly during the first half of the decade, due largely to a sharp increase in the number of beneficiaries. Higher unemployment appears to have encouraged applications for disability, and government efforts to pare the rolls were largely unsuccessful. The absence of alternatives forced the Thatcher government to resort to the politically damaging strategy of cutting benefits. As in many other arenas, the ability to lower the visibility of cutbacks was crucial to the government's limited success in this area. The government had one major victory: the change of indexation rules. As with the Basic Pension, changing the basis for upratings from earnings to prices froze real benefit levels, producing a gradual reduction of replacement rates. It also did so at little cost. By contrast, the government was forced to restore a 5 percent "abatement" of benefits introduced in 1980 after persistent opposition, and proposals to tax disability benefits were dropped. As a result, real expenditures grew along with the rise in recipients.

The government laid claim to more substantial reforms in sickness pay. The Statutory Sickness Pay (SSP) scheme adopted in 1982 transferred authority for short-term sickness-benefit payments from the government to the private sector. On its face, the reform of sick pay represented a notable example of successful privatization. In reality, it revealed how reliance on compensation strategies can undermine a government's retrenchment ambitions. As in the case of pension reform, the government found that obtaining the acquiescence of employers was expensive. As Michael O'Higgins noted, "In a series of attempts to meet . . . [employer] objections, the government announced five successive versions of the scheme, each offering more or different forms of compensation."[30] The Thatcher government's repeated concessions ultimately produced tax expenditures that roughly offset the public-expenditure costs of the original program.

Because sick pay was made taxable, the new plan did somewhat reduce benefits to workers. In essence, the change redistributed resources from employees to employers. By obscuring the nature of state subsidies, the shift also gave employers the chance to claim credit for the benefits provided. The scheme's advantages for employers were revealed in 1986, when SSP was extended from the first eight weeks of sickness to twenty-eight weeks. Although the original legislation had generated employer opposition and lengthy negotiations, the extension was accepted without protest.

But what did the government gain from the reform? Although probably not displeased with the modest shift of resources to employers, the tangible policy impact of the program was limited. As two close observers concluded, "Far from privatizing sick pay, the benefit is, in effect, paid from the National Insurance Fund. . . . From an economic viewpoint, compensation for sickness remains firmly in the public sector."[31] Because the government's costs took the form of tax expenditures rather than on-budget outlays, however, the expense would no longer appear in public-expenditure figures. Even though this accounting convenience was of some use to the government, it hardly amounts to a case of successful retrenchment.

The United States has no public sick-pay program, but it has a well-established system of disability insurance (DI). Part of the Social Security system, DI paid $15.4 billion in benefits to about 3 million disabled workers in

1980.[32] The Reagan administration saw disability insurance, like most facets of the American welfare state, as a costly, inefficient program that weakened work incentives while requiring ever-higher outlays. Unlike many other programs, in this case the administration seemed to be in a strong position to act. Having been authorized by Congress to review the disability rolls, the administration for once had the institutional high ground. It would take positive action from Congress to curtail Reagan's retrenchment efforts, and the Republicans held a majority in the Senate.

The outcome reveals that a strong institutional position was not enough. The administration's harsh and highly visible cutbacks led to an embarrassing reversal. Faced by a rapidly mobilized and fierce opposition that led its congressional allies to desert, the Reagan administration reluctantly gave up its retrenchment ambitions and settled for much less dramatic cutbacks.

Reagan's push for retrenchment in the DI program took advantage of an initiative introduced before he took office. The program had expanded rapidly after 1965, with the number of recipients increasing from just under a million to almost 2.5 million in 1975. Tighter standards of evaluation led to sharply lower approval rates for applications thereafter, but high costs and concerns about the prospect of trust-fund insolvency led to continuing pressures for retrenchment during the Carter administration.[33] In 1980, Congress authorized the Social Security Administration to reexamine the existing disability rolls to see if some recipients could now be declared ineligible. Expectations were limited. The congressional conference report on the bill projected savings of only $10 million over the first four years.[34]

Enforcement of the new requirements, however, fell to an eager Reagan administration. The result indicated how vigorously the administration would pursue retrenchment when given the opportunity. As Martha Derthick observed, the administration's enthusiasm "alter[ed] . . . the spirit of the undertaking. What had been conceived by Congress in 1980 was deliberate invigoration of a review procedure that had been too feeble to have much effect. What was set in motion in 1981 was more like a purge."[35]

Congress had expected the evaluations to begin in early 1982. Instead, the administration began reviews within three months of coming to office, casting its net far more widely than had been anticipated. The Social Security Administration proceeded to drop a staggering share of those evaluated – nearly 50 percent – from the rolls. By 1984, nearly 500,000 participants had been removed from the program, although more than 200,000 (well over half of those who appealed) had their benefits reinstated.

The result was chaos. Administrative law judges and the appellate court system were flooded with appeals. By 1984, twenty-eight states had stopped carrying out the disability reviews either on their own initiative or in response to court orders.[36] The political pressure to reverse course accelerated rapidly. The abrupt and absolute nature of the cutbacks, combined with the clear deservingness of many of those affected, made this a clear instance of highly visible retrenchment. The administration's actions lent themselves perfectly to extensive media coverage of those adversely affected. Congress had to confront evidence of severe hardships (including a number of suicides by those losing benefits) and widespread complaints from constituents.

Powerful institutional actors pitched in as well.[37] There were loud demands for relief from an overburdened court system flooded with disability appeals. Agency decisions were overturned in a majority of cases. The Social Security Administration's refusal to accept a wave of circuit-court decisions challenging its procedures led to sharp attacks from the judiciary, putting the SSA in an increasingly difficult position. Finally, the disability-insurance review met growing pressure from state governors concerned that terminated recipients would turn to state assistance programs. Because disability insurance had never been fully federalized, the SSA continued to rely on state bureaucracies to administer the program. In response to the raging conflict – or under court order – state governors began to announce their unwillingness to cooperate in the administration's review. In this context, legislators acted quickly to reverse the administration's efforts. Despite administration insistence that mistakes could easily be corrected, Congress voted overwhelmingly (410–1 in the House, 96–0 in the Senate) to sharply curtail the administration's ability to take people off the rolls.[38]

When the dust had settled, the administration had managed to achieve a moderate cutback in spending on the DI program but at a considerable political price.[39] Even with Congress's substantial grant of authority, the Reagan administration found radical retrenchment an elusive goal. The outcome of the administration's efforts confirms that a concentration of authority represents a mixed blessing for retrenchment advocates. The administration was in a strong position to act, but it was also highly exposed. By inflicting such sharp cutbacks in a highly visible way, the Reagan administration induced a quick and effective response from supporters of the DI program, raising the political costs of reform and forcing conservatives to dramatically scale back their efforts.

PROGRAMMATIC RETRENCHMENT: THE REAGAN AND THATCHER RECORDS

The two programs considered in this section confirm the main conclusions of the preceding three chapters. Programmatic retrenchment has generally proven to be difficult, but the degree of success has varied significantly from program to program and between the two countries. Table 6.1 offers a rough summary of the outcomes in each country, with the success of retrenchment efforts in each program rated high, moderate, or low. These judgments are based on the extent to which reforms seem likely to produce long-term changes in benefits, and on the balance between public and private sectors.

In the United States, only housing policy could be considered an area of major retrenchment, and judged by expenditure levels, it is the least important

Table 6.1. *Programmatic retrenchment outcomes (ratings indicate approximate level of success)*

Retrenchment type	Britain	United States
Pensions	High	Low
Housing	High	High
Income support	Low	Low
Health care	Low	Low/moderate
Disability/sickness	Low/moderate	Low/moderate

American policy area covered by this study. In the cases of disability insurance and health care, the Reagan administration demonstrated some capacity to curb program expenditures, but it would be hard to argue that in either case the administration produced dramatic long-term changes in the nature or scope of the programs. Regarding income support and old-age pensions, the administration's record is even less impressive. Although there has been a modest erosion of benefit levels and eligibility rules, these programs have on the whole been durable.

In Britain the government's record is more mixed. In a number of areas – such as health care, most components of income support, and sickness pay – the amount of retrenchment has been modest. However, in the cases of housing and pensions, the Conservatives have engineered reforms that have reduced public expenditures and substantially increased the role of the private sector. What stands out in the British situation is the variation in results between programs.

Nor do the overall expenditure records of the two governments show much sign of radical reform. As Table 6.2 indicates, real spending on welfare state programs has increased in both countries. The share of gross domestic product (GDP), which is probably a better measure of the scope of the welfare state, has held steady. The expenditures indicate a shifting of resources among programs, but not an overall curtailment of expenditures.

Of course, I argued in Chapter 1 that expenditure estimates provide an inadequate basis for reaching conclusions about retrenchment outcomes. To gain a more complete picture, I suggested, one needs to consider long-term as well as short-term effects of policy shifts, changes in program structure along with size, and systemic reforms in addition to as programmatic ones. This last issue is taken up in the next section of this chapter, but it is necessary to say more about the first two points here.

Because retrenchment advocates often pursue strategies that hide the magnitude of cuts by minimizing short-term negative consequences, it is important to consider the long-term implications of policy changes. Indeed, important reforms such as the changed indexation rules on pension and disability benefits in Britain confirm the need to remember this. Where possible, my investigation

Table 6.2. *Public and social expenditure trends, 1978–92*

	1978	1980	1982	1984	1986	1988	1990	1992
Total Public Expenditure								
Real Spending (1978=100)								
Britain	100.0	105.1	109.4	114.4	116.3	113.4	117.4	121.5
United States	100.0	108.8	116.0	121.8	132.6	133.5	144.2	148.0
% of GDP								
Britain	44.0	46.6	47.5	46.9	43.9	39.3	40.1	44.8
United States	21.3	22.3	23.9	23.1	23.5	22.1	22.9	23.3
Total Social Expenditure								
Real Spending (1978=100)								
Britain	100.0	104.0	108.2	114.1	119.7	117.6	122.4	142.7
United States	100.0	109.2	114.5	117.0	122.0	127.0	135.0	156.8
% of GDP								
Britain	24.1	25.2	25.7	25.6	24.7	22.2	23.0	27.0
United States	11.2	11.9	12.5	11.7	11.4	11.1	11.3	13.0
% of Total Outlays								
Britain	54.7	54.1	54.1	54.6	56.3	56.7	57.0	60.1
United States	52.8	53.0	52.1	50.7	48.6	50.1	49.4	53.9

Notes: Total Expenditure refers to General Government Expenditure minus privatization proceeds for Britain, total federal outlays for the United States. For Britain, Social Expenditures refers to the following budget functions: employment and training, housing, education, health and personal social services, and social security. For the United States, Social Expenditure includes the following budget functions: education, training, employment and social services (ETESS), health, medicare, income security, social security, and veterans' benefits. For Britain, "1978" refers to the 1978/79 budget year. British figures for 1992 are estimated outturns.

Sources: HM Treasury, *Public Expenditure Analyses to 1995–96: Statistical Supplement to the 1992 Autumn Statement* (London: HMSO, January, 1993, Tables 2.1, 2.3, 2.4; Congressional Research Service, *1995 Budget Perspectives: Federal Spending for Social Welfare Programs* (Washington, D.C.: Library of Congress), Report #94-215 EPW, March 1994, Tables 1.5, 1.6, 2.3, 2.4, 2.5; author's calculations.

of individual programs has included such examples of lagged cutbacks in reaching conclusions about programmatic change. More than a decade has passed since Reagan and Thatcher were first elected – an ample period for hidden time bombs to explode, or at least be located. Nevertheless, incorporation of this dimension does not change the basic conclusions regarding outcomes.

I further argued that an analysis of retrenchment must consider the welfare state's structure as well as its size. Spending levels aside, has reform pushed toward more residual designs of social programs? Table 6.3 provides some evidence on this score, indicating the changing shares of means-tested and non-means-tested expenditures in the U.S. and Britain. The American pattern reveals little evidence of residualization. Even if one factors out Medicare, which reflects exploding health-care costs rather than an attempt to improve middle-class benefits, little shift occurs in relative weight toward means-tested programs.

Table 6.3. *The role of means testing in Britain and the United States*

Britain (% of social-security expenditures)	1980–1	1985–6	1990–1
Contributory benefits	64	53	55
Noncontributory, non-income-related	17	15	16
Income-related	15	28	24
Administration	4	4	5
United States (% of combined total)	1980	1985	1990
Means-tested benefits[a]	18.2	17.1	18.5
Social insurance benefits[b]	81.8	82.9	81.5

[a]Federal spending only on Medicaid, food stamps, EITC, AFDC, and Supplemental Security Income.
[b]Medicare, Social Security, unemployment compensation.
Sources: HM Treasury, *Government's Expenditure Plans* (London: HMSO, Cmnd 9702–II), p. 229; Department of Social Security, *Government's Expenditure Plans* (London: HMSO, Cmnd 1514, February 1991); House Ways and Means Committee, *1991 Green Book*, pp. 614, 1524–5.

In Britain, on the other hand, the role of means testing has grown. As Table 6.3 demonstrates, within the social security budget, the share of means tested expenditures rose from 15 percent to 28 percent from 1980–1 to 1985–6, before declining to 24 percent in 1990–1. The major causes of this shift have been changes in the composition of the beneficiary population – the rising unemployment rate and increasing number of people on low incomes – combined with the declining reach of universal benefits (especially the shrinking of unemployment benefit) for these groups. The decline in the role of means testing after 1986 reflects falling unemployment rates. None of the major social-security programs have been means tested, but there has been a shift in the relative weight of programs toward more targeted alternatives.

Of course, social-security expenditures represent only about three-fifths of British welfare-state spending. If one extends the scope of discussion, one would have to say that there has been considerable residualization in housing, and very little, if any, in health care. A balanced assessment would suggest a significant but not fundamental shift away from universal programs in the British welfare state.

What constitutes radical change? Different readers are likely to give different answers. Although it would be hard to argue that the changes in the United States have been dramatic, the British outcome is less clear-cut. One could make a case that the considerable erosion of universal programs in Britain is of great importance, and one could argue that many programs have been sufficiently weakened that a dynamic of retrenchment has been set in place. Eroded by cutbacks, these programs might be unable to withstand further assaults. Such predictions of future collapse are very difficult to evaluate, though I have tried to look for signs that would bear them out. On the whole, however, the evidence concerning programmatic change points in the other direction. Spending levels have not diminished, privatization initiatives have been limited, and program structures show more signs of continuity than of change. With few exceptions, the major programs of the welfare state have survived a decade of retrenchment. The evidence on systemic retrenchment, to which I now turn, confirms this general conclusion for Britain, but it complicates the picture for the United States.

SYSTEMIC RETRENCHMENT IN BRITAIN AND THE UNITED STATES

If signs of extensive programmatic retrenchment are lacking, there remains the possibility that something has happened outside the welfare state to alter the political balance. The welfare state's political position is influenced not only by the structure and dynamics of existing programs, but by the context within which decisions about those programs are made. This context is neither stable nor entirely beyond the control of policymakers. Systemic retrenchment refers to policy changes that encourage future cutbacks and residualization by altering that context. Such policy changes can act either to weaken the political strength of program supporters or to enhance the position of retrenchment advocates. A full account of Thatcher and Reagan's retrenchment efforts must add an evaluation of systemic retrenchment to the preceding discussion of programmatic retrenchment.

I argued in Chapter 1 that four sets of possible changes should be distinguished. First, an administration might successfully alter public opinion, weakening popular attachment to the welfare state. Second, a government could defund the welfare state by constraining the flow of revenues to future administrations. Third, policy changes might modify political institutions, changing the way decision making about the welfare state is carried out and thus potentially changing policy outcomes. Fourth, an administration might weaken pro-welfare state interest groups. This section considers the extent to which these four types of systemic retrenchment have occurred in Britain and the United States, and draws on the empirical findings of the preceding chapters to consider the likely impact of these developments on the welfare state.

Public opinion

The political health of the welfare state is dependent upon popular attitudes. In an otherwise unchanged context, a growing hostility toward social programs could be expected to facilitate retrenchment. There was some reason for both governments to hope that their policies would encourage such a realignment of public opinion. Growing inequality might encourage the "haves" to dissociate themselves from the "have-nots," leading to a rejection of public expenditures in which they no longer perceived themselves as having a stake. Successful privatization initiatives might also lead to a growing orientation toward private rather than public consumption. Some analysts of public opinion, particularly in Britain, have advanced the idea of "consumption sector" cleavages, claiming that those without strong, multiple consumption links to the public sector will be less supportive of public spending.[40] Thus, shifts in public policy might generate a self-reinforcing pattern: growing inequality and expanding private provision leading to declining public support for social programs, encouraging further erosion of the welfare state.

To what extent has such a shift in popular attitudes occurred? Accurately gauging public opinion is difficult, but what evidence there is strongly suggests that public support for the welfare state did not diminish in either country during Thatcher and Reagan's tenures.[41] Indeed, in almost every respect, the patterns of public opinion are similar in Britain and United States, and provide strong confirmation for my emphasis on the precariousness of retrenchment initiatives. On the whole, social programs never became unpopular, but the late 1970s revealed growing disquiet about taxation and declining levels of support for particular programs. These attitudes clearly contributed to Reagan and Thatcher's initial electoral success. Once retrenchment initiatives began, however, a pro-welfare state backlash occurred almost immediately. Visible cutbacks were quite unpopular, and by the mid-1980s levels of support for public programs had returned to roughly the levels of the early 1970s.

It is in Britain that one would most expect to see a substantial shift in public attitudes toward the welfare state. It was Britain that witnessed the greater increase in inequality during the 1980s, the greater shift toward means testing, and the larger expansion of private systems of social provision. All of these developments might be expected to drive a wedge between rich and poor, undermining popular support for the welfare state. Nevertheless, the evidence on this issue is clear-cut. The highest levels of discontent with social policy preceded Thatcher's rule, and public opinion quickly recoiled in the face of her retrenchment efforts. As Peter Taylor-Gooby summarized a careful analysis of opinion surveys, "Support for state welfare increased among all social and political groupings and became more unified as the 1980s progressed . . . there is no support for the view that growing income inequality in Britain in the 1980s has reduced support for the welfare state, especially among the more contented groups in society. The evidence points in an entirely contrary direction."[42]

Thatcher initially benefited from increasing voter concern about social policy nerally and means-tested programs in particular. The British electorate already thought welfare benefits were too generous rather than too stingy in 1974 (34 percent to 24 percent); by 1979, that perception had become overwhelming (50 percent to 17 percent).[43] If core welfare state programs remained far more popular than these figures indicate, there were nevertheless signs of public ambivalence. Thatcher might have hoped that this backlash could be extended or at least consolidated, but public opinion moved sharply in the other direction after her election. Even when the attention of voters is explicitly drawn to the tax costs of public programs, already-strong support for program expansion has grown. This suggests that public opinion about the welfare state is durable and highly sensitive to indications of even moderate cutbacks in public programs. If Thatcher had a mandate to curb the growth of social expenditures, the electorate remained opposed to radical shifts in priorities.[44]

The prospect that policy shifts may yet produce long-term changes in public opinion is obviously harder to evaluate. Some studies have suggested that "consumption sectors" – the extent of an individual's reliance on public or private provision of health care, housing, education, pensions, etc. – have a significant impact on voting behavior. If so, successful privatization might gradually shift opinion against the welfare state. Although the ambitious privatization efforts of the Thatcher administration were rarely realized, there was a noticeable shift toward private consumption in a number of areas. Homeownership rates increased from 55 percent in 1978 to 65 percent of the population a decade later; the number of people covered by private medical insurance tripled between 1979 and 1990, from just over 2 million to 7.2 million; more than 4 million people have taken out the new private, personal pensions.[45]

Overall evidence for the impact of consumption-sector cleavages remains limited, however, and is difficult to reconcile with the continuing signs of strong public support (indeed generally growing support among the most affluent) for extended state provision. As Taylor-Gooby argues, the idea of consumption-sector cleavages probably overestimates the extent to which voters see a clear trade-off between public and private provision. Although support for the private sector has grown in some cases, this seems to be in addition to, rather than at the expense of, support for the public sector.[46] Only in the case of housing does private provision necessarily substitute for rather than supplement public provision, and it is in this sphere that one might expect the biggest attitudinal shift to result from privatization. Even here, however, the evidence is less than overwhelming. Although homeowners have indeed exhibited more conservative attitudes, the causal connection is far from clear. For that matter, even though there is a widespread belief that council-house sales were a major vote winner for the Conservatives, the evidence suggests otherwise. As Heath and Garrett have determined, although those purchasing council homes voted Conservative more often than those who continued to rent, these voting differences largely preceded the purchase decision, and hence could not be the result of privatization itself.[47]

It is difficult to disprove the contention that policy trends in Britain may be generating a gradual but silent erosion of support for the welfare state. What evidence there is, however, supports the opposite interpretation. As I have argued throughout this volume, retrenchment initiatives, unless they are very carefully designed, are likely to activate attachments to social programs. On the whole, this would seem to be the legacy of Thatcher's retrenchment efforts.

In the United States, there is equally little evidence of a shift away from support for social programs. Indeed, public-opinion trends are remarkably similar to those in Britain. Before Reagan's election there were some indications of increased hostility toward the federal government in general and toward social programs in particular. Far from cementing or accelerating these trends, however, Reagan's term in office reversed them. After declining markedly in the late 1970s, public support for social programs began to recover in 1981, returning to levels not seen since the early 1970s.[48] Attitudes toward programs for the poor in the United States provide a striking example. There had been a particularly strong rightward shift in public opinion toward these programs during the 1970s. However, the well-publicized cutbacks in AFDC and other programs during 1981 produced an immediate reaction. Within months, poll results indicated a liberal turn in public opinion – a trend that was to continue throughout the 1980s.[49]

As Hugh Heclo has summarized the evidence, "Public attitudes in the 1980s showed little sign of a conservative conversion toward what commentators called the 'Reagan Revolution.' In fact the opposite was more the case."[50] James Stimson's careful study of public attitudes showed that the conservative mood peaked around the time of Reagan's election in 1980 and has been moving in a more liberal direction ever since. Faye Cook's more detailed investigation of attitudes toward social-welfare programs indicated that all such programs, even such frequently criticized ones as food stamps and AFDC, retained broad popular support. Although food stamps received the lowest ratings of any program, 76 percent of respondents said that they wished spending on the program to be maintained or increased.[51]

Nor has the Reagan administration been able to produce policy shifts likely to weaken public support for social expenditures. There have been no privatization initiatives like those Thatcher produced in housing and pension provision. Indeed, homeownership levels have reached a plateau, while participation in private-pension schemes actually declined in the 1980s. In any event, there is little evidence in American survey research to suggest that consumption-sector cleavages have a dramatic effect on mass opinion.[52]

The impact of Thatcher and Reagan on popular attitudes toward the welfare state has been nearly identical. Conservative shifts in public opinion preceded rather than followed the elections of conservative governments. Subsequent opinion trends confirm the hazardous nature of retrenchment politics. Visible cutbacks activate a strong negativity bias. The spending cuts that these administrations introduced triggered a rapid erosion of popular support for further retrenchment. If the welfare state's vulnerability has increased, factors other than changing popular attitudes toward social programs must be responsible.

Defunding the welfare state

One of the most effective strategies for welfare state retrenchment over the long run is defunding, that is, a curtailment of the flow of revenues on which social programs rely. As Theda Skocpol has noted, "A state's means of raising and deploying financial resources tell us more than could any other single factor about its . . . capacities to create or strengthen state organizations, to employ personnel, to coopt political support, to subsidize economic enterprises, and to fund social programs."[53]

At least three different avenues to defunding are possible. First, policy shifts could increase the public sector's reliance on unsustainable sources of finance (such as asset sales), jeopardizing the long-term financial support for programs. Second, spending on non-welfare state items could be expanded, generating a process of fiscal "crowding out" in which less money is left for social spending. Finally, policy changes could reduce the government's revenue-generating capacity by lowering taxes, or increasing the difficulty of raising taxes in the future.

The divergence between the Thatcher and Reagan administrations' records in these areas is striking, and likely to have considerable consequences for the future of social policy in the two countries. If anything, Thatcher seems to have had a positive impact on the financial position of central government, whereas Reagan had considerable success in defunding the welfare state. Indeed, if the Reagan administration's programmatic-retrenchment record is generally one of failure, its success in constraining the flow of federal revenues is likely to be its most lasting social-policy legacy.

Although some developments in Britain have worsened the prospects for future spending, the overall atmosphere created by revenue conditions has improved. The government has utilized one approach that might produce defunding: increased reliance on unsustainable sources of finance. Thatcher inherited one such source, North Sea oil revenues. Taxes on oil production created a significant flow of revenues, temporarily easing the pressure for lower spending or higher taxes on individuals. The Conservatives also shrewdly exploited a second source of unsustainable revenues: privatization proceeds. The government has gradually sold off a large share of Britain's sizable array of public enterprises (as well as council housing). Privatization has provided important political benefits beyond the profits it has offered to buyers. Revenues generated were used to sustain spending in the short run, but each sale depleted the government's assets while providing only a one-time infusion of funds.

Table 6.4 shows that privatization and North Sea oil income provided a significant share of revenues during the Thatcher years, and that as the oil money fell, privatization proceeds rose to fill the gap. Nevertheless, although these sources indicate a certain weakness in the revenue position of the British government, they do not invalidate the basic conclusion that Thatcher's revenue policies have not defunded the welfare state. Even excluding the contribution of North Sea oil and asset sales, the British government claimed a higher percentage of gross domestic product in revenues and had a lower borrowing requirement in 1988 than it did in 1979 (see Table 6.5).

The British Conservatives might also have been able to reduce the revenues

Table 6.4. *Reliance on unsustainable finance in Britain (in billions of pounds, 1988–9 prices)*

	1979–80	1988–9	% Change
Public-sector borrowing	18.4	−3.2[a]	NA
Privatization proceeds	0.7	5.0	+614.3
Oil revenues	4.3	4.1[b]	−4.7
Total	23.4	5.9	−74.8

NA = Not applicable
[a]Surplus
[b]1987–8
Sources: House of Commons, *Hansard*, June 16, 1988, cols. 275–6w; Treasury, *Government's Expenditure Plans*, 1988, vol. 1, pp. 90–1; Board of Inland Revenue, *Inland Revenue Statistics*, 1987, Table 1.3.

available to welfare state programs through a process of fiscal crowding out – that is, expanding other programs to leave less money available for social programs. However, such a shift has simply not occurred. The budget shares obtained by defense and law enforcement have grown somewhat, but interest payments have fallen. Overall, social expenditure's share of the government's budget expanded from 48.8 percent in 1978–9 to 52.8 percent in 1991–2.[54]

The final possible source of retrenchment, a restriction on the central government's revenue-generating capacity, has not been pursued. Thatcher's commitment to monetarism made a reduction in public borrowing her top economic priority. As Table 6.4 indicates, the public-sector borrowing requirement has been driven down, but at the cost of higher tax rates.[55] Not only did revenues as a percentage of GDP grow, but the government actually lowered the visibility of taxes. As shown in Table 6.5, the share of revenues produced by highly visible (and unpopular) income taxes was reduced, whereas the less visible National Insurance contributions and value-added tax were raised to more than make up the difference. This shift in the visibility of taxes had significant political advantages for Thatcher. It allowed her to build a reputation as a tax cutter when she was actually increasing the government's revenues, and transferred resources to her supporters by diminishing the progressivity of the tax system. From the perspective of systemic change, however, the government's tax policies bolstered the welfare state's position. The restructured tax base will make it easier for future governments to impose heavy taxes without generating a political outcry.

If there is little in the Thatcher record to suggest an erosion of the welfare state's finances, the outcome has been quite different in the United States. By indexing tax brackets, the administration raised the visibility of the tax system, making it extremely difficult to generate new taxes. Whereas once governments could let inflation-induced bracket creep raise new revenues, now politicians had

Table 6.5. *Taxation in Britain, 1979–80 to 1988–9 (in billions of pounds, 1988–9 prices)*

	1979–80	1988–9	% Change
Income tax	38.6	43.4	+12.4
Value-added tax	15.0	25.2	+68.0
Excise duties	15.3	18.6	+21.6
Customs duties and agriculture levies	2.1	1.7	−19.0
Other central government taxes and royalties	27.7	31.7	+14.4
Other central government receipts[a]	28.5	41.4	+45.3
Total central government receipts	127.3	162.0	+27.3
Share of gross domestic product	33.8%	37.0%	+ 3.2

[a]Includes National Insurance contributions.
Sources: House of Commons, *Hansard*, June 16, 1988, cols. 275–6w; Treasury, *Government's Expenditure Plans*, 1988, vol. 2, p. 91.

to vote openly for tax increases. This policy change contributed to the emergence and continuation of large deficits, which has forced the diversion of a growing share of government spending to cover debt-finance charges. The Reagan administration's success in limiting the availability of revenues for social programs clearly represents its most significant change in the political position of the welfare state.

The administration had little luck in utilizing Thatcher's one successful defunding tool: increased reliance on unsustainable sources of funds. The United States has not benefited from a temporary infusion of funds from oil holdings, and it simply does not possess the enormous assets that the British government sold off to widen the scope of its tax cuts. In other respects, however, the American administration had far greater success.

The climate of austerity needed to impose constraints on social expenditure stemmed partly from fiscal crowding out: the growing demand of competing functions on available revenues. Defense spending increased rapidly during the Reagan years, as did interest payments – the latter another consequence of the fiscal deficit. These two budgetary items accounted for 30.1 percent of federal outlays in FY1981, a figure that increased to 41.9 percent in FY1987.[56] The rapid upward trajectory of defense spending stopped after Reagan's first term, and the Pentagon has since become a source of spending cutbacks. Nevertheless, much defense spending is hard to cut: Once contracts have been signed and budget authority granted, reductions are hard to impose. Interest payments are even more uncontrollable, given that the government's influence is limited to its indirect and unreliable control over interest rates.

The contribution of interest payments to the crowding-out phenomenon reflects the growing role of the federal deficit, which looms over any discussion of contemporary American domestic politics. The emergence of the deficit, in turn, is related to the Reagan administration's most important domestic policy triumph: the impairment of the federal government's ability to generate tax revenues. In each of the two Reagan terms, the president's single most important domestic-policy initiative concerned taxation. In both cases, the result restricted the federal government's revenue-raising capacity.

This was especially clear in the 1981 Economic Recovery Tax Act (ERTA) legislation, which combined a sharp cut in personal income-tax rates with major new tax breaks for business. The already-massive handouts backed by the administration escalated when the Democratic leadership of the House, determined not to lose again after the Reagan administration's victories in the just-completed budget rounds, tried to outbid the administration. The result was, in David Stockman's words, an "accident of fiscal governance that decimated the nation's fiscal equilibrium."[57]

A critical if underappreciated provision of ERTA was the introduction of tax indexation, automatically adjusting tax brackets in line with changes in the cost of living. Although originally opposed by the Reagan administration as an obstacle to ERTA's quick passage, the indexation provision's implications were quickly recognized. Embracing indexation as an integral part of the Reagan Revolution, the president promised to veto any bill tampering with its introduction.

The enactment of indexation provides a striking example of how radical change sometimes hangs on precarious events.[58] Indexation enjoyed only a brief window of political opportunity; by 1982 the mounting budget deficits would have made the change impossible. Once enacted, however, it had truly revolutionary effects. By eliminating inflation-generated bracket creep, indexation ended the politically convenient dynamic that had traditionally allowed Congress to simultaneously increase spending and hand out tax "cuts." If the government wished to spend more, it would now have to vote openly for higher taxes. Moreover, because increasing revenues now required positive action, the president's veto power put him in a strong bargaining position. As Stockman noted, this constituted a "second tax cut," far more radical in its effects than the heralded "Kemp-Roth" reduction of tax rates.[59]

Indexation also fueled political preoccupation with the budget deficit. In the past, budget forecasts had always shown shrinking deficits, as the assumption of "no policy change" in a nonindexed tax system assured that revenues would rise to meet shortfalls. Indexation eliminated this effect, and the projection of deficits far into the future helped make austerity the dominant political concern.

The mounting deficits led many key participants, including David Stockman and Senate Finance Committee chairman Robert Dole, to seek a change of course. The Tax Equity and Fiscal Responsibility Act of 1982 (TEFRA), and the Deficit Reduction Act of 1984 (DEFRA), recouped some of the lost revenues, largely at the expense of the most generous provisions affecting business in the 1981 legislation. ERTA was projected to lower federal revenues by $261 billion in FY1988; TEFRA and DEFRA combined to offset $83 billion of that reduction.[60] Nevertheless, even these tax hikes, much smaller than the 1981 cuts, showed how difficult it had become to raise revenue. President Reagan fought hard against any "revenue enhancement," and across-the-board increases in tax rates were politically unthinkable. Instead, Congress had to resort to eliminating or reducing particular tax expenditures, an approach bound to become more difficult as the most vulnerable loopholes were closed.

In Reagan's second term, an unusual cross-party coalition attracted by the prospect of lower rates produced another major piece of tax legislation, with important ramifications including the sharply lower tax burdens on the poor discussed in Chapter 5.[61] For current purposes, however, the question is how the 1986 Tax Reform Act influenced the government's ability to raise revenues. Although any judgment is necessarily speculative, the act probably further impeded the prospects for revenue generation.

The 1986 Reform was carefully crafted to be "revenue neutral": Lower taxes would have worsened the deficit, and higher taxes would have made reform unpalatable. Although the specific provisions of the act were designed to balance out over a five-year period, changing the tax system affected the prospects of repeating the tax-raising efforts of TEFRA and DEFRA. Some analysts have argued that by making the tax system fairer, tax reform will make rate increases easier to legislate.[62] The arguments for believing the opposite are compelling. Recent revenue increases have generally come from curtailing various tax breaks, not from raising tax rates. The 1986 reform cut those preferences by $120 billion without generating any revenue. Furthermore, the struggle over the legislation was a kind of policy Darwinism: Preferences that were politically weak lost out while the strongest survived. In short, the easiest roads to higher taxes were effectively blocked.[63]

By increasing the visibility of the tax system and forcing Congress to gain presidential approval for a tax hike, policy changes during the Reagan years contributed significantly to the emergence of a "politics of deficits" in the United States. The connection between Reagan's tax policies and the federal government's precarious fiscal position needs to be carefully stated. Although some critics, such as Senator Daniel Moynihan, have argued that the tax cuts were a "Trojan horse" designed to undercut the policy capacities of the federal government, a more balanced assessment suggests that a major fiscal crunch was inevitable in the early 1980s.[64] The maturation of the major entitlement programs created considerable momentum toward higher spending. At the same time, excepting the last years of the Carter administration, the level of federal taxation had hovered around 18–19 percent of GNP for two decades. The Reagan tax cuts only returned federal taxes to that level. Unless one believes that in Reagan's absence taxes would have easily moved upward to the new, higher levels required – a difficult argument to sustain in light of the significant antitax movements of the late 1970s – there was bound to be a sizable increase in the deficit.

The administration's contribution was to engineer a substantial change in the political dynamics once fiscal constraints set in. As mentioned, indexation of tax brackets increased the cost to Congress of raising taxes, forcing it to do openly what before would have been less visible. To raise taxes, Congress would also have to obtain the president's agreement or assemble a veto-proof majority in both the House and Senate. The result has been an enduring impasse. If the political strength of social programs has made it difficult to obtain cuts on the spending side, the tax reforms greatly increased political resistance to deficit reduction on the revenue side.

Thus, the Reagan administration had a considerable impact on the fiscal capacities of the federal government. The combination of limited revenues and expanded outlays for debt interest solidified the place of retrenchment issues on Congress's agenda, as the last three chapters have all indicated. As the rest of this chapter demonstrates, defunding has also had important ripple effects on political institutions and the lobbying capacities of program advocates.

Political institutions

A third avenue of systemic retrenchment would be to alter the political institutions that frame future decision making about the welfare state. As I argued in Chapter 1, retrenchment advocates face a choice when it comes to institutional reforms: centralization or decentralization. The case materials presented in the past three chapters provide a stronger basis for establishing some general propositions about institutional design and retrenchment. Centralizing authority offers something of a mixed blessing: It makes it easier to control the design and implementation of cuts, but it also concentrates accountability, which may increase the political dangers associated with retrenchment initiatives. The merits of decentralization strategies seem more straightforward: the ability to shift blame for cutbacks, the potential to generate competitive deregulation in social policy, and the fragmentation of pro-welfare state interest groups.

Institutional reform represents a case in which the two administrations diverged not just on outcomes but on basic strategies. The Reagan administration favored decentralization, attempting to shift responsibility for social policy to states and localities. The Thatcher government sought to further centralize an already centralized system. This divergence reflected preexisting institutional differences. Placed in different institutional contexts, Thatcher and Reagan reached different conclusions about the desirable route of institutional change.

In Britain, a number of factors made a centralizing strategy appealing. Local councils have no constitutionally guaranteed status. In contrast to federal systems, there is no division of jurisdiction between levels of government that makes it possible for the central government to shift the political responsibility for austerity to subnational governments. Thatcher's desire to remove Labour's local power base rendered a strategy of decentralization even less attractive. If decentralization was less appealing to Thatcher, the benefits of centralizing efforts were also far greater. Thatcher could reasonably expect to gain control over traditional local powers, increasing her ability to pursue a reform agenda.

The Thatcher government had some success in restructuring relations between central and local government, but the consequences for retrenchment are at best ambiguous. As I have indicated, the Conservatives aggressively curbed local political authority, tilting an already lopsided relationship further toward the center. The Thatcher government imposed increasingly stringent reforms designed to limit local councils' capacities for autonomous action. From tighter subsidy rules, to rate capping, to the introduction of the poll tax, central government acted to sharply curtail the financial independence of local authorities. The metropolitan counties and the Greater London Council – the latter a particularly vocal opponent of Thatcher's policies – were abolished. The government's dogged pursuit of the poll tax, which was clearly intended to shackle local government spending, was perhaps the clearest signal of a commitment to centralization. The willingness to pay a tremendous political cost – indeed the poll tax probably contributed as much as any other factor to Thatcher's fall from power – indicated the priority placed on institutional reform.

The government's success in further centralizing power in an already centralized system is unquestioned.[65] Local governments became increasingly dependent on grants from the national government. At the same time, local authorities took greatly diminished roles in areas like housing and education. Even where they continued to provide services, they were often forced to operate within tight constraints imposed from London.

There is, however, little reason to expect that these changes will produce a heightened capacity for retrenchment in the long run. Increasing the Conservative government's power may have strengthened immediate pressures for retrenchment, but Conservative governance will not last forever. There is little evidence that local governments are generally more expansionist than national governments. Indeed, the opposite is almost certainly the case. Despite Thatcher's complaints about free-spending local authorities, it was national rather than local expenditure that proved most resistant to retrenchment during her tenure. Short-term efforts to transfer authority from local councils may benefit a Conservative government, but not by permanently installing an environment more hostile to social expenditures.

In the United States, institutional reform moved in the opposite direction. In a federal system, the arguments for further decentralization were compelling. Given the protections for states built into the American Constitution (e.g., the role of the Senate in protecting state interests), a strategy of radical centralization would have been a political nonstarter. Decentralization, on the other hand, would make it difficult for future governments to coordinate interventionist policies. It would create fiscal competition between jurisdictions that would restrict the prospects for extensive social policy. Furthermore, it might diminish the organizational resources of welfare state supporters, which were concentrated in Washington. Finally, it could shift the responsibility (and blame) for cutbacks to local administrations.

The Reagan administration recognized that the transfer of major social obligations from the federal government to the states would represent a significant change in the country's institutional environment that would be detrimental to the welfare state. As a result, Reagan moved quickly to decentralize institutional responsibility for social policy. In his first year, he asked that a wide range of federal grants to states, localities, and individuals be consolidated into block grants.

Block grants offered the administration four potential advantages. First, the process of consolidation provided some political cover for an actual reduction in the size of the affected programs. Second, by providing states with greater discretion, block grants were expected to reduce the role of redistributive programs. Third, block grants contained spending caps, rather than the matching formulas of categorical grants, which encouraged higher state outlays. Finally, block grants circumscribed the room for specific project grants, which networks of interest groups, bureaucrats, and politicans had used to encourage higher spending.[66] In all these respects, the block-grant strategy offered a promising avenue for systemic retrenchment. For much the same reason, Congress generally opposed these changes. The linkage of consolidation to program cuts also dissipated much of the potential state-government support for Reagan's initiatives. Some block-grant consolidations took place in 1981, but far fewer than Reagan had requested.

As in many policy areas, Reagan was unable to follow up on the steps taken in 1981. Reagan's 1982 New Federalism initiative, discussed in Chapter 5, went nowhere. His vision of a swap of responsibilities between the federal government and the states would have had dramatic repercussions for social programs, especially those targeted at the able-bodied poor. America's fragmented political system no doubt contributed to the failure of Reagan's radical proposal, but the president's insistence on using the plan as a tool for immediate spending restraint undermined any conceivable political coalition that might have emerged to support it.

There is a strong consensus among students of intergovernmental relations that Reagan was relatively unsuccessful in consolidating a major shift of programs toward the states.[67] If change took place, it was largely the indirect result of the changing budgetary climate at the federal level. Federal aid to the states declined somewhat. In the general competition between programs produced by budgetary stress, federal grants to states proved relatively vulnerable.[68] The discretionary status of such programs was a major weakness. The reshaping of institutional responsibilities resulting from the harsh fiscal climate of the 1980s should not be trivialized, but it fell far short of both the president's aspirations and of anything that could be considered a radical institutional shift. With the federal government strapped for resources, demands for social initiatives have fallen increasingly on the relatively healthy budgets of the states. This strengthened state role is likely to favor retrenchment. Although Reagan's reforms at least pushed in the desired direction, it remains true that none of the core social-policy functions of the federal government were transferred to the states. If Reagan succeeded in halting the fifty-year trend toward a nationalization of social policy, he did not reverse it.

Interest groups

My analysis of the politics of social policy strongly suggests that the impact of an administration dedicated to retrenchment depends in part on the political influence of welfare state supporters. Those supporters include groups of beneficiaries, producer interests with a stake in either the provision of specific services (housing or health care) or in a pattern of public intervention in the marketplace (e.g., labor unions), and public-interest organizations dedicated to advancing programs for the underprivileged and underrepresented. Although the strength of such groups is clearly only one determinant of retrenchment outcomes, a government seeking cutbacks could be expected to try to weaken the political position of its potential opponents.

Both the Reagan and Thatcher governments pursued such a strategy, with mixed results. Direct assaults were generally unsuccessful excepting those on trade unions, which were quite effective. In the United States, the most dramatic change is again probably a result of new fiscal realities. Austerity has not so much reduced the resources of interest groups as it has "devalued" them. The overwhelming pressure of budget deficits makes it more difficult for social-program supporters to translate those resources into policy successes.

Because the role of public interest groups in Britain has traditionally been more limited than in the United States, reducing their power was not a top priority for the Thatcher government. Thatcher attempted to lower the credibility of such groups by portraying them as selfish seekers of special favors. The government's dominant response, however, was to ignore such groups rather than combat them directly. Groups such as the Child Poverty Action Group found their access to politicians diminished. Nevertheless, the influence such organizations enjoy has always depended more on their capacity to rouse public opinion and embarrass a government than to lobby it directly. The Thatcher government's animosity probably simply reinforced this emphasis among social-policy pressure groups.[69]

As I argued in Chapter 4, the government had some success in breaking up the local corporatist networks that traditionally played an important role in pushing for an expansion of public-sector housing programs. Reform of local-government finance was wedded to policies of council-house sales, capital spending cuts, and increased reliance on housing associations. All of these policies led not only to retrenchment in housing programs, but to the weakening of the interest groups that might have lobbied for a reversal of the government's policies. In housing, retrenchment advocates succeeded in establishing a self-reinforcing dynamic in which cutbacks led to weaker opposition, allowing further cutbacks. Had the government been able to apply these strategies effectively in other domains, the repercussions for the welfare state would have been serious; but housing was the exception rather than the rule.

The Conservatives were equally assertive in challenging the power of trade unions. Historically, the unions, frequently speaking through the Trades Union Congress (TUC), were prominent advocates of the welfare state, providing support for the expansion of a range of social programs. That influence, along with the unions' visible impact on British economic policy in the 1960s and 1970s, made the restriction of labor-union power a central ambition of the Thatcher government.

That goal was pursued vigorously and with a substantial degree of success. The approach was incremental: The government gradually introduced more restrictive laws to reduce the ability of unions to act as a collective political force. Carefully planned and aggressively waged contests with major unions put the labor movement on the defensive. These trends culminated in the government's enormously important defeat of the National Union of Mineworkers in 1984. Extremely high unemployment levels during the early Thatcher years gave the government a critical boost in its struggles with the unions. The heart of union power – the threat to withdraw labor – is greatly reduced in a slack labor market. In this context, and with a government committed to avoiding any encumbering negotiations with labor, union influence dwindled. Union membership dropped by one-fifth in the decade after 1979, and union density fell from 58.9 percent in 1978 to 46.5 percent in 1988. Peter Riddell hardly exaggerated when he wrote that the union movement was, "at the national level, in its weakest position in fifty years."[70]

The critical question is whether that sharp reduction in trade-union influence is likely to be sustained. If in fact the slackness of the labor market was a critical ingredient in the government's success, labor's weakness might not outlast the period of high unemployment.[71] There is, however, evidence to suggest more lasting change. The steep fall in levels of union organization will weaken the labor movement's capacity to reassert its interests. The backwardness of British industry has left it highly vulnerable to international competition, and the efforts of unions to adapt to this challenge have greatly divided the TUC. A new focus on flexible, plant-level arrangements seems to be supplanting older, corporatist patterns of union behavior.[72] This shift leaves little room for a focus on national "political" concerns like social-welfare policy. Indeed, it is difficult to imagine circumstances that would restore the level of union influence that existed in the late 1960s and early 1970s.

This change represents a significant modification in the context for future policy-making about the welfare state. Unions are unlikely to play the kind of role they held during the welfare state's expansionary phase. However, there is to date little evidence that suggests these diminishing political resources will undermine the welfare state's position. Individual programs in most cases have developed powerful new constituencies that guard against radical retrenchment. Except in the case of housing, even an extended period of conservative rule has done little to weaken these bases of support.

The Reagan administration's direct attacks on interest groups supporting the welfare state also had limited effect. As observers have long noted, the diffusion of authority exhibited by the American political system allows such groups to flourish and makes them relatively resistant to centralized control.[73] Nevertheless, these groups have frequently found their political resources diminished as an indirect consequence of changes introduced during the Reagan years.

Two direct interventions were of some significance. First, the administration pursued a strategy of "defunding the left." Many groups with an interest in domestic policy rely on federal funds to support their activities, and where possible the administration stopped the flow of these resources. Although access to diverse sources of income made most groups immune to these shifts, some, such as organizations representing states and localities, were vulnerable. The National League of Cities saw federal grants drop from 50 percent of its budget to almost nothing between 1981 and 1983, and was forced to cut its staff by more than half. The U.S. Conference of Mayors and the National Conference of State Legislators suffered similar cutbacks.[74] Public-interest and nonprofit groups that relied heavily on government funds were also put in a difficult position. Most, however, appear to have been able to shift over to new sources of revenues, and indeed Reagan's assault on domestic spending often provided a useful rallying cry for mobilizing private funding. Far from contracting, the already crowded world of Washington interest groups continued to expand during the Reagan years.[75]

The second major target of the Reagan administration's direct efforts to undermine welfare state supporters was the labor movement. Although weaker than their European counterparts, American unions played a considerable role in supporting expansions of the postwar welfare state.[76] By the late-1970s, however, unions were clearly on the defensive. Under the Reagan administration, organized labor found itself hard pressed to protect its most immediate interests in wages, jobs, and labor legislation. Reagan's aggressive response to public-sector unions (vividly symbolized by his breaking of the air traffic controllers' strike) and his success in shifting the composition of the National Labor Review Board sharply in favor of those sympathetic to business heightened labor's vulnerability. Organized labor was generally unable to take much initiative on public policy issues, although it succeeded in holding off conservative efforts to achieve statutory (as opposed to administrative) changes in industrial relations.[77]

Labor struggled hard to maintain political influence in the 1980s. Although labor political action committee (PAC) contributions did not grow as fast as those generated by business groups, they nonetheless rose from 5.6 percent of total congressional campaign receipts in 1979–80 to 7.3 percent of a much larger total in 1987–8.[78] In many respects, however, labor's organizational base was clearly in decline. Union membership fell from 22.4 million in 1979–80 to 17 million in 1987–8.[79] Given the importance of a broad electoral base for labor's political clout, this decline indicated serious trouble. Under such direct pressures, the capacity of unions to lobby strenuously against social-policy retrenchment diminished.[80]

The welfare state's defenders have also been weakened by the institutional changes already discussed. Reagan's social-policy proposals, though far from fully implemented, somewhat decentralized decisions about social spending, weakening the ability of interest groups to lobby effectively. The administration was clearly aware of this consequence. As Reagan himself said in 1981, "It's far easier for people to come to Washington to get their social programs. It would be a hell of a lot tougher if we diffuse them and send them out to the states. All their friends and connections are in Washington."[81]

However, as with institutional shifts, it is the indirect consequences of the new "deficit politics" rather than any direct reform effort that has most damaged the political position of welfare state supporters.[82] Increased budget pressures and the more centralized congressional budget-making process developed in response to those pressures further constrained interest group influence. Austerity and centralization of congressional and administration decision-making had the effect of moving policy discussions from what Theodore Lowi has called a "distributive" framework to a "redistributive" one.[83] Distributive policy involves the handing out of divisible goods in a way that enhances the role of interest groups and facilitates accommodations (such as log-rolling arrangements) among them. Redistributive policy heightens the visibility of the costs to other groups of providing benefits to a few. Clearly, both austerity (which clarifies the dependence of each interest on the treatment accorded to other groups) and centralized budgeting (which illuminates the trade-offs between taxes, deficit levels, and the provision of benefits to specific interests) push policy-making in a redistributive direction.[84]

These conditions have circumscribed some of the major political assets of interest groups. Powerful groups – for example, in the health-care industry – have been unable to prevent the adoption of objectionable policies. This has been especially true when deficit concerns have been dominant, and when policy-making has occurred through centralized budgeting mechanisms. Nevertheless, the change in the position of interest groups should not be exaggerated. On occasions when groups were able to force votes on specific programs, they were far more successful in protecting their interests.[85] As the Reagan administration's reluctance to pursue strategies of direct cutbacks indicates, interest groups retain a substantial ability to inflict political retribution for such visible assaults on programs they favor. The record in the United States thus parallels that in Britain. Labor unions excepted, there is little sign that conservatives were able to dislodge the extensive interest-group networks that have grown up around social programs.

Conclusion

As in the case of programmatic retrenchment, the results of systemic retrenchment efforts provide a mixed picture. Of the two governments, the Reagan
administration was clearly the more successful. Indeed, in three of the four areas,
one could make a case that Conservative governance in Britain strengthened the
welfare state's long-term position. Only in the case of interest groups did the
Conservatives have some success, weakening welfare state advocates in general
and trade unions in particular. Public opinion, financial conditions, and institutional arrangements all seem more favorable to social expenditures than they
did before 1979. This conclusion should not be taken too far, but it serves as a
useful corrective to suspicions of an invisible but far-reaching erosion of the
British welfare state's foundations.

Like those of the Thatcher government, the Reagan administration's actions
appear to have solidified public support for social programs. Although Reagan
was more successful in reforming institutions and weakening his political opponents, the changes achieved were marginal. The truly important divergence
between his record and that of Thatcher lies in the fourth area, defunding of the
welfare state. Here, the Reagan administration produced major changes, significant not only in their direct impact but because of ripple effects on the position
of interest groups and the functioning of political institutions.

The evidence presented in this chapter is likely to prove disappointing both
to those who believe the Reagan and Thatcher administrations represented radical disjunctures from the past, and to those who argue that their initiatives were
thwarted by the "tyranny of the status quo." Both administrations demonstrated
that their professed antipathy to the welfare state was not mere rhetoric. Efforts
to cut benefits, restrict eligibility, and expand the role of the private sector were
persistent. More often than not, these efforts ran up against stiff resistance,
however, and retrenchment advocates had to settle for marginal changes. In a
few areas, social policies proved vulnerable, and more dramatic initiatives were
possible.

Extending the analysis to consider the long-term implications of policy
change both inside and outside the welfare state permits a more accurate evaluation of retrenchment efforts. Although projecting future trends is difficult, it
seems likely that in the United States major changes in the government's fiscal
capacities will have lasting repercussions. In both countries, the ability of program advocates to press their cases was somewhat reduced. In other respects,
however, the foundations of the welfare state look relatively secure. In particular,
popular support for social provision is more solid than it was a decade ago. Far
from introducing a self-reinforcing dynamic of retrenchment leading to greater
political alienation from social programs and further retrenchment, the conservative assault generated a backlash in support of the welfare state.

The evidence suggests significant but not radical retrenchment in both countries. Three important insights emerge from this detailed review. First and most

striking, there is a marked difference in the vulnerability of individual programs that is not always easily explained. Second, programmatic retrenchment has been somewhat more extensive in Britain. Finally, systemic retrenchment was more successful in the United States. Chapter 7 considers the reasons for this particular pattern of policy change.

7

Social policy in an era of austerity

The resurgence of conservatism in the late 1970s marked an important development for western industrial democracies. The electoral triumphs of Reagan and Thatcher signaled a juncture of economic, social, and political pressures that challenged the Keynesian settlement of the postwar period.[1] The resulting clash between committed reform administrations and an established set of institutions, organizations, and policies led to a decade of turbulent domestic politics in both Britain and the United States. This chapter suggests why, within this turbulence, the welfare state remained an area of relative calm.

THE SOURCES OF PROGRAMMATIC DURABILITY

Both Reagan and Thatcher found that cutting social programs posed an extraordinary challenge. If they were able to achieve occasional successes, the more frequent outcome was one of initially aggressive efforts giving way to embarrassed retreat. On the whole, welfare state programs demonstrated considerable resilience during the tenures of both leaders. The proximate reasons for this pattern were suggested in Chapter 1. Unlike many parts of the conservative agenda, the pursuit of welfare state retrenchment was an unpopular undertaking. Imposing losses on specific groups usually generated such a vigorous response and such limited political benefits that governments were forced to adopt a more cautious posture, picking their opportunities for reform carefully and shifting their emphasis to other policy goals.

Nevertheless, if the immediate causes of programmatic stability are evident, it remains true that some programs proved vulnerable. To understand why requires a reexamination of the three contextual factors discussed in Chapter 2: organized interests, institutions, and program designs. The Reagan and Thatcher records provide considerable evidence for evaluating the role of each in the new politics of the welfare state.

From power resources to programmatic networks: the transformation of welfare state support

Because retrenchment requires the minimization of opposition, the role of groups committed to mobilizing program supporters is of clear significance. Two distinct sets of groups are potential influences on retrenchment politics: trade unions, which view welfare state programs as a protection against the unfettered market, and the clientele and advocacy groups that cluster around particular programs. Although evidence of union involvement in the welfare state's expansion is extensive, there is no doubt that this role diminished considerably in the period of retrenchment. During the 1980s, unions were threatened on many fronts. Dwindling political resources and the press of higher priorities left unions unable to push effectively for the maintenance of social programs. Unions continued to participate in these political battles, but with significantly reduced influence. It is difficult to identify examples where unions took the lead role in the mobilization against programmatic cutbacks.

This finding raises important issues for theories of social-policy change. Of course, the importance of case selection in a study limited to two countries needs to be taken into account. Perhaps the examination of countries with stronger labor movements would have yielded different conclusions. Nonetheless, the continued durability of the American and British welfare states despite the declining political influence of organized labor suggests an important shift in the politics of social policy. Had the fate of these welfare states truly depended on the strength of unions, the outcome of recent struggles would have been very different.

With the role of organized labor shrinking, however, the primary responsibility for direct opposition to programmatic retrenchment shifted to the client groups with a stake in each program. In many cases, the groups themselves were largely products of the programs. The emergence of these new networks of support for the welfare state is one of the most important illustrations of the role of policy feedback in contemporary politics. As pointed out in past chapters, program structure plays a critical role in determining the political strength of clientele groups. For example, there was nothing about the characteristics of the elderly per se that made this group a stronger lobby in the United States than in Britain. Rather, this difference developed in significant part because the structure of Social Security unified pensioner interests, whereas the design of British pensions fragmented its potential clientele.

Indeed, the emergence of these program-based interest networks has been a major part of the conservative brief against the modern welfare state. The expansion of public activity, conservatives argue, has given rise to a range of actors who struggle to redistribute wealth rather than produce it.[2] Whether this objection is justified is a matter of heated dispute. The relevant issue here is the extent to which these networks of program clienteles have been able to shore up support for a welfare state that organized labor itself would have been hard pressed to defend. If there is controversy over the economic consequences of these group efforts, the political consequences are more straightforward: Their presence dramatically increases the cost of pursuing retrenchment initiatives.

Broad, "institutional" welfare state programs could count on significant support from such groups, and their presence has made up for the diminishing strength of organized labor. The important exception has been unemployment insurance. Because unemployment is not an experience all workers expect to share, their commitment to the program is likely to be limited. Of course, this changes if they lose their jobs; but even then, their reliance on the program is likely to be temporary and their political influence modest. Unemployment insurance, then, is the exception that proves the rule. It is not surprising that the one universal program that remained dependent on the kind of encompassing interest-group represented by trade unions has declined along with the political influence of the labor movement.

Even though the contribution of these networks of interests has been evident, it has been far from determinative. There have been cases where even extensive interest-group structures proved vulnerable – pensions and housing in Britain being the most notable examples. The varied fate of means-tested programs provides further evidence that the strength of program clienteles is not everything. Means-tested programs, with politically marginalized beneficiaries, have had to rely primarily on public-interest groups and providers (e.g., state governments in the United States) to generate opposition to retrenchment. In general, these groups have less clout than those connected to universal programs. Consequently, means-tested programs have depended on other supports (e.g., their unattractiveness as retrenchment targets, or politicians' concern with the fairness issue).

The continuing durability of many means-tested programs, and the vulnerability of some universal programs, suggests that other factors besides the organizational resources of interest groups are at work. Even relatively weak groups often give retrenchment advocates pause, and potentially strong groups have on occasion been outflanked. To account for these patterns, my analysis has stressed the critical role of the rules of the game governing the political competition between program supporters and opponents. In particular, the structure of political institutions and the design of individual programs may create opportunities for retrenchment advocates to prevent or limit the mobilization of program supporters.

Political institutions and programmatic retrenchment

Students of policy formation have begun to stress that the structure of political institutions plays a major part in determining policy outcomes. The usual claim of institutionalists regarding social policy is that centralized state structures, which limit opportunities for the exercise of minority vetoes, will permit greater innovation and public-sector expansion; in other words, that strong states will generate strong welfare states.[3] Does a similar dynamic apply to the politics of retrenchment? The evidence indicates that the connection between the structure of political institutions and retrenchment success is far more complex.

It is too simple to claim that the tremendous concentration of political authority in the British system gave the Thatcher government an overwhelming advantage in pursuing a reform agenda. Although this was probably true in many other policy arenas, the distinctive character of social-policy retrenchment complicates the picture. Recognizing the distinctiveness of retrenchment means moving toward more multidimensional accounts of institutional effects. As Kent Weaver and Bert Rockman have recently argued, analyses of institutional consequences must remain sensitive to the diverse tasks of governments.[4] Governments, for example, seek to manage social cleavages as well as to respond to majority demands; they wish to be able to reallocate resources to new needs as well as to establish lasting commitments. Institutional features that enhance some capabilities are likely to diminish others.

If Thatcher had the advantage of being able to do more or less as she chose – subject only to the impact on her prospects at the next election – she had the disadvantage of being the recipient of whatever blame her efforts generated.[5] Indeed, a striking feature of the Thatcher government's record was the frequency of retreats in the face of opposition. To name but a few cases, radical retrenchment strategies advanced for the NHS, Child Benefit, and SERPS (the green-paper proposal) were all dropped when they provoked popular hostility. These retreats occurred despite the government's strong electoral position and an institutional structure that virtually prohibited the translation of this opposition into an effective political barrier against the enactment of government proposals.

The government's modest retrenchment success generally depended on an ability to fashion acceptable alternatives rather than on a capacity to ignore opposition.[6] As my discussion of pensions, housing, and income-support policies suggested, the particular characteristics of existing policies heavily influenced the prospects for identifying viable retrenchment strategies. The contribution of institutional features, however, was substantial in two respects. First and most important, the concentration of authority in Britain meant that a government able to identify appropriate retrenchment strategies would be in a strong position to pursue them. In several cases in which the Thatcher government's initial efforts led to defeats, the concentration of political authority made it possible to refashion reforms in ways that weakened potential opposition. In this respect, I will argue, the Thatcher government did enjoy a considerable advantage over its American counterpart.

Furthermore, features of institutional design made some retrenchment strategies more promising than others, and therefore had an important effect in channeling government efforts in particular directions. Specifically, unlike their American counterparts, British retrenchment advocates rarely directed their efforts toward lowering the traceability of policy reforms. As the massive public reaction against the poll tax demonstrated, the concentration of political authority made it difficult for the Thatcher government to duck responsibility for unpopular policies. Instead, the government's obfuscation efforts usually focused on diminishing the visibility of negative effects and obscuring the links between negative effects and public policies.

Political institutions in the United States, of course, present a sharp contrast.

Whereas the British system concentrates political authority and facilitates strong government action, the American system – designed in part as a reaction to British practices – seeks to decentralize political power. The critical question concerning how institutions affected retrenchment politics in the United States centers on the role of "divided government." Although one often hears general arguments about the functioning of checks-and-balances systems, it has become increasingly clear in recent years that the functioning of American political institutions is likely to depend in part on electoral results.[7] In an already fragmented political system, the absence of unified partisan control of both the legislative and executive branches meant that power was even more dispersed than it would otherwise have been. Although the Republicans held the White House throughout the 1980s, Democrats maintained a majority in the House and regained control of the Senate in 1986. How important a role did this arrangement play in political struggles over the welfare state?

The impact of divided government has been the subject of considerable controversy, and recent analyses have suggested that the effects of this arrangement on policy may not be especially large.[8] This investigation provides some support for the view that divided government was not of overwhelming importance. Reagan's limited ability to achieve retrenchment would at first glance suggest otherwise. The Thatcher government's record demonstrates that a greater concentration of authority would not have made the Reagan administration's task a simple one, however. Reagan would have had to deal with the concentration of accountability that accompanies such a position. There is little reason to think that he would have been any more eager than Thatcher was to accept the political costs of a radical retrenchment strategy.

One should not overstate the effects of the relative fragmentation of American politics. Governments can sometimes take steps that partly mitigate the effects of institutional arrangements. Cutback efforts in the United States have sometimes taken advantage of opportunities for more centralized decision making. The use of reconciliation procedures to force a single vote on budget cuts in 1981, the appointment of a special commission to design a cutback package for Social Security in 1983, and the adoption of the Gramm-Rudmann budget reduction mechanisms (and later deals such as the 1990 deficit agreement) are important examples. If these cases suggest the occasional utility of centralizing the retrenchment process, they also indicate that it is not impossible to establish such mechanisms in the American political system in which an acceptable package can be formulated. Again, the importance of identifying politically acceptable cuts becomes prominent.

If the strongest case for the role of divided government is unpersuasive, it nonetheless remains true that the system of checks and balances in the United States, and the strong institutional position of the Democratic Party, did impose considerable constraints on the Reagan administration's efforts. Thatcher found that designing strategies that would minimize an electoral reaction was generally sufficient to allow reform. By contrast, the Reagan administration also had to overcome institutional barriers that were often strongly defended by Democrats

This meant that the administration's position was strongest when it did not have to confront these obstacles on a regular basis.

Reagan's greatest successes came when his opposition needed to take positive action to avoid the negative effects of retrenchment. Under these circumstances, institutional fragmentation strengthened the president's bargaining position. As I argued in Chapter 6, this was the key to Reagan's defunding strategy. The indexation of tax brackets changed the "status quo option" from one of buoyant revenues to one of fiscal stringency. In the case of individual social programs as well, the Reagan administration often did best when it could play defense. Success was most common where programs were not entitlements and therefore required annual authorizations (e.g., housing programs); were not indexed and therefore relied on regular benefit adjustments (a main source of AFDC's troubles at the state level); or rested not on statutory requirements but rather on traditions of expansion during times of greater need (as with unemployment insurance). In addition, circumstances in which trust funds operated as focusing events, forcing even program supporters to contemplate reform, sometimes allowed retrenchment. In these cases again, the unacceptability of the status quo improved the Reagan administration's bargaining position.

The second dimension of institutional fragmentation in the United States, federalism, also had implications for programmatic retrenchment. The intergovernmental lobby emerged as an important support for social programs, blocking some of Reagan's most strenuous reform efforts. Although state governments lacked the formal veto power over policy change that they sometimes possess in other federal systems, they were formidable opponents.[9] Nonetheless, the administration had some success in harnessing the retrenchment-facilitating characteristics of federalism: opportunities for burden-shifting and the competitive pressures that hold down state-level spending. Again, however, programmatic rules were critical. The policy legacies of the New Deal, when reformers failed to fully nationalize systems of income support, left AFDC and unemployment insurance vulnerable to these strategies, whereas programs like food stamps and Social Security were not.

These examples suggest a final important conclusion about the complex impact of institutional context. Rather than operating in a single, unidirectional way, institutional effects are often mediated by programmatic characteristics. The rules of the game that structure retrenchment politics involve complex interactions between institutional requirements and the specific features of individual programs. With this point in mind, it is appropriate to consider what has been a central theme of this study: the role of programmatic features in retrenchment politics.

Policy arenas and programmatic structures

Again, policies produce politics. One of the most distinctive qualities of contemporary political life is the pervasiveness of government activity. Just as the specific features of formal institutions have important consequences, so do the particular patterns of policy intervention that have developed in an age of big government. Nowhere is this more true than in the case of the welfare state itself, which epitomizes government's expanded role.

How do policies exert influence on welfare state politics? I wish to answer first by outlining the problems with several broad arguments about the political impact of policies. Some studies have emphasized the differences between universal and means-tested programs as well as those between programs based on transfer payments and service provision. Although these perspectives draw relevant distinctions, each has considerable limitations.

Means-testing vs. universalism. Robert Kuttner has termed the weakness of targeted programs "the most fundamental principle in the political economy of social spending."[10] This is, indeed, a widely held view. Many have argued that universal programs, with a far larger constituency to draw on for support, will be less vulnerable to retrenchment than means-tested programs.[11] The Reagan and Thatcher records confirm some of the logic behind this expectation, but suggest that its application to retrenchment politics is far from straightforward. Universal programs do tend to be stronger, but because of this they also are much larger and more generous. Because they are often directly in competition with private alternatives, they also present a much more serious challenge to the market-oriented preferences of conservative governments. Means-tested programs tend to remain small, stingy, and restricted to groups unable to afford private provision. The result of these differences is that a government committed to radical change finds its attention naturally drawn to universal programs. The same features that make universal programs politically strong make them likely targets for major retrenchment efforts.

It is important not to misunderstand the claim being made here. It is not that universal programs are somehow "weaker." Rather, the key point is that they generally offer more room for a dramatic shift in policy. Beyond a point, it becomes difficult to make means tests meaner. In short, knowing whether a program is targeted or universal by itself tells us relatively little about its political prospects in a period of retrenchment.

Services vs. transfers. What about the relative vulnerability of programs based on transfer payments and service provision? Analysts starting from a public-choice perspective that emphasizes the empire-building proclivities of bureaucrats have sometimes implied that service provision will produce more durable programs.[12] Not only do these programs create larger "empires" for bureaucrats, but they generate two important constituencies. Like transfer programs, service programs benefit recipients, but in addition they offer benefits to providers. This alliance of recipients, providers, and policymakers might seem to insulate service programs from retrenchment efforts.[13]

The preceding chapters provide little support for the idea that service-providing programs are more immune to retrenchment than are transfer programs. If anything, the evidence suggests that service programs may be slightly more vulnerable. First, any service-providing program is likely to face at least potential private competition. Private income support for the able-bodied is limited, but there are private markets in housing, health care, and education. These private alternatives may provide opportunities for compensation strategies that facilitate retrenchment.

Second, a program's reliance on consumer and producer interests may offer opportunities for divide-and-conquer tactics. Retrenchment can be designed in ways that hurt one program clientele much more than another. This approach has been used effectively in housing policy in both countries, and in health care in the United States. The vulnerability of service programs to this divide-and-conquer strategy again reveals the distinctive dynamics of retrenchment. Factors that encourage welfare state expansion at one stage may cause problems in different circumstances. Joining disparate interests together may foster program growth in an era of rising expenditures, but leave the program vulnerable at a time of austerity. For example, the Johnson administration's efforts to bring the private-housing industry into the public-housing coalition gave the latter a political boost in the late 1960s. In the early 1980s, however, the diverse interests of the coalition greatly facilitated the use of strategies of division.

Programmatic structure and retrenchment strategies. I have argued throughout that the emergence of the welfare state itself has transformed the nature of struggles over social policy. Earlier policy choices feed back into the policy-making process, altering the balance of political resources among interest groups and modifying the rules governing future decision making. Analysts interested in the connection between policies and politics have sometimes developed broad typologies that associate specific policy "types" with particular political outcomes. The arguments of Theodore Lowi and James Q. Wilson are prominent examples.[14] The current discussion suggests two problems with such efforts. First, individual policies may have a number of politically relevant characteristics, and these characteristics may have a multiplicity of consequences. Second, policy characteristics rarely operate in isolation from features of the broader political environment (such as the structure of formal institutions). The impact of policies is likely to occur in interaction with other variables. For both of these reasons, it seems doubtful that we can develop sweeping theories that link a few policy types to clearly defined political outcomes.

A more promising strategy is to develop middle-range theories that acknowledge both the complexity of feedback and its context-specific qualities. A useful starting point is to distinguish between the long-term and short-term consequences of policy design. Many of the most important social-policy-feedback effects occur over extended periods of time. When Reagan and Thatcher began to seek cutbacks in social programs, the legacies of previous decision makers profoundly influenced their prospects for success. Interest group structures, such as the far more unified and powerful lobby for the elderly in the United States, and Britain's corporatist-style housing networks, were in considerable part an outgrowth of previous policy choices.

Another important example is the prevalence of policy-induced lock-in effects. The cumulative outcome of millions of individual commitments resulting from public policy choices has received limited attention. However, Chapter 3 suggested that sunk costs resulting from previous decisions in pension policy created lock-in effects that greatly constrained Reagan's options on Social Security.

The long-term consequences of preexisting policies helped to structure private social provision as well.[15] The availability of private alternatives is often crucial to retrenchment success. Given that universal programs have strong constituencies, the ability to compensate some of those hurt by cutbacks by fashioning attractive private options is a critical component of retrenchment efforts. This is most obviously evident in the divergent fates of privatization initiatives for health care and old-age pension provision in Britain. In the case of British pensions, public policy helped create a private system that was well integrated with public provision. This legacy made a strategy of compensation based on increased reliance on private pensions relatively simple to implement and lowered the visibility of sharp cutbacks in public pensions.

These long-term effects of policy feedback helped determine both the array of interests that retrenchment advocates had to contend with and the reform options available to them. Specific features of program structures also influenced the immediate viability of different retrenchment strategies. Whether Reagan or Thatcher could devise strategies of obfuscation, division, or compensation often depended on structures of existing programs. The diversity of the linkages discussed in the previous chapters suggests again the difficulties of any sweeping argument about the vulnerability of broad types of policies. Nonetheless, particular aspects of programmatic structure are of such importance that they deserve special emphasis: the presence of lag times, opportunities for burden shifting, indexation structures, and financing provisions.

A critical programmatic feature concerns the existence of lag times in individual programs. As the previous chapters have stressed, the temporal link between the enactment of retrenchment policies and the imposition of costs on recipients may vary widely from program to program. In some cases such as housing construction and contribution-based pensions, the existence of lag times permits the introduction of retrenchment policies with deferred repercussions for beneficiaries. Such circumstances greatly enhance the prospects for political success.

Programs also vary widely in their openness to burden shifting. In health care, for example, the Reagan administration succeeded in shifting some of the burden for imposing cutbacks onto providers – an option that the virtual absence of consumer fees-for-service in the NHS made impossible in Britain. Where program responsibilities are shared between different levels of government, it may be possible to impose cutbacks so that at least some of the blame is transferred from central government to local government. Of course, this tactic requires that program responsibilities be shared. The prominent role of federalism has made this an attractive and plausible strategy for a number of programs in the United States.

Indexation rules are also important. In a political venture in which lowering visibility enhances prospects for success, rising earnings and prices in the broader economy may provide crucial opportunities. If retrenchment advocates can hold benefits or expenditures constant in an inflationary context, they can achieve dramatic reductions in real terms. Such decremental cuts require limited legislative initiatives. If a program is not indexed, it is simply a matter of preventing ad hoc adjustments, giving retrenchment advocates the strategic advantage of defending the status quo. If a program is indexed, a one-time shift in policy will result in mounting expenditure reductions over time. Even if price indexation cannot be removed, economic growth provides opportunities for "implicit privatization." Holding public provision constant in real terms means that additional provision must be provided privately. This strengthening of the private sector may open opportunities for a more aggressive attack on the public sector at a later date.

Whether the approach taken is one of decremental cutbacks or implicit privatization, the indexing provisions of existing programs become important. In Britain, Wilson's Labour governnment fought to institute protections against implicit privatization, generally establishing benefit upratings in line with "the higher of earnings or prices." The Thatcher government's shift to indexation against price increases only presented a very significant example of implicit privatization.

As Weaver's recent research has demonstrated, the application of indexation in the United States is extremely uneven.[16] One American program contains extremely strong protections against benefit erosion: Social Security. Benefit adjustments are linked to prices, and these COLAs are sometimes identified as potential targets for cutbacks. Nevertheless, initial benefit determinations are based on a formula linked explicitly to earnings. The formula is designed to maintain constant replacement rates: As average earnings increase, benefits increase as well. This provides an important protection against implicit privatization, and is deeply embedded in the structure of Social Security. On the other hand, many programs are not indexed at all. The widely disparate fates of AFDC and food stamps during the high inflation years of the late 1970s indicate the tremendous repercussions of this single aspect of program design.

Finally, the structure of finances for universal programs may play an important role. Contributory insurance systems are usually seen as a major source of program support because they produce a strong sense of entitlement. However, if contributions are used to set up a distinct trust fund for particular programs, the result may be to heighten vulnerability under some circumstances. In the United States, successful cutbacks (though not radical overhauls) in unemployment insurance, Social Security pensions, and Medicare were all produced at times of heightened concern over trust-fund balances.[17] Trust-fund crises reshape the political debate in ways that facilitate cutbacks. The threat of financial shortages prevents program supporters from keeping cutbacks off the agenda and allows retrenchment advocates to argue that reductions are necessary to save the programs.[18] Britain's different system of financing social-insurance programs has left no room for this particular strategy. The treasury makes a flexible contribution to social-insurance programs, assuring that revenues and payments will balance. The result is that trust-fund crises do not appear, and provide no particular leverage for lowering benefits.

The way that cutback efforts have lost force when surpluses developed in programs demonstrates the important role that trust funds play in structuring debates over programs in the United States. The growing Social Security surplus has undermined calls for cuts in this largest American social program. The recent removal of the program from the unified budget is likely to reinforce its image as a separate entity, untouchable unless its own finances are precarious.

It is worth stressing that many of these critical programmatic features are relevant to retrenchment because they have implications for the application of obfuscation strategies. This emphasis is in keeping with the broad finding that programmatic retrenchment often involves struggles over the distribution of information. Policy structures often have a major impact on the ability of policymakers to minimize public awareness of negative outcomes, of the links between those outcomes and public policies, or of individual politicians' responsibility for those policies.

Previous work on policy feedback has often stressed the effects of policy structures on elite capacities and learning processes, and the material resources available to social groups. Increasingly, political scientists have recognized that the staggering complexities of modern life make information a critical factor in politics. There has been growing attention to the ways in which institutional structures facilitate or impede information flows, and to the role of politicians, parties, and interest groups as transmitters of information to various actors.[19] Nevertheless, we still know relatively little about the contribution of policies themselves to such processes. Because both the visibility and traceability of policies can vary so widely, the informational content of policies is likely to have significant effects on the mobilizing potential of political actors. The current analysis suggests that in retrenchment politics, the effects of policy structures on the informational resources available to large segments of the public are critical.

Historical institutionalist analysis has largely missed the impact of policies on mass publics, whether in the form of information asymmetries or the development of lock-ins. It is no accident that both of the arguments I have advanced about the effects of policy feedback on such groups draw heavily on work in rational-choice theory. Although historical institutionalists have studied state structures and social groups, the use of microeconomic theory leads naturally to a focus on individual behavior. Economists have developed powerful models for exploring how different institutional frameworks and resource distributions influence both individual choices and the ways in which individual choices produce particular aggregate outcomes. Wedded to historical-institutionalist arguments about the prominence of public policies and the importance of tracing historical processes, these insights from rational choice can produce powerful tools for the study of policy feedback on mass publics.

The development of the welfare state clearly has had extensive economic, social, and political implications. Over the long term, processes set in motion by earlier policy enactments, such as the accumulation of sunk costs and the development of interest-group structures, have important consequences for subsequent struggles over social policy. In the short run, policy structures also establish specific decision rules that affect the difficulty of pursuing reform and influence the distribution of information among relevant actors. The structures of welfare states themselves now have a tremendous impact on struggles over the future of social policy.

Institutional analysis and programmatic retrenchment

Welfare state retrenchment involves struggles by social groups and their political representatives over the content of social policy. This investigation has stressed, however, the ways in which institutional circumstances condition these struggles. Institutional features have profound consequences for the distribution of political resources and help to establish the incentives that channel individual behavior in particular directions.

Formal political institutions and policy designs constitute two closely linked aspects of the institutional environment, and should be studied together. Each, I have argued, has important consequences. Often, how the two interact establishes the prospects for social-policy reform. The authority relations established by formal institutions frequently take on a distinctive character in different programs. The role of central and local authorities in both countries differed depending on policy design (compare housing and pensions in Britain or AFDC and Social Security in the United States).

This interplay between formal institutions and policy design is the reason I have stressed a focus on individual programs. "The welfare state" is an analytical concept, a construct that joins together a range of distinctive public policies. Because the design of individual policies matters, a careful analysis of retrenchment requires disaggregation. The wide variation in outcomes among programs provides clear evidence of the need to incorporate aspects of program design into our explanations of policy change. The system-level variables that have been dominant in social-policy research operate in different ways depending upon the structure of the program in question.

CHANGING THE CONTEXT: THE RESTRICTED SCOPE
OF SYSTEMIC RETRENCHMENT

Most of this investigation has concentrated on the political struggles between
conservatives and welfare state supporters over individual social programs. The
dynamics of programmatic retrenchment, however, reveal the importance of institutional settings, interest-group influence, and the broader budgetary and political climate. I have argued that evaluating the impact of conservative
governance on the welfare state also requires the adoption of a wider frame of
reference. Without considering aspects of systemic change, one might attribute
greater stability to the welfare state than is justified. The examination of systemic
retrenchment in Chapter 6, however, generally did not challenge the picture of
relative resilience. Interest groups remain well entrenched. Institutional reforms
have been limited. Public opinion has become, if anything, more supportive of
social provision.

Providing a full explanation for these results would require a more far-
reaching analysis of the two administrations than is offered here. Nevertheless,
it is important to comment briefly on two key outcomes: the two governments'
sharp divergence in their revenue policies, and the Thatcher government's general inability to achieve systemic reform. Both of these are particularly instructive for evaluating the welfare state's current circumstances.

The political basis for a defunding strategy

No other divergence between Reagan and Thatcher's records is as striking – or
as important – as their differing treatment of government revenues. The Reagan
administration's taxation policies were its major policy achievement, substantially altering the federal government's long-term financial position. The results
have already been felt, and not just in the area of social policy. The federal
deficit was *the* domestic policy issue of the 1980s in the United States, and
looks to be the issue of the 1990s as well. By contrast, the Thatcher government
produced a balance between British spending and revenue levels last experienced
in the 1960s. Avoiding deficits rather than restraining revenues was the order
of the day. Indeed, during the years of peak economic growth in the late 1980s,
the British government ran a substantial budget surplus.[20]

In most areas of social policy, divergence between the American and British
experiences reflected unequal success at achieving similar goals; both governments sought cutbacks wherever possible. In this case, however, the divergence
in results reflected distinctive goals. Each government sought to strengthen the
private economy by restricting governmental interventions and restoring a sense
of dynamism and entrepreneurship in the marketplace. Nevertheless, the two
governments identified quite different policy levers for bringing about this transformation. Faced with broadly similar climates of high inflation and budgetary

difficulties when coming to power, the Thatcher government raised taxes and lowered the budget deficit, whereas the Reagan administration did the opposite.

In Britain, monetarism reigned, and managing the money supply was seen as the overriding economic objective.[21] This analysis in turn led to a focus on the key variable directly subject to government control, the Public Sector Borrowing Requirement (PSBR). Once this goal of reduced borrowing had been established, it required budgetary priorities that precisely reversed the pattern developing in the United States. Lowering revenues became dependent on success in controlling expenditures. When cutbacks failed to be sufficient, Thatcher chose to increase the level of revenues.

In the United States, supply-side economic advisors identified tax cuts rather than monetary stability or balanced budgets as the key to economic success. True "supply-siders" argued that tax cuts need not increase deficits; indeed, they argued that the removal of heavy tax burdens would unleash such entrepreneurial energies that revenues would actually rise. The actual result of these policies was a sharp divergence of revenues and expenditures that is likely to limit domestic policy options for the foreseeable future.[22]

The difference between the fundamental economic theories guiding policymakers in the two countries was substantial. Throughout this analysis, I have downplayed the independent role of ideas and learning processes in policy formation. In the politics of programmatic retrenchment, hostility toward public provision has been uniform among conservative policymakers, and it has been difficult to establish cases in which aspects of ideology or learning processes might explain why some programs survived and others did not. There were, however, considerable differences during the critical period of the early 1980s in the assumptions guiding economic policy-making in the two countries.

Although it is useful to note that the divergence between Reagan and Thatcher's revenue policies can be linked to their different economic priorities, these priorities were in turn shaped by the different circumstances facing the two administrations. As Peter Hall has argued, to gain political relevance, economic ideas need to pass tests of economic, political, and administrative viability.[23] We are led back, then, to the particular context in which these governments operated.

The defunding strategy was one case in which Reagan clearly benefited from the fragmentation of responsibility endemic to American political institutions. Once the deficits were in place, responsibility for reducing them was dispersed throughout the federal government. Reagan was remarkably successful in passing the buck, blaming Congress for the large deficits. Even had the Thatcher government wished to pursue a defunding strategy, political circumstances would have made such an approach extremely dangerous. In Britain's political system, the Thatcher government's responsibility for an unbalanced budget would have been clear. This would have sharply increased political pressure to cut the deficit, even if higher taxes were necessary. As Paul Peterson and Mark Rom have noted in explaining the contrast with Reagan's experience, "That the

Conservative party had full control of Parliament as well as the cabinet precluded Thatcher from pursuing a potentially more popular course of proposing large deficit-producing tax cuts while blaming Parliament for any failure to cut expenditures by a comparable amount."[24]

Britain's position in the international economy also made a high deficit policy unattractive. As a middle-ranking power with a relatively uncompetitive economy, Britain would have been far more vulnerable than the United States to international pressures to reduce deficit spending. The economic crisis of 1974–5, which led to a loan agreement with the International Monetary Fund, demonstrated just how limited Britain's room to sustain large deficits had become.[25]

Thus, the divergent situations facing the Reagan and Thatcher governments produced quite different prospects for a retrenchment effort focused on government revenues. In the United States, economic and political circumstances limited the costs of such a strategy. Different conditions in Britain made a path of deficit-led reduction unattractive to the Conservatives.

Contradictions of the conservative reform agenda

The absence of defunding efforts in Britain, and of broad examples of systemic retrenchment more generally, highlights an important if rarely noted aspect of the conservative resurgence of the 1980s: the pressure facing policymakers to choose among competing priorities for reform. Thatcher's broader effort to reshape the political landscape had a surprisingly mixed impact on the welfare state. In some cases, other policy goals dovetailed nicely with retrenchment objectives. However, the government frequently was forced to set priorities. Welfare state retrenchment fits less comfortably into a broad conservative agenda than is usually assumed. As a result, Thatcher has left the welfare state in healthier condition than one might have expected.

Discussions of conservative governance usually suggest that the goal of welfare state retrenchment was an integral part of a general strategy to reshape mixed economies in a more market-oriented fashion. In certain respects, there is indeed a good fit here; cuts in social benefits generally support the goal of increasing labor-market flexibility, for example, because they remove alternatives to low-wage employment.[26] Similarly, efforts to weaken organized labor furthered both the government's economic policies and its goal of restricting the welfare state.

Nevertheless, the Thatcher record reveals several instances in which promoting welfare state retrenchment conflicted with key conservative objectives. The most important case of this, already discussed, was taxation. By reducing revenues, Thatcher would have placed serious pressures on welfare state development. In response, a future Labour government would have been forced to enact major tax increases to fund social programs. Sharp tax cuts, however, conflicted with other aspects of the Thatcher agenda, namely the desire to run a tight monetary policy to fight inflation and diminish union power. Forced to choose between tax cuts and a low public sector borrowing requirement, the government chose the latter. It did manage to avert a popular outcry against its tax policies, largely by shifting from obvious to less visible tax sources. By raising the level of politically sustainable taxation, however, this shift also helped the welfare state in the long run.

The clash between central and local government provides a second example of conflicting policy goals. Arguably, a focus on retrenchment would have dictated a decentralization of authority in order to promote the fiscal competition among local jurisdictions that exerts strong downward pressure on spending. The Reagan administration chose precisely this course in many of its social-policy initiatives, although with only modest success. By contrast, the Thatcher government decided to put a higher priority on weakening Labour Party enclaves in local governments.

It is important to emphasize these conflicting objectives because of the common assumption that retrenchment is part of a logically coherent conservative project. Although conservatives have enunciated clear policy goals – greater reliance on the market, lower government spending, and weaker "redistributive coalitions," for example – along with the obvious goal of reelection, some aspects of the conservative agenda can be achieved only at the expense of others. Pressure for trade-offs in such objectives has left the welfare state less vulnerable than it might otherwise have been. At the same time, the sources of welfare state strength discussed later in this section help explain why conservative governments, when forced to choose, have often given higher priority to tasks other than retrenchment.

WELFARE STATE RESILIENCE AND THE FUTURE OF SOCIAL POLICY

Social scientists are drawn to the study of variation, and this chapter has considered the causes of considerable variations within the records examined in this study. Despite these important differences, however, a fundamental similarity in outcomes also cries out for comment: the dominant pattern of continuity in social policy. Despite the aggressive efforts of retrenchment advocates, the welfare state remains largely intact. As I said at the outset, any attempt to understand the politics of welfare state retrenchment must start from a recognition that social policy remains the most resilient component of postwar domestic policy.

In many respects, this stability is surprising. Talk of "welfare state crisis" began in earnest two decades ago. The intervening period has witnessed dramatic shifts in the international system, in structures of economic organization, in the political complexion of many governments, in the balance of power between labor and capital, and in the capacities of nation-states. Nevertheless, the welfare state has endured. Before summarizing the sources of continuity, it is worth reviewing the reasons why many believed the welfare state to be so vulnerable.

Pressures on the welfare state mounted following the first oil shock. One source of stress was fiscal, a result of the upward momentum of spending in a maturing welfare state, of demographic pressures, and of poor economic performance. Fiscal strain and changing economic conditions were not the only sources of pressure on the welfare state. Political challenges were evident as well. Business interests were increasingly influential, and appeared eager to question the old social contract. The enhanced mobility of capital in an increasingly integrated world economy, combined with slack labor markets, strengthened the position of employers while devaluing the bargaining chips of unions (e.g., promises of wage restraint) and of the nation-state (effective demand management). This shift in the political balance was reflected partly in the resurgence of conservative parties and partly in a rightward drift of left-of-center parties.

Observers who questioned the welfare state's durability also pointed to growing political challenges within traditional welfare state constituencies. The welfare state was portrayed as a victim of its own success. Although poverty and economic insecurity remained a major problem for those in the secondary labor market, the welfare state managed to assure a degree of affluence and stability for much of the working class. This very success, it was argued, made these same groups more open to electoral recruitment by conservative parties. Affluence clouded memories of the uncertainties and hardship that had made the postwar expansion of welfare states so popular. Conservative, consumer-oriented appeals could be an attractive alternative to traditional, class-based platforms based on workers' status as wage earners. The massive growth of the (relatively sheltered) public sector created new opportunities for conservative parties to generate anti-welfare state backlashes among blue-collar workers in the private sector. Finally, the welfare state's expansion fueled growing criticism of its rigidifying, bureaucratic tendencies. The agendas of new social movements, which appealed to groups traditionally supportive of social expenditures, were often ambivalent if not hostile to major elements of the welfare state.

These economic, political, and social pressures combined to foster an image of welfare states beset by crisis. Nevertheless, if one turns from a description of context to an examination of actual policy change, it becomes impossible to sustain the proposition that these strains have generated fundamental shifts. Even in Thatcher's Britain, where an ideologically committed conservative party controlled one of Europe's most centralized political systems for more than a decade, reform was generally incremental rather than revolutionary. The British welfare state is battered but intact. In the United States, the evidence of continuity is equally apparent. Thus, to understand what has been happening, one must move from an examination of the pressures on the welfare state to a consideration of enduring sources of support.

The main source of durability comes from the high political costs associated with retrenchment initiatives. Despite scholarly speculation about declining popular support for the welfare state, there remains little evidence of such a shift in opinion polls, and even less in actual political struggles over social spending. On the contrary, efforts to dismantle the welfare state have exacted a high political price. The costs associated with cutbacks are concentrated and immediate, whereas benefits are likely to be diffuse and to appear only over time. Furthermore, voters generally are quicker to respond negatively to losses than they are to laud commensurate gains.

The welfare state's political position does not seem to have been seriously eroded by the decline of its key traditional constituency, organized labor. The maturation of social programs has produced a new network of organized interests – the consumers and providers of social services – that are well placed to defend the welfare state. Recent research on "path dependency" has revealed an additional way in which the networks associated with mature welfare state programs constitute a barrier to radical change. Certain courses of development, once initiated, are hard to reverse. Organizations and individuals adapt to particular arrangements, making investments of human and financial capital that render the costs of change (even to some potentially more efficient alternative) far higher than the costs of continuity. Existing commitments, then, often lock in policymakers.

If the barriers to retrenchment have given would-be reformers pause, so has a growing awareness of the continuing persuasiveness of the case for the welfare state. This is another way of saying that the absence of attractive private alternatives is often a source of strength for social programs. Although some of the macroeconomic arguments for social expenditure have lost credibility, many of the microeconomic arguments remain compelling. Whatever their shortcomings, key aspects of social provision remain more efficient than free-market alternatives. Health care provides a good example. The relatively market-oriented American system is increasingly seen as a drag on economic competitiveness – a recognition that contributed to the demise of Reagan and Thatcher's most radical market-based proposals for health-care reform. The efficiency argument for many aspects of social insurance remains persuasive, as does the case for many public-sector programs (e.g., education and training, child care, and health and safety issues) that the private sector is inclined to treat as externalities.

In short, the standard arguments for a welfare state crisis resulting from rapid political, social, and economic change must be weighed against the fact that there remain very substantial sources of strength. Once these sustaining factors are taken into account, the durability of the welfare state is easier to understand. The evolution of public opinion provides the clearest sign that, barring the onset of much more serious pressures, the welfare state is unlikely to undergo radical change. Expectations that retrenchment would be self-reinforcing – as weakened and divided program supporters became increasingly isolated from a middle class won over to private consumption – have largely failed to materialize. Instead, mass publics remain strongly attached to the central features of modern welfare states. The stances of Reagan and Thatcher's successors are equally instructive. Although both were conservatives, George Bush and John Major moved quickly to temper their predecessors' positions on social policy; and though they generally sought to preserve the modest retrenchment successes already achieved, they showed little inclination to pursue aggressive new initiatives of their own.

None of this is meant to downplay the significant changes that have occurred. The position of those on the margins of the labor market has deteriorated considerably. To a significant extent, this shift is driven by transformations in the global economy that have affected all industrial democracies. Even so, public policy in Britain and the United States has played an important role. As welfare state supporters struggle to hold on to existing resources, the capacity to address new social problems has suffered. This is especially true in the United States, where deficit politics did not roll back the welfare state, but nevertheless became a considerable barrier to new initiatives.

All institutions undergo change over time. This is bound to be true for very large ones, which must necessarily be influenced by broad social developments. The welfare state is no exception, but there is little basis for the claim that the Reagan and Thatcher era was one of radical transformation in the provision of social benefits. Although certain parts of the welfare state are vulnerable to cutbacks or partial privatization, the fundamental structure of social policy remains comparatively stable. Given the ambitions of retrenchment advocates and the concerns of their opponents, the considerable signs of continuity are worth emphasizing. They stand as a clear testament to the pervasive consequences of large-scale social policies for contemporary political life.

Notes

INTRODUCTION: CONSERVATIVES AND THE WELFARE STATE

1. R. Kent Weaver, "The Politics of Blame Avoidance," *Journal of Public Policy*, 6, no. 4 (1986), 371–98.
2. Christine L. Day, *What Older Americans Think: Interest Groups and Aging Policy* (Princeton, N.J.: Princeton University Press, 1990), pp. 25–6.
3. Rudolf Klein and Michael O'Higgins, "Defusing the Crisis of the Welfare State: A New Interpretation," in Theodore R. Marmor and Jerry L. Mashaw, eds., *Social Security: Beyond the Rhetoric of Crisis* (Princeton, N.J.: Princeton University Press, 1989), pp. 203–25.
4. Suzanne Berger, "Politics and Antipolitics in Western Europe in the Seventies," *Daedalus*, 108, no. 1 (Winter 1978), 27–49.
5. Peter Taylor-Gooby, *Social Change, Social Welfare and Social Science* (Toronto: University of Toronto Press, 1991), ch. 4; Department of Social Security, *Households Below Average Incomes, 1981–1987: A Statistical Analysis* (London: HMSO, 1990); House Ways and Means Committee, *1990 Green Book: Background Material and Data on Programs Within the Jurisdiction of the Committee on Ways and Means* (Washington, D.C.: Government Printing Office [hereafter GPO], 1990), pp. 1069–1145.
6. This is especially true in Britain, where change in a number of policy arenas was quite significant. See Paul Pierson and Miriam Smith, "Bourgeois Revolutions? The Policy Consequences of Resurgent Conservatism," *Comparative Political Studies*, 25, no. 4 (January 1993), 487–520.
7. Walter Korpi, "Social Policy and Distributional Conflict in the Capitalist Democracies," *West European Politics*, 3 (1980), 296–316; Theda Skocpol, "Targeting Within Universalism: Politically Viable Policies to Combat Poverty in the United States," in Christopher Jencks and Paul E. Peterson, eds., *The Urban Underclass* (Washington, D.C.: Brookings Institution, 1991), pp. 411–36.
8. Peter Jenkins, *Mrs. Thatcher's Revolution: The Ending of the Socialist Era* (Cambridge, Mass.: Harvard University Press, 1987); Geoff Garrett, "The Politics of Structural Change: Swedish Social Democracy and Thatcherism in Comparative Perspective," *Comparative Political Studies*, 25, no. 4 (January 1993), 521–47.
9. See for example Douglass North, *Institutions, Institutional Change, and Economic Performance* (Cambridge University Press, 1990); Sven Steinmo, Kathleen Thelen, and Frank Longstreth, eds., *Structuring Politics: Historical Institutionalism in Comparative Analysis* (Cambridge University Press, 1992); Theda Skocpol, *Protecting*

Soldiers and Mothers: The Origins of Social Policy in the United States (Cambridge, Mass.: Harvard University Press, 1992), ch. 1.

1. THE LOGIC OF RETRENCHMENT

1. Sara A. Rosenberry, "Social Insurance, Distributive Criteria and the Welfare Backlash: A Comparative Analysis," *British Journal of Political Science*, 12 (1982), 421–47; Ray Robinson, "Restructuring the Welfare State: An Analysis of Public Expenditure, 1979/80–1984/85," *Journal of Social Policy*, 15, no. 1 (January 1986), 1–21; and John L. Palmer, "Income Security Policies in the United States: The Inevitability and Consequences of Retrenchment," *Journal of Public Policy*, 7, no. 1 (1987), 1–32.
2. Gøsta Esping-Andersen, *The Three Worlds of Welfare Capitalism* (Cambridge University Press, 1990). For a thoughtful extension of this argument see Diane Sainsbury, "Analysing Welfare State Variations: The Merits and Limitations of Models Based on the Residual-Institutional Distinction," *Scandinavian Political Studies*, 14, no. 1 (1991), 1–30.
3. See for example John D. Stephens, *The Transition from Capitalism to Socialism* (London: Macmillan Press, 1979).
4. Richard Titmuss, *Social Policy* (New York: Pantheon, 1974).
5. Esping-Andersen, *Three Worlds of Welfare Capitalism*, p. 21.
6. Text of Reagan's February 5, 1981, speech in *New York Times*, February 6, 1981, p. A12.
7. For discussions of the impact of changes in consumption patterns on public opinion toward the welfare state see Patrick Dunleavy, "The Urban Basis of Political Alignment," *British Journal of Political Science*, 9 (1979), 409–43; and Peter Taylor-Gooby, "Consumption Cleavages and Welfare Politics," *Political Studies*, 34 (1986), 592–606.
8. An excellent treatment of the relationship between the extent of centralization and social-policy development can be found in Keith G. Banting, *The Welfare State and Canadian Federalism* (Montreal: McGill-Queen's University Press, 2d ed., 1987).
9. On the concept of "blame avoidance" see Weaver, "Politics of Blame Avoidance."
10. The contrast will not always be this stark. There may be concentrated benefits for those who gain from reduced social expenditures – e.g., employers who profit from weaker unemployment protection, or private providers of social services for whom restricted public provision may create new opportunities.
11. Mancur Olson, *The Logic of Collective Action: Public Goods and the Theory of Groups* (Cambridge, Mass.: Harvard University Press, 1965); James Q. Wilson, *Political Organizations* (New York: Basic, 1973), pp. 330–7; and James Q. Wilson, *American Government* (Lexington, Mass.: Heath, 4th ed., 1989), pp. 422–47, 590–604.
12. Daniel Kahneman and Amos Tversky, "Prospect Theory: An Analysis of Decision Under Risk," *Econometrica*, 47 (March 1979), 263–91; Amos Tversky and Daniel Kahneman, "The Framing of Decisions and the Psychology of Choice," *Science*, 211 (1981), 453–8; and Daniel Kahneman and Amos Tversky, "Choices, Values and Frames," *American Psychologist*, 39 (April 1984), 341–50.
13. Howard S. Bloom and H. Douglas Price, "Voter Response to Short-Run Economic Conditions: The Asymmetric Effect of Prosperity and Recession," *American Polit-*

ical Science Review, 69 (December 1975), 1240–54; Samuel Kernell, "Presidential Popularity and Negative Voting: An Alternative Explanation of the Midterm Congressional Decline of the President's Party," *American Political Science Review*, 71 (1977), 44–66; Gerald Wright, "Constituency Responses to Congressional Behavior: The Impact of the House Judiciary Committee Impeachment Votes," *Western Political Quarterly*, 30, no. 3 (September 1977), 401–10; and Richard R. Lau, "Negativity in Political Perception," *Political Behavior*, 4 (1982), 353–77.

14. See Richard R. Lau, "Two Explanations for Negativity Effects in Political Behavior," *American Journal of Political Science*, 29 (February 1985), 119–38. In a thoughtful review of the literature on loss aversion and the framing of decisions, Jack Levy argues that the evidence challenges several important assumptions of rational-choice theory. Jack S. Levy, "Prospect Theory and International Relations: Theoretical Applications and Analytical Problems," *Political Psychology*, 13 (June 1992), 283–310. For an imaginative effort – relying on principal-agent theory – to reconcile negative voting with rational-choice assumptions see Morris P. Fiorina and Kenneth A. Shepsle, "A Positive Theory of Negative Voting," in John A. Ferejohn and James H. Kuklinski, eds., *Information and Democratic Processes* (Urbana: University of Illinois Press, 1990), pp. 219–39.

15. Derthick's discussion of social-security expansion offers an excellent analysis of this bidding process; Martha Derthick, *Policymaking for Social Security* (Washington, D.C.: Brookings Institution, 1979).

16. For an argument linking the capacity of governments to pursue radical reform to the preexistence of relatively safe majorities see Geoff Garrett, "The Politics of Structural Reform: Swedish Social Democracy and Thatcherism in Comparative Perspective," *Comparative Political Studies* (January 1993), 521–47.

17. W. Mishler, M. Hoskin, and R. Fitzgerald, "British Parties in the Balance: A Time Series Analysis of Long-Term Trends in Labour and Conservative Support," *British Journal of Political Science*, 19 (1989), 211–36.

18. James H. Kuklinski, "Information and the Study of Politics," in Ferejohn and Kuklinski, eds., *Information and Democratic Processes*, p. 391.

19. Hugh Heclo, *Modern Social Politics in Britain and Sweden* (New Haven, Conn.: Yale University Press, 1974).

20. One strand of contemporary social science that has taken the study of asymmetric information seriously is transaction-cost economics. I have found this work helpful in developing the following discussion. For an introduction see Oliver Williamson, *Markets and Hierarchies: Analysis and Antitrust Implications* (New York: Free Press, 1975); Terry M. Moe, "The New Economics of Organization," *American Journal of Political Science* 28 (1984), 739–77; John W. Pratt and Richard J. Zeckhauser, eds., *Principals and Agents: The Structure of Business* (Boston: Harvard University Press), 1985; and James E. Alt and Kenneth A. Shepsle, eds., *Perspectives on Positive Political Economy* (Cambridge University Press, 1990).

21. R. Douglas Arnold, *The Logic of Congressional Action* (New Haven, Conn.: Yale University Press, 1990).

22. Ibid, p. 48n. For interesting efforts to explore this issue see Paul M. Sniderman et al., "Reasoning Chains: Causal Models of Policy Reasoning in Mass Publics," *British Journal of Political Science*, 16 (1986), 405–30; and Deborah Stone, "Causal Stories and the Formation of Policy Agendas," *Political Science Quarterly*, 104, no. 2 (1989), 281–300.

23. David Cameron, "The Expansion of the Public Economy: A Comparative Analysis," *American Political Science Review*, 72 (1978), 1243–61; Douglas A. Hibbs and Henrik Jess Madsen, "Public Reactions to the Growth of Taxation and Government Expenditure," *World Politics* (1981), 413–45; Harold Wilensky, "Leftism, Catholicism, and Democratic Corporatism: The Role of Political Parties in Recent Welfare State Development," in Flora and Heidenheimer, eds., *The Development of Welfare States*, pp. 345–82.

24. Weaver, "Politics of Blame Avoidance."

25. On indexation as a mechanism of blame avoidance see R. Kent Weaver, *Automatic Government* (Washington, D.C.: Brookings Institution, 1988).

26. R. Kent Weaver's work is singular in this respect.

27. This explains why there is no incompatibility between my claim here and the earlier suggestion that concentrated interests have advantages over diffuse ones. If retrenchment advocates have already targeted a group that is concentrated enough to permit easy information flow and collective action, the advantages to exploiting divisions within the group may outweigh any costs of further concentrating opponents.

28. This issue plagued the development of pension reforms in Britain, with employers and insurance companies arguing strenuously against the proliferation of separate categories of pensioners that the initial proposals would have generated (see Chapter 3). Similarly, the provision of transitional benefits accounted for much of the complexity and confusion surrounding Britain's 1982 Housing Benefit reforms (Chapter 4) and the 1988 social-security reforms (Chapter 5).

29. Weaver, *Automatic Government*, pp. 79–80, 86–7.

2. INTERESTS, INSTITUTIONS, AND POLICY FEEDBACK

1. Useful review articles include Michael Shalev, "The Social Democratic Model and Beyond: Two Generations of Comparative Research on the Welfare State," *Comparative Social Research*, 6 (1983), 315–51; Hannu Uusitallo, "Comparative Research on the Determinants of the Welfare State: The State of the Art," *European Journal of Political Research*, 12 (1984), 403–22; and Theda Skocpol and Edwin Amenta, "States and Social Policies," *Annual Review of Sociology*, 12 (1986), 131–57.

2. For prominent examples see Stephens, *The Transition from Capitalism to Socialism*; Walter Korpi, *The Democratic Class Struggle* (London: Routledge & Kegan Paul, 1983); and Gøsta Esping-Andersen, *Politics Against Markets: The Social Democratic Road to Power* (Princeton, N.J.: Princeton University Press, 1985).

3. Esping-Andersen, *Three Worlds of Welfare Capitalism*.

4. One might argue that there is a lag effect, and that a shift in the distribution of power resources will be followed by welfare state retrenchment only after some intervening period. Because this argument implies retrenchment at some future time it is difficult to test. However, the argument suggests that retrenchment should have accelerated over the course of Reagan and Thatcher's terms in office – a proposition for which there is, again, little evidence.

5. In Esping-Andersen's typology Britain emerges as a borderline case, but seems to be closest to the liberal type. To put the methodological issue more formally, by minimizing the variation across cases, the study decreases the likelihood that the distribution of power resources will emerge as a prominent independent variable. For a study of retrenchment based on different case selection that reaches results

more supportive of power-resources arguments, see Ramesh Mishra, *The Welfare State in Capitalist Society: Policies of Retrenchment and Maintenance in Europe, North America and Australia* (University of Toronto Press, 1990). Mishra's conclusions of substantial retrenchment in the United States and Britain, however, are based on a much wider definition of social policy than that utilized here.

6. Esping-Andersen, *Three Worlds of Welfare Capitalism*, p. 32.

7. Jack L. Walker, Jr., *Mobilizing Interest Groups in America: Patrons, Professions and Social Movements* (Ann Arbor: University of Michigan Press, 1991), p. 54.

8. The distinctive burdens falling on political organizations heavily dependent on the mobilization of large numbers of individuals are clearly outlined in Claus Offe and Helmut Wiesenthal, "Two Logics of Collective Action," in Claus Offe, *Disorganized Capitalism* (Cambridge, Mass.: MIT Press, 1984), pp. 170–220. Although Offe and Wiesenthal's presentation focuses on the particular problems confronting labor unions, much of the analysis can be extended to other labor-intensive mobilization efforts.

9. For a variety of New Institutionalist approaches see for example, Peter Evans, Dietrich Reuschemeyer, and Theda Skocpol, eds., *Bringing the State Back In* (Cambridge University Press, 1985); James G. March and Johan P. Olsen, *Rediscovering Institutions: The Organizational Basis of Politics* (New York: Free Press, 1989); North, *Institutions*; Kenneth A. Shepsle, "Studying Institutions: Some Lessons from the Rational Choice Approach," *Journal of Theoretical Politics*, 1, no. 2 (April 1989), 131–47; and Stephen Skowronek, *Building a New American State: The Expansion of National Administrative Capacities, 1877–1920* (Cambridge University Press, 1982).

10. See in particular Margaret Weir, Ann Shola Orloff, and Theda Skocpol, eds., *The Politics of Social Policy in the United States* (Princeton, N.J.: Princeton University Press, 1988). In addition, see Theda Skocpol and John Ikenberry, "The Political Formation of the American Welfare State," *Comparative Social Research*, 6 (1983), 87–118; and Skocpol, *Protecting Soldiers and Mothers*. For a comparative study that explicitly criticizes the power-resources approach, see Margaret Weir and Theda Skocpol, "State Structures and Political Responses to the Great Depression," in Evans et al., eds., *Bringing the State Back In*, pp. 107–63. Hugh Heclo's work represents another important contribution; see his *Modern Social Politics*.

11. For comparatively informed introductions to its most peculiar features and some of their consequences, see Samuel P. Huntington, *Political Order in Changing Societies* (New Haven, Conn.: Yale University Press, 1968), ch. 2, and Walter Dean Burnham, *The Current Crisis in American Politics* (New York: Oxford University Press, 1982).

12. Martin Shefter, "Party, Bureaucracy, and Political Change in the United States," in Louis Maisel and Joseph Cooper, eds., *The Development of Political Parties: Patterns of Evolution and Decay* (Beverly Hills, Calif.: Sage, 1979), pp. 211–65; Robert H. Salisbury, "Why No Corporatism in America?" in Philippe C. Schmitter and Gerhard Lehmbruch, eds., *Trends Toward Corporatist Intermediation* (Beverly Hills, Calif.: Sage, 1979), pp. 213–30.

13. The following argument was developed in collaboration with R. Kent Weaver. For an extended discussion see Paul Pierson and R. Kent Weaver, "Political Institutions and Loss Imposition: The Case of Pensions," in R. Kent Weaver and Bert A. Rockman, eds., *Do Institutions Matter? Government Capabilities in the United States and Abroad* (Washington, D.C.: Brookings Institution, 1993). The essays in this volume contain a great deal of evidence and analysis of how the impact of institutional design influences policy development.

14. See for example Lloyd Cutler, "To Form a Government," *Foreign Affairs*, 59, no. 1 (Fall 1980), 126–43.
15. Weir et al., eds., *Politics of Social Policy in the United States*. Ellen Immergut, "Institutions, Veto Points, and Policy Results: A Comparative Analysis of Health Care," *Journal of Public Policy*, 10 (1991), 391–416.
16. Paul Starr, *The Transformation of American Medicine* (New York: Basic, 1982).
17. R. Kent Weaver, "Are Parliamentary Systems Better?" *The Brookings Review*, 3, no. 4 (Summer 1985), 16–25; Weaver, "Politics of Blame Avoidance."
18. David R. Cameron, "The Expansion of the Public Economy: A Comparative Analysis," *American Political Science Review*, 72 (1978), 1243–61; Banting, *The Welfare State and Canadian Federalism*; Weir, "Citizenship, Localism and Poverty."
19. For a good introduction see Paul E. Peterson, *City Limits* (University of Chicago Press, 1981); and Paul E. Peterson and Mark Rom, *Welfare Magnets* (Washington, D.C.: Brookings Institution, 1990). For historical accounts stressing this argument in the United States see David Brian Robertson, "The Bias of American Federalism: The Limits of Welfare State Development in the Progressive Era," *Journal of Policy History*, 1, no. 3 (1989), 261–91; and Colin Gordon, "New Deal, Old Deck: Business and the Origins of Social Security, 1920–1935," *Politics and Society*, 19, no. 2 (1991), 165–207.
20. Fritz Scharpf, "The Joint-Decision Trap: Lessons from German Federalism and European Integration," *Public Administration*, 66 (1988), 239–78; Keith Banting, "Institutional Conservatism: Federalism and Pension Reform," in J. Ismael, ed., *Canadian Social Welfare Policy: Federal and Provincial Dimensions* (Montreal: McGill-Queen's University Press, 1985).
21. For a thoughtful elaboration of this point see R. Kent Weaver and Bert Rockman, "Introduction" and "Conclusion" in *Do Institutions Matter?*
22. Theda Skocpol, "Bringing the State Back In: Strategies of Analysis in Current Research," in Evans et al., eds., *Bringing the State Back In*, p. 16.
23. Weir and Skocpol, "Political Responses to the Great Depression." See also Margaret Weir, "The Federal Government and Unemployment: The Frustration of Policy Innovation from the New Deal to the Great Society," in Weir et al. eds., *Politics of Social Policy*, pp. 149–97; G. John Ikenberry, *Reasons of State: Oil Politics and the Capacities of American Government* (Ithaca, N.Y.: Cornell University Press, 1988).
24. See for example Theodore Marmor, "Policy Entrepreneurship in Government: An American Study," *Journal of Public Policy*, 6, no. 3 (1986), 225–53.
25. Heclo's *Modern Social Politics* remains the most articulate argument for the role of autonomous bureaucratic action. For the case that bureaucratic influence is greatest during the process of specifying policy alternatives, see John W. Kingdon, *Agendas, Alternatives and Public Policies* (Boston: Little, Brown, 1984), pp. 32–7.
26. See Chapter 1, note 23.
27. Pierson and Smith, "Bourgeois Revolutions?"
28. This section draws heavily on Paul Pierson, "When Effect Becomes Cause: 'Policy Feedback' and Political Change," *World Politics* (July 1993), 595–628.
29. E. E. Schattschneider, *Politics, Pressures and the Tariff* (New York: Prentice-Hall, 1935), p. 288.
30. Weir and Skocpol, "Keynesian Responses to the Great Depression," pp. 143–4. New initiatives may also fuel counter-mobilizations by opponents. David Vogel, for example, traces the resurgence of business activism to a range of regulatory policies

adopted in the 1960s and 1970s; David Vogel, *Fluctuating Fortunes: The Political Power of Business in America* (New York: Basic, 1989), pp. 13–14.

31. On the importance of political entrepreneurs see Olson, *Logic of Collective Action*; Russell Hardin, *Collective Action* (Baltimore: Johns Hopkins University Press, 1982), pp. 35–7; and Moe, *Organization of Interests*, pp. 37–9.

32. See for example Day, *What Older Americans Think*. Thanks to Kent Weaver for bringing this example to my attention.

33. Bo Rothstein, "Labor-Market Institutions and Working-Class Strength," in Sven Steinmo, Kathleen Thelen, and Frank Longstreth, eds., *Structuring Politics: Historical Institutionalism in Comparative Analysis* (Cambridge University Press, 1992), pp. 33–56.

34. On corporatism, see Suzanne Berger, ed., *Organizing Interests in Western Europe* (Cambridge University Press, 1981); Phillipe Schmitter and Gerhard Lehmbruch, eds., *Trends Toward Corporatist Intermediation* (Beverly Hills, Calif.: Sage, 1979); and John H. Goldthorpe, ed., *Order and Conflict in Contemporary Capitalism* (Oxford University Press, 1984). On regulatory capture see Grant McConnell, *Private Power and American Democracy* (New York: Random House, 1966); and George J. Stigler, "The Theory of Economic Regulation," *Bell Journal of Economics and Management Science*, 2 (Spring 1971), 3–21.

35. Heclo, *Modern Social Politics*; Amenta et al., "The Political Origins of Unemployment Insurance in Five American States," *Studies in American Political Development*, 2 (1987), 137–82; and Peter A. Hall, "Policy Paradigms, Social Learning and the State: The Case of Economic Policy-Making in Britain," *Comparative Politics* (forthcoming). See also March and Olsen, *Rediscovering Institutions*, pp. 39–52.

36. Herbert A. Simon, *Models of Man* (New York: Wiley, 1957); Charles E. Lindblom, "The 'Science' of Muddling Through," *Public Administration Review*, 19 (1959), 79–88; and James G. March, "Bounded Rationality, Ambiguity, and the Engineering of Choice," *Bell Journal of Economics*, 9 (1978), 587–608.

37. Heclo, *Modern Social Politics*, p. 305.

38. Ibid., pp. 315–16.

39. For a more detailed critique see Pierson, "When Effect Becomes Cause."

40. Kingdon, *Agendas, Alternatives and Public Policies*.

41. The following draws on the discussion in North, *Institutions*, pp. 92–104.

42. Paul David, "Clio and the Economics of QWERTY," *American Economic Review*, 75 (1985), 332–7.

43. W. Brian Arthur, "Self-Reinforcing Mechanisms in Economics," in Philip W. Anderson, Kenneth J. Arrow, and David Pines, eds., *The Economy as an Evolving Complex System* (Reading, Mass.: Addison-Wesley, 1988); W. Brian Arthur, "Competing Technologies, Increasing Returns, and Lock-In by Historical Events," *Economic Journal*, 99 (1989), 116–31. See also the discussion in North, *Institutions*, pp. 92–104.

44. North, *Institutions*, p. 3.

45. Ibid., p. 97.

46. Kenneth T. Jackson, *Crabgrass Frontier: The Suburbanization of the United States* (New York: Oxford University Press, 1985), especially ch. 11. Michael N. Danielson, *The Politics of Exclusion* (New York: Columbia University Press, 1976).

47. Interestingly, within political science the idea of "lock-ins" (though focusing on institutions rather than policies) has mainly been utilized in the field of international relations. See for example Robert O. Keohane, *After Hegemony: Cooperation and*

Discord in the World Political Economy (Princeton, N.J.: Princeton University Press, 1984), pp. 100–6. Keohane draws on Arthur Stinchcombe's analysis of "sunk costs." See Stinchcombe, *Constructing Social Theories* (New York: Harcourt, Brace, 1968), pp. 120–5.

48. Peter Bachrach and Morton Baratz, "Two Faces of Power," *American Political Science Review*, 56 (1962), 947–52.

49. For a pathbreaking study of networks of social interdependence see Thomas C. Schelling, *Micromotives and Macrobehavior* (New York: Norton, 1978). The contribution of public policies to the development of these social networks is discussed in more detail in Fred Hirsch, *Social Limits to Growth* (Cambridge, Mass.: Harvard University Press, 1976); and in Alfred E. Kahn, "The Tyranny of Small Decisions," *Kyklos* (1966), 23–45.

50. This is much more likely to be true in an institutional setting like that of the United States, where the location of accountability is often uncertain. See Pierson and Weaver, "Political Institutions and Loss Imposition."

51. R. Kent Weaver, *Automatic Government: The Politics of Indexation* (Washington, D.C.: Brookings Institution, 1988).

52. Ann Shola Orloff and Theda Skocpol, " 'Why Not Equal Protection?': Explaining the Politics of Social Spending in Britain, 1900–1911, and the United States, 1880s–1920," *American Sociological Review*, 49 (1984), 726–50; Ann Shola Orloff, "The Political Origins of America's Belated Welfare State," in Weir et al., eds., *Politics of Social Policy*, pp. 37–80; and Skocpol, *Protecting Soldiers and Mothers*, part 2.

53. Weir et al., eds., *Politics of Social Policy*; William Julius Wilson, *The Truly Disadvantaged: The Inner City, the Underclass, and Public Policy* (University of Chicago Press), 1987; Theda Skocpol, "Targeting within Universalism: Politically Viable Policies to Combat Poverty in the United States," in Jencks and Peterson, *Urban Underclass*, pp. 411–36. Gøsta Esping-Andersen, *Politics Against Markets: The Social Democratic Road to Power* (Princeton, N.J.: Princeton University Press, 1985).

54. Kingdon, *Agendas, Alternatives, and Public Policies*, pp. 99–105.

3. RETRENCHMENT IN A CORE SECTOR: OLD-AGE PENSIONS

1. On the political strength of middle-class social programs, see Robert E. Goodin and Julian Le Grand, eds., *Not Only the Poor: The Middle Classes and the Welfare State* (London: Allen & Unwin, 1987). Thatcher's attempts to reform the NHS are reviewed in Rudolf Klein, *The Politics of the NHS* (London: Longman Group, 2d ed., 1989), chs. 6 and 7.

2. John Myles, "Postwar Capitalism and the Extension of Social Security into a Retirement Wage," in Weir et al., eds., *Politics of Social Policy*, pp. 265–84.

3. On the history of Social Security see especially W. Andrew Achenbaum, *Social Security: Visions and Revisions* (Cambridge University Press, 1986); Jerry Cates, *Insuring Inequality: Administrative Leadership in Social Security* (Ann Arbor: University of Michigan Press, 1983); and Martha Derthick, *Policymaking for Social Security* (Washington, D.C.: Brookings Institution, 1979).

4. On British pension development see Heclo, *Modern Social Politics*, ch. 4; and Michael O'Higgins, "Public/Private Interaction and Pension Provision," in Martin Rein and Lee Rainwater, eds., *Public/Private Interplay in Social Protection* (Armonk, N.Y.: Sharpe, 1986), pp. 99–148.

5. The Wilson government's 1969 plan was never introduced; it was moving through Parliament when the Conservative Party won the June 1970 election.

6. In 1980, 8.7 percent of the elderly participated in the means-tested SSI program, though the majority of these recipients also received Social Security benefits. Committee on Ways and Means, U.S. House of Representatives, *Background Material and Data on Programs Within the Jurisdiction of the Committee on Ways and Means*, (Washington, D.C.: GPO, WMCP 102–9, 1991), p. 756.

7. In 1980, replacement rates for a pensioner couple averaged 66 percent of pre-retirement earnings in the United States but only 47 percent in Britain. Jonathan Aldrich, "The Earnings Replacement Rate of Old-Age Benefits in 12 Countries, 1969–1980," *Social Security Bulletin*, 45, no. 11 (1982), 3–11.

8. In 1981–2, 19 percent of the elderly were in receipt of the means-tested supplementary pension. Department of Treasury, *The Government's Expenditure Plans, 1983/4–1985/6* (London: HMSO, Cmnd 8789, 1983), p. 64.

9. Another policy feedback has probably played an even more important role. Holes in the Medicare health-insurance program for the elderly allowed AARP to provide "medigap" insurance, offering an important "selective incentive" for individuals to join. On the importance of these benefits see Day, *What Older Americans Think*, pp. 25–6 and 65–6.

10. Figures for AARP from Day, *What Older Americans Think*, pp. 25–6. On the weakness of the British pensioner lobby see Wyn Grant, *Pressure Group Politics and Democracy in Britain* (New York: Allan, 1989); and Paul F. Whiteley and Stephen J. Winyard, *Pressure for the Poor: The Poverty Lobby and Policy Making* (London: Methuen, 1987).

11. Robert M. Ball, "The Original Understanding on Social Security: Implications for Later Developments," in Theodore R. Marmor and Jerry L. Mashaw, eds., *Social Security. Beyond the Rhetoric of Crisis* (Princeton, N.J.: Princeton University Press, 1988), p. 25.

12. O'Higgins, "Public/Private Interaction," p. 139. See also Richard Hemming and John Kay, "The Costs of the State Earnings Related Pension Scheme," *Economics Journal*, 92 (1982), 300–21.

13. Derthick, *Policymaking for Social Security*, ch. 19.

14. *Guardian*, April 25, 1988, p. 8.

15. *Report by the Government Actuary on the First Quinquennial Review* (London: HMSO, HC Paper 445, 1982), p. 21.

16. London *Times*, March 28, 1986, p. 4.

17. Quoted in Sue Ward, "Pensions," in Richard Silburn, ed., *The Future of Social Security* (London: Fabian Society, 1985), pp. 34–5.

18. HM Treasury, *The Next Ten Years: Public Expenditure and Taxation into the 1990s* (London: HMSO, Cmnd 9189, 1984), p. 14; *New York Times*, January 24, 1984, p. 13A.

19. London *Times*, April 8, 1984, p. 1.

20. House of Commons, *Hansard*, April 2, 1984, col. 652–60.

21. Nicholas Deakin, *The Politics of Welfare* (London: Methuen, 1987), p. 139. *Financial Times*, February 7, 1985, p. 10.

22. *Financial Times*, February 11, 1985, p. 11.

23. DHSS, *Reform of Social Security* (London: HMSO, Cmnd 9517–9, 3 vols., 1985).

"Green papers" usually offer broad discussions of policy issues, whereas "white papers" contain detailed legislative proposals.

24. *Economist*, June 22, 1985, p. 25.
25. *Financial Times*, September 4, 1985, p. 11.
26. Evan Davis et al., *1985 Benefit Reviews: The Effects of the Proposals* (London: Institute for Fiscal Studies, 1985), pp. 25–7. The Confederation of British Industry, not usually a strong defender of public-social provision, provided even more pessimistic projections. If, as seemed likely, most personal-pension investments went into safe, short-term assets, the eventual pensions would be less than half those offered by SERPS. *Financial Times*, September 20, 1985, p. 22.
27. *Reform of Social Security* (London: HMSO, Cmnd. 9517, 1985), p. 25.
28. *Financial Times*, May 13, 1985, p. 32.
29. London *Times*, April 30, 1985, p. 12.
30. *Financial Times*, March 1, 1985, p. 6.
31. Ibid., August 3, 1985, p. 4; September 5, p. 7; and September 12, p. 7.
32. DHSS, *The Reform of Social Security: Program for Action* (London: HMSO, Cmnd 9691, 1985).
33. Among other changes, SERPS benefits would now be based on average lifetime earnings, rather than the best twenty years, though there would be some allowance for breaks in employment to care for children or the disabled. SERPS pensions would be equal to 20 percent of qualifying earnings, rather than 25 percent. Widows and widowers would be entitled to 50 percent rather than 100 percent of a deceased spouse's pension.
34. Rudolf Klein and Michael O'Higgins, "Defusing the Crisis of the Welfare State: A New Interpretation," in Marmor and Mashaw, eds., *Social Security*, pp. 216–18.
35. Author's calculations from data in Cmnd 9691, Technical Annex, Tables P1, P3 and P5; *Hansard*, February 21, 1986, col. 384–88w, Tables P1A, P3A and P5A; *Hansard*, January 17, 1986, col. 743–44w.
36. The cost of these incentives in 1990–1 was estimated at £615 million; *Report by the Government Actuary on the Drafts of the Social Security Benefits Up-Rating Order 1990 and the Social Security (Contributions) (Re-Rating) Order 1990* (London: HMSO, Cmnd 948, January 1990), Appendix 7.
37. *Independent*, December 5, 1990, p. 2; *Hansard*, May 23, 1989, p. 447w.
38. Figures in 1988 prices; Vanessa Fry, Stephen Smith, and Stuart White, *Pensions and the Public Purse: Public Spending Policies and Population Aging* (London: Institute for Fiscal Studies, 1990), p. 24.
39. *Economist*, December 21, 1985, p. 15.
40. Paul Light, *Artful Work: The Politics of Social Security Reform* (New York: Random House, 1985), p. 49.
41. Lawrence I. Barrett, *Gambling with History: Reagan in the White House* (New York: Doubleday, 1983), p. 155.
42. For example, J. J. Pickle, the Democratic chairman of the House Ways and Means Committee subcommittee with jurisdiction over Social Security, was working on his own package of major Social Security cuts.
43. Light, *Artful Work*, p. 121. For Stockman's recollections see David Stockman, *The Triumph of Politics* (New York: Harper & Row, 1986), pp. 199–209.
44. Quoted in William Greider, *The Education of David Stockman and Other Americans* (New York: Dutton, 1982), p. 46.

45. Ibid., p. 43.
46. Light, *Artful Work*, p. 121.
47. Stockman, *Triumph of Politics*, pp. 204–6; Barrett, *Gambling with History*, pp. 154–9.
48. On the administration's deliberations see Stockman, *Triumph of Politics*, pp. 304–17; *New York Times*, September 21, 1981, p. A21, and September 22, 1981, p. A1.
49. Richard E. Neustadt and Earnest R. May, *Thinking in Time: The Uses of History for Decision-Makers* (New York: Free Press, 1986), pp. 22–5.
50. For a detailed account of the negotiations, see Light, *Artful Work*, pp. 163–228.
51. This change had broad appeal because it could be sold as "all things to all people." It could be called a benefit cut or a tax increase, but in fact it was a benefit cut. Quite simply, it meant that for those taxed the real value of benefits would decline.
52. John A. Svahn and Mary Ross, "Social Security Amendments of 1983: Legislative History and Summary of Provisions," *Social Security Bulletin*, 46, no. 7 (1983), 44.
53. Henry J. Aaron, Barry P. Bosworth, and Gary Burtless, *Can America Afford to Grow Old?* (Washington, D.C.: Brookings Institution, 1989), p. 28.
54. For a detailed discussion of this episode see *Congressional Quarterly Almanac* (Washington, D.C.: Congressional Quarterly Press, 1985), pp. 441–57.
55. Elizabeth Wehr and John R. Cranford, "Crippled Market Spurs Budget Breakthrough," *Congressional Quarterly Weekly Report*, October 24, 1987, p. 2571.
56. See for example Anthony King, "Ideas, Institutions and the Policies of Governments," *British Journal of Political Science* (1973), 291–313 and 409–23.
57. See for example Lloyd Cutler, "To Form A Government," *Foreign Affairs*, 59, no. 1 (1980), 126–43.
58. House of Commons, *Hansard*, May 19, 1986, col. 105. Even the reforms of the still-immature SERPS schemes have forced the government to absorb a significant share of the double-payment burden in order to limit the political outcry. According to the National Audit Office, by 1993 increased tax costs associated with the reform are expected to outweigh reduced expenditures on SERPS by £5.9 billion. *Independent*, December 5, 1990, p. 2.
59. Peter J. Ferrara, for example, advocated radical privatization reforms through publications for two conservative think tanks, the Heritage Foundation and the Cato Institute. Ferrara was a senior staff member in the White House's Office of Policy Development, but he was not a major participant in Social Security reform. He later acknowledged that the double-payment problem was a major political impediment to privatization initiatives. See Peter J. Ferrara, "Social Security and the Super IRA: A Populist Proposal," in Peter J. Ferrara, ed., *Social Security: Prospects for Real Reform* (Washington, D.C.: Cato Institute, 1985), pp. 193–220.

4. RETRENCHMENT IN A VULNERABLE SECTOR:
HOUSING POLICY

1. For background see Bruce Headey, *Housing Policy in the Developed Economy* (London: Croom Helm, 1978), pp. 201–27; and Peter Malpass and Alan Murie, *Housing Policy and Practice* (London: Macmillan Press, 3d ed., 1990).
2. For background see Headey, *Housing Policy*; and R. Allen Hays, *The Federal Government and Urban Housing* (Albany, N.Y.: SUNY Press, 1985).
3. John C. Weicher, "Halfway to a Housing Allowance?" in John C. Weicher, ed.,

Maintaining the Safety Net: Income Redistribution Programs in the Reagan Administration (Washington, D.C.: American Enterprise Institute, 1984), p. 94.

4. Jill Khadurri and Rajmond J. Struyk, "Housing Vouchers for the Poor," *Journal of Policy Analysis and Management*, 1 (1982), 197.

5. Julien LeGrand, *The Strategy of Equality: Redistribution and the Social Services* (London: Allen & Unwin, 1982), ch. 5.

6. Cushing N. Dolbeare, "Federal Housing Assistance: Who Needs It? Who Gets It?" in U.S. Congress, Hearings, Subcommittee on Housing and Community Development, Committee on Banking, Finance and Urban Affairs, *Housing Act of 1985* (Washington, D.C.: GPO, 1985), pp. 449, 453.

7. See William C. Apgar, Jr., et al., *The State of the Nation's Housing*, 1991 (Cambridge, Mass.: Harvard University, Joint Center for Housing Studies, 1991).

8. Ibid., p. 424; Khadurri and Struyk, "Housing Vouchers for the Poor," p. 204.

9. Treasury, *Government's Expenditure Plans*, 1987, vol. 2, p. 157.

10. *Conservative Manifesto, 1979* (London: Conservative Central Office, April 1979).

11. Jennifer Dale, "Privatization and Politics: A Case Study of Housing," in Maria Brenton and Clare Ungerson, *The Year Book in Social Policy, 1984/5* (London: Longman Group, 1985).

12. House of Commons, *Hansard*, May 15, 1979, cols. 79–80.

13. Jim Bulpitt, *Territory and Power in the United Kingdom: An Interpretation* (Manchester University Press, 1983); Carolyn T. Adams, "The Politics of Privatization," in Bengt Turner, Jim Kemeny, and Lennart J. Lundquist, eds., *Between State and Market: Housing in the Post-Industrial Era* (Stockholm: Almqvist and Wiksell, 1987), pp. 127–55; Nathan H. Schwartz, "The Relation of Politics to the Instruments of Housing Policy," in Turner et al., eds., *Between State and Market*, pp. 156–85.

14. Ray Forrest and Alan Murie, "If the Price is Right," *Roof* (March–April 1986), 23–5.

15. A. D. H. Crook, "Privatisation of Housing," *Environment and Planning A*, 18 (1986), 643.

16. John Hills and Beverley Mullings, "Housing: A Decent Home for All at a Price within their Means?" in John Hills, ed., *The State of Welfare: The Welfare State in Britain since 1974* (Oxford University Press, 1989), p. 171.

17. Duncan Maclennan and Kenneth Gibb, "Housing Finance and Subsidies in Britain after a Decade of 'Thatcherism,' " *Urban Studies*, 27, no. 6 (1990), 909.

18. For a good discussion see Anthony Heath (with Geoff Garrett), "The Extension of Popular Capitalism," in Anthony Heath et al., *Understanding Political Change: The British Voter, 1964–1987* (Oxford: Pergamon Press, 1991), pp. 126–30.

19. Ray Forrest and Alan Murie, *Selling the Welfare State: The Privatization of Public Housing* (London: Routledge, 1988), p. 101, quoting R. Jowell, S. Witherspoon, and L. Brook, *British Social Attitudes: The 1986 Report* (London: Gower, 1986).

20. Maclennan and Gibb, "Housing Finance and Subsidies in Britain," p. 912.

21. Ray Forrest and Alan Murie, *An Unreasonable Act? Central-Local Government Conflict and the Housing Act of 1980*, SAUS Study No. 1, University of Bristol, School for Advanced Urban Studies.

22. Tony Travers, *The Politics of Local Government Finance* (London: Allen & Unwin, 1986), pp. 79–149.

23. Peter Esam, "The Bottom Line: Has Conservative Social Security Protected the

Poor?'' in Alan Walker and Carol Walker, eds., *The Growing Divide: A Social Audit, 1979–1987* (London: Child Poverty Action Group, 1987), p. 113.

24. John Hills et al., "Shifting Subsidy from Bricks and Mortar to People: Experiences in Britain and West Germany," *Housing Studies*, 5, no. 3 (June 1990), 156.
25. Glen Bramley, "Incrementalism Run Amok: Local Government Finance in Britain," *Public Administration*, 63 (Spring 1985), 100–7; Glen Bramley, "Paying for Local Government," in Brenton and Ungerson, eds., *Year Book, 1986–7*, pp. 178–95; Travers, *Politics of Local Government Finance*.
26. Department of Environment, *Housing: The Government's Proposals* (London: HMSO, Cmnd 214, 1987); Peter Malpass, "Ridley's One-Way Ringfence," *Roof* (September–October 1987), 23–4.
27. Hills and Mullings, "A Decent Home for All," p. 147.
28. Ibid., pp. 191–4.
29. Treasury, *Government's Expenditure Plans*, 1987, p. 241.
30. Stephanie Cooper, *Public Housing and Private Property: 1970–1984* (London: Gower, 1985).
31. On the general issue of how changes in individual "micromotives" can generate major shifts in social structures, see Schelling, *Micromotives and Macrobehavior*.
32. Hills and Mullings, "Decent Home for All," pp. 148, 174.
33. Ray Forrest and Alan Murie, "Marginalization and Subsidized Individualism: The Sale of Council Houses in the Restructuring of the British Welfare State," *International Journal of Urban and Regional Research*, 10 (1986), 46–65; Forrest and Murie, "If the Price is Right," p. 23.
34. Department of Environment, *Government's Proposals*.
35. Nick Raynsford, "Reviving the Private Landlord: The Recurrent Tory Delusion," *Roof* (September–October 1987), 30.
36. Crook, "Privatisation of Housing," p. 1035. See also *Economist*, January 7, 1989, pp. 56–7.
37. Hills and Mullings, "Decent Home for All," p. 159.
38. William Waldegrave, speech in Bristol, August 28, 1987. Conservative Central Office, London.
39. Department of Environment, *Government's Proposals*, p. 14.
40. William Waldgrave, speech to the Institute of Housing annual conference, June 19, 1987, mimeo.
41. Anne Power, "Dismantling the Fiefdoms," *New Statesman and Society*, June 17, 1989, p. 28.
42. "Privatising Britain's Housing," *Economist*, February 24, 1990, pp. 17–20.
43. Ivor Crewe, "The Electorate: Partisan Dealignment Ten Years On," *West European Politics*, 6 (October 1983), 183–215.
44. *Economist*, December 26, 1987, p. 26. Bob Widdowson, "Homelessness in the International Year of Shelter for the Homeless," in Brenton and Ungerson, eds., *Year Book, 1986–7*, pp. 215–30.
45. Quoted in Tim Dwelly, "Homes for Some," *New Statesman and Society*, June 7, 1991, p. 23.
46. Weicher, "Halfway to a Housing Allowance?" p. 97.
47. Hays, *Federal Government and Urban Housing*, pp. 246–8.
48. President's Commission on Housing, *The Report of the President's Commission on Housing* (Washington, D.C.: GPO, 1982), ch. 1.

49. For background see Hays, *Federal Government and Urban Housing*, and R. Allen Hays, "The President, Congress, and the Formation of Housing Policy: A Reexamination of Redistributive Policy-Making," *Policy Studies Journal*, 18, no. 4 (Summer 1990), 847–69.
50. See for example Margaret Weir, "American Social Policy and the Politics of Race and Localism," unpublished manuscript, October, 1992.
51. Mary K. Nenno, "H/CD after Reagan: A New Cycle of Policies and Partners," *Journal of Housing*, 46 (March–April 1989), 76.
52. *National Journal*, September 9, 1989, p. 2260; Charles H. Moore and Patricia A. Hoban-Moore, "Some Lessons from Reagan's HUD: Housing Policy and Public Service," PS, 23 (March 1990), 13–18; B. J. Reed, "The Changing Role of Local Advocacy in National Politics," *Journal of Urban Affairs*, 5 (Fall 1983), 294.
53. Unekis and Rieselbach ranked the House Banking and Urban Affairs Committee as having a relatively high level of partisan cleavage; Joseph K. Unekis and Leroy N. Rieselbach, *Congressional Committee Politics: Continuity and Change* (New York: Praeger, 1984). See also Hays, "President, Congress, and Housing Policy."
54. Raymond J. Struyk, John A. Tucillo, and James P. Zais, "Housing and Community Development," in John L. Palmer and Isabel V. Sawhill, eds., *The Reagan Experiment* (Washington, D.C.: Urban Institute, 1982), pp. 393–417.
55. Ibid., p. 411.
56. *Washington Post*, November 6, 1981.
57. Olson, *Logic of Collective Action*; Adams, "Politics of Privatization," pp. 127–55.
58. The preliminary results of this demonstration project are outlined in David F. Linowes, *Privatization: Toward More Effective Government* (Urbana: University of Illinois Press, 1988), pp. 16–18.
59. Robert Kuttner, "Bleeding Heart Conservative," *The New Republic*, June 11, 1990, p. 23
60. Ann B. Schnare, "The Preservation Needs of Public Housing," *Housing Policy Debate*, 2, no. 2 (1991), 294.
61. *National Journal*, August 3, 1985, p. 1798.
62. *National Journal*, April 8, 1989, p. 852. See also Robert Guskind and Carol F. Steinbach, "Sales Resistance," *National Journal*, April 6, 1991, pp. 798–803.
63. Moore and Hoban-Moore, "Lessons from Reagan's HUD," p. 15.
64. George J. Mitchell, quoted in *Congressional Quarterly*, August 5, 1989, p. 2043 (statement August 2). Dean's comments were in the *Wall Street Journal*, May 25, 1989.
65. Moore and Hoban-Moore, "Lessons from Reagan's HUD," p. 15.
66. See the essays in "Preserving Low-Income Housing Opportunities: Principles for a 1990s Strategy," *Housing Policy Debate*, 2, no. 2 (1991).
67. *Congressional Quarterly Weekly Report*, March 4, 1987, p. 631.
68. Ibid., December 26, 1987, pp. 3205–6.
69. Carolyn T. Adams, "Housing Policy," in Arnold J. Heidenheimer, Hugh Heclo, and Carolyn T. Adams, eds., *Comparative Public Policy* (New York: St. Martin's, 2d ed., 1983), pp. 88–121; Adams, "Politics of Privatization," pp. 133–9.
70. See for example "Conference Discussion," in Downs and Bradbury, eds., *Do Housing Allowances Work?*, pp. 402–4.
71. Henry J. Aaron, "Policy Implications: A Progress Report," in Downs and Bradbury, eds., *Do Housing Allowances Work?*, pp. 67–98.

72. Schwartz, "Relation of Politics," pp. 162–3.
73. Travers, *Politics of Local Government Finance*, pp. 150–91.
74. On these networks see Patrick Dunleavy, *The Politics of Mass Housing in Britain, 1945–1975* (Oxford University Press [Clarendon Press], 1981); and Adams, "Politics of Privatization."
75. Albert O. Hirschman, *Exit, Voice and Loyalty: Responses to Decline in Firms, Organizations and States* (Cambridge, Mass.: Harvard University Press, 1970).
76. Ulf Torgerson, "Housing: The Wobbly Pillar under the Welfare State," in Turner et al., eds., *Between State and Market*.

5. RETRENCHMENT IN A RESIDUALIZED SECTOR: INCOME-SUPPORT POLICY

1. The term "able-bodied" is used to distinguish efforts for those generally expected to participate in the labor force from programs for the elderly, handicapped, or disabled, whose absence from the labor market is considered less problematic. The prominence of work-incentive issues in the politics of income maintenance makes this analytic separation crucial. The main American expenditure programs discussed in this chapter are AFDC, food stamps, the Earned Income Tax Credit, and unemployment insurance. For Britain, the chapter focuses on Supplementary Benefit (since 1988, "Income Support"), Family Income Supplement (now "Family Credit"), Child Benefit, and Unemployment Benefit.
2. See for example Palmer and Sawhill, eds., *Reagan Experiment*.
3. Department of Social Security, *Households Below Average Incomes, 1981–87: A Statistical Analysis* (London: HMSO, 1990). Ways and Means, *Background Material and Data* (Washington: GPO, 1992), p. 1275.
4. Rosenberry, "Social Insurance", Skocpol, "Targeting Within Universalism," pp. 411–36; Goodin and Le Grand, *Not Only the Poor*.
5. The intractability of these constraints can be judged from the fact that they were widely recognized two decades ago. See for example Theodore Marmor, "On Comparing Income Maintenance Alternatives," *American Political Science Review*, 65 (1971), 83–96.
6. On the development of income-support policies in Britain see Heclo, *Modern Social Politics*, ch. 3; Alan Deacon and Jonathan Bradshaw, *Reserved for the Poor: The Means Test in British Social Policy* (Oxford: Martin Robertson, 1983); Keith Banting, *Poverty, Politics and Policy* (London: Macmillan Press, 1979); and Michael S. Lund, "The Politics of a National Minimum Income: The Poor Law Coalition in Postwar Britain," in Douglas E. Ashford and E. W. Kelley, eds., *Nationalizing Social Security in Europe and America* (Greenwich, Conn.: JAI, 1986), pp. 25–58. For the United States, see Weir et al., eds., *Politics of Social Policy*; Frances Fox Piven and Richard A. Cloward, *Regulating the Poor: The Functions of Public Welfare* (New York: Random House, 1971); and Hugh Heclo, "The Political Foundations of Anti-Poverty Policy," in Sheldon H. Danziger and Daniel H. Weinberg, eds., *Fighting Poverty: What Works and What Doesn't* (Cambridge, Mass.: Harvard University Press, 1986), pp. 312–40.
7. Theda Skocpol, "The Limits of the New Deal System and the Roots of Contemporary Welfare Dilemmas," in Weir et al., eds., *Politics of Social Policy*, pp. 293–311.

8. Theda Skocpol and John Ikenberry, "The Political Formation of the American Welfare State in Historical and Comparative Perspective," *Comparative Social Research*, 6 (1983), 293–311; Edward J. Harpham, "Federalism, Keynesianism and the Transformation of the Unemployment Insurance System in the United States," in Ashford and Kelly, *Nationalizing Social Security*, pp. 155–79.

9. Based on OECD-standardized unemployment measures. OECD, *Economic Outlook*, 43 (June 1988), 170.

10. A. Dilnot and N. Morris, "Private Costs and Benefits of Unemployment: Measuring Replacement Rates," in C. A. Greenhalgh, P. R. G. Layard, and A. J. Oswald, eds., *The Causes of Unemployment* (Oxford University Press, 1984).

11. In 1985, 90 percent of the lowest-income quartile supported more spending on health care compared with 84 percent of the highest quartile (a gap of just 6 percent); on the other hand, 59 percent of the lowest quartile wanted more spending on unemployment benefits, compared with only 25 percent of the top quartile (a difference of 34 percent); Taylor-Gooby, *Social Change*, p. 133. See also data on pp. 114 and 124 in that work.

12. Quoted in McCarthy, *Campaigning for the Poor*, p. 295.

13. CPAG, *Poverty*, no. 40 (August 1980), 4.

14. Tony Atkinson and John Micklewright, "Turning the Screw: Benefits for the Unemployed 1979–1988," in Dilnot and Walker, *Economics of Social Security*, pp. 17–51.

15. Ibid., p. 18.

16. Dilnot and Morris, "Costs and Benefits of Unemployment."

17. John Moore, speech to the Conservative Political Center, September 26, 1987; *Hansard*, October 27, 1987, col. 180.

18. London *Times*, May 25, 1990.

19. Peter Taylor-Gooby, *Public Opinion, Ideology and State Welfare* (London: Routledge & Kegan Paul, 1985), pp. 42–5; Deakin, *Politics of Welfare*, p. 134.

20. Fran Bennett, "Closed Doors and Closing Options," in Sue Ward, ed., *DHSS in Crisis: Social Security Under Pressure and Under Review* (London: Child Poverty Action Group, 1985), pp. 130, 140.

21. *Financial Times*, October 7, 1985, p. 36, and April 15, 1985, p. 5. A survey of Conservative MPs conducted between September 1986 and August 1987 found that less than one-third advocated means testing Child Benefit. Peter Taylor-Gooby and Hugh Bochel, "Public Opinion, Party Policy and MPs' Attitudes to Welfare," *Political Quarterly*, 59, no. 2 (April–June 1988), 55–6.

22. On these lobbying efforts see Ruth Lister, "The Politics of Social Security: An Assessment of the Fowler Review," in Andrew Dilnot and Ian Walker, eds., *The Economics of Social Security* (Oxford University Press, 1989), pp. 200–23.

23. *Hansard*, November 6, 1989, cols. 459–60.

24. See Fran Bennett, "Foreword," in Joan C. Brown, *Child Benefit: Options for the 1990s* (London: Save Child Benefit, 1990), pp. 3–5.

25. David Willetts, "Time to Cut Child Benefit to Help the Under-fives," *Sunday Correspondent*, May 22, 1990.

26. DHSS, *Social Assistance: A Review of the Supplementary Benefit Scheme in Britain* (London: HMSO, 1978). On the review process see David Donnison, *The Politics of Poverty* (Oxford: Martin Robertson, 1982).

27. On the reviews see Carol Walker, *Changing Social Policy: The Case of the Supplementary Benefits Review* (London: Bedford Square, 1983).

28. Peter Kemp, "The Reform of Housing Benefit," *Social Policy and Administration*, 21, no. 2 (Summer 1987), 181; HM Treasury, *Public Expenditure Plans*, 1987.

29. HM Treasury, *Public Expenditure Plans*, 1987, vol. 2, p. 245; House of Commons, *Hansard*, July 28, 1988, cols. 515–16w.

30. *Financial Times*, June 4, 1985, p. 18.

31. A. W. Dilnot, J. A. Kay, and C. N. Morris, *The Reform of Social Security* (London: Oxford University Press [Clarendon Press], 1984).

32. DHSS, *Reform of Social Security* (London: HMSO, Cmnd 9517–19, 1985), vol. 1, p. 19.

33. House of Commons, *The Government's Green Paper, 'Reform of Social Security'* (London: HMSO), Seventh Report of the Social Services Committee, HC 451, 1984–5 session, p. 3.

34. HM Treasury, *The Reform of Personal Taxation* (London: HMSO, Cmnd 9756, 1986), pp. 31–2, 38–9. On Lawson's opposition to tax/benefit integration see *Financial Times*, August 5, 1985, p. 1.

35. On the history of these schemes see Leslie Lenkowsky, *Politics, Economics and Welfare Reform: The Failure of the Negative Income Tax in Britain and the United States* (Washington, D.C.: American Enterprise Institute, 1986).

36. HM Treasury, *Personal Taxation*, pp. 37–8.

37. Ibid., p. 37. On the issue of tax visibility see B. Guy Peters, "The Development of the Welfare State and the Tax State," in Ashford and Kelley, *Nationalizing Social Security*, pp. 219–43.

38. Lister, "Assessment of the Fowler Review," p. 218. See also the comments of a CPAG interviewer in "Frankly Speaking," *Poverty* (Summer 1986), 8.

39. Berthoud, "New Means Tests for Old," p. 13. Richard Berthoud, "The Social Fund – Will it Work?" *Policy Studies*, 8, pt. 1 (July 1987), 15.

40. Berthoud, "New Means Tests for Old," p. 17.

41. Evan Davis, Andrew Dilnot, and John Kay, "The Social Security Green Paper," *Fiscal Studies*, 6, no. 3 (August 1985), 7–8.

42. HM Treasury, *Public Expenditure Plans* (London: HMSO, 1987), vol. 2, p. 247.

43. Except at the "notches" created by the tax reforms of 1985, which introduced national insurance thresholds at £55 and £90 per week.

44. For detailed discussions see Deakin, *Politics of Welfare*; Lister, "Assessment of the Fowler Review"; and Kay Andrews and John Jacobs, *Punishing the Poor: Poverty Under Thatcher* (London: Macmillan Press, 1990).

45. *Economist*, March 12, 1988, p. 51; HM Treasury, *Government's Expenditure Plans* (HMSO, Cmnd 288, 1988), vol. 2, Table 15.8, p. 267.

46. The government had eventually agreed to make up the 20 percent rates requirement by increasing Income Support, but the new scales were insufficient to do so. This could be regarded as either a failure to compensate for the rates requirement, or as an insufficient uprating for inflation during the period of transition from Supplementary Benefit to Income Support. The debate over "winners" and "losers" from the reform was hopelessly muddled by such maneuvers, and further complicated by an almost indecipherable series of government figures. For a summary of the debate and a partisan but nonetheless useful attempt to sort out the facts see Andrews and Jacobs, *Punishing the Poor*, pp. 24–49.

47. Berthoud, "New Means Tests for Old," p. 22.
48. Ibid., p. 18.
49. *Economist*, March 12, 1988, p. 51.
50. *Financial Times*, "Lack of Vision on Benefits," April 5, 1988.
51. For balanced assessments, see Allen Schick, "The Budget as an Instrument of Presidential Policy," in Solamon and Lund, eds., *Reagan and the Governing of America*, pp. 91–125; and Robert D. Reischauer, "The Congressional Budget Process," in Mills and Palmer, eds., *Federal Budget Policy*, pp. 385–413.
52. *New York Times*, April 8, 1981, p. 25A. *Congressional Quarterly Weekly Report*, February 7, 1981, p. 275.
53. Thomas Ferguson and Joel Rogers, *Right Turn: The Decline of the Democrats and the Future of American Politics* (New York: Hill & Wang, 1986), ch. 5; Stockman, *Triumph of Politics*, ch. 6.
54. *Congressional Quarterly Weekly Report*, February 13, 1982, pp. 240–1. *Congressional Quarterly Almanac*, 1982, p. 477.
55. Ways and Means, *Background Data*, 1988, p. 462. *Congressional Quarterly Almanac 1982*, p. 476.
56. The one significant cutback after 1982 was the subjection of all UI benefits to taxation in the Tax Reform Act of 1986. That UI continued to be cut back after retrenchment in other programs had ceased provides further evidence of its relative vulnerability. See later in this section.
57. Palmer and Sawhill, *Reagan Record*, p. 367.
58. Ways and Means, *Background Data*, 1991, p. 1401.
59. In 1981, the period between uprating the Thrifty Food Plan was lengthened for the next few years. In 1982, benefits for the next three years were linked to 99 percent of the TFP.
60. Because for most indexed programs such as Social Security, upratings are linked to the current year's benefits rather than some independent base, a COLA delay produces a permanent reduction in real benefits. For a more thorough discussion see Weaver, *Automatic Government*, ch. 5.
61. For a summary see Ways and Means, *Background Data*, 1991, pp. 1401–4.
62. Ways and Means, *Background Data*, 1991, pp. 1403, 1401; Robert Greenstein, "Universal and Targeted Approaches to Relieving Poverty: An Alternative View," in Jencks and Peterson, *Urban Underclass*, p. 441.
63. Ways and Means, *Background Data*, 1988, pp. 459–63.
64. See Paul E. Peterson, "Why State Welfare Policy Making Has Grown Increasingly Conservative," *Center for American Political Studies* occasional paper, Harvard University, #92–16, September 1992.
65. See Russell L. Hanson, "The Expansion and Contraction of the American Welfare State," in Goodin and Le Grand, *Not Only the Poor*, pp. 169–99; and Peterson and Rom, *Welfare Magnets*.
66. Congressional Budget Office estimates cited in Wayne Vroman, "The Aggregate Performance of Unemploymant Insurance, 1980–1985," in W. Lee Hansen and James F. Byers, eds., *Unemployment Insurance: The Second Half-Century* (Madison: University of Wisconsin Press, 1990), p. 23.
67. Vroman, "Aggregate Performance," p. 29. See also Gary Burtless, "Why is Insured Unemployment So Low?" *Brookings Papers on Economic Activity*, no. 1 (1983), 225–54; and Walter Corson and Walter Nicholson, "Unemployment Insurance Dur-

ing the 1981–83 Recession: Were the Lessons of 1974–76 Learned Too Well?'' Paper prepared for the 1984 meeting of the Association for Public Policy Analysis and Management.

68. Ways and Means, *Background Data*, 1991, p. 491.
69. For details see Vroman, ''Aggregate Performance of Unemployment Insurance,'' pp. 21–7.
70. Data from Ways and Means, *Background Data*, 1991, p. 482. For a summary of the MPR study, see ibid., pp. 482–4. For a study that emphasizes demographic shifts (particularly the increasing proportion of unemployment occurring in states with weak UI programs) see Rebecca M. Blank and David E. Carol, ''Record Trends in Insured and Uninsured Unemployment: Is There an Explanation?'' *Quarterly Journal of Economics*, 106 (1991), 1157–90.
71. *National Journal*, February 27, 1982, p. 363. An excellent appraisal of Reagan's New Federalism initiatives can be found in Timothy Conlan, *New Federalism: Intergovernmental Reform from Nixon to Reagan* (Washington, D.C.: Brookings Institution, 1988), pp. 95–238.
72. Although the goal of retrenchment was not stressed in public, it was clearly on the minds of administration officials. According to Carleson: ''We have consciously set out to force political decisions and the struggles that accompany them down to the state and local level. The so-called iron triangles in Washington for too long have had a virtual monopoly on political influence in Congress and the agencies.'' Quoted in Claude E. Barfield, *Rethinking Federalism* (Washington, D.C.: American Enterprise Institute, 1981), p. 24.
73. Peterson and Rom, *Welfare Magnets*.
74. Quoted in *National Journal*, February 27, 1982, p. 368. An econometric analysis by Edward Gramlich estimated that these competitive pressures would sharply reduce AFDC spending if the New Federalism proposals were adopted. Edward M. Gramlich, ''An Econometric Examination of the New Federalism,'' *Brookings Papers on Economic Activity*, no. 2 (1982), 327–60.
75. Conlan, *New Federalism*, pp. 179–98.
76. Ibid., p. 198. Nixon's New Federalism plans for returning authority to the states had contained budgetary ''sweeteners'' to make proposals attractive to congressional liberals. This contrast is brought out in Richard P. Nathan, ''The Reagan Presidency in Domestic Affairs,'' in Fred I. Greenstein, ed., *The Reagan Presidency: An Early Assessment* (Baltimore: Johns Hopkins University Press, 1983), pp. 53–6.
77. Berkowitz, ''Changing the Meaning of Welfare Reform''; Robert B. Carleson, ''The Reagan Welfare Reforms,'' *Journal of the Institute for Socioeconomic Studies* (Summer 1980), 1–13.
78. David L. Kirp, ''The California Work/Welfare Scheme,'' *The Public Interest*, 83 (Spring 1986), 39.
79. On the state experiments see Michael Wiseman, ''Workfare and Welfare Reform,'' in Harrel R. Rodgers, ed., *Beyond Welfare: New Approaches to the Problem of Poverty in America* (New York: Sharpe, 1988), pp. 14–38; and Kirp, ''California Work/Welfare Scheme.'' The feedback effects are discussed in Michael Wiseman, ''Research and Policy: An Afterword for the Symposium on the Family Support Act of 1988,'' *Journal of Policy Analysis and Management*, 10, no. 4 (Fall 1991), 657–66; and Julie Rovner, ''Welfare Reform: The Issue that Bubbled up from the States to Capitol Hill,'' *Governing* (December 1988), 17–21.

80. An important contribution to this renewed interest in work-based approaches has been Lawrence Mead, *Beyond Entitlement: The Social Obligations of Citizenship* (New York: Free Press, 1986). Prominent reports include *A New Social Contract: Rethinking the Nature and Purpose of Social Assistance*, submitted to Governor Mario Cuomo by the Task Force on Poverty and Welfare, December 1986; *Ladders Out of Poverty*, by the Project on the Welfare of Families, co-chaired by Bruce Babbitt and Arthur Flemming, December 1986; and *A Community of Self-Reliance: The New Consensus on Family and Welfare*, by the Working Seminar on Family and American Welfare Policy, Marquette University and the American Enterprise Institute, March 1987. For a discussion see Robert D. Reischauer, "Welfare Reform: Will Consensus Be Enough?" *Brookings Review* (Summer 1987), 3–8.

81. On the impact of research see the symposium on the Family Support Act in the *Journal of Policy Analysis and Management*, 10, no. 4 (Fall 1991), especially Peter L. Szanton, "The Remarkable 'Quango': Knowledge, Politics and Welfare Reform," 590–602; Erica B. Baum, "When the Witch Doctors Agree: The Family Support Act and Social Science Research," 603–15; and Ron Haskins, "Congress Writes a Law: Research and Welfare Reform," 616–32. See also Lawrence M. Mead, *The New Politics of Poverty: The Nonworking Poor in America* (New York: Basic, 1992), pp. 195–8.

82. The phrase "making work pay" comes from David T. Ellwood, *Poor Support: Poverty in the American Family* (New York: Basic, 1988), which contains a detailed discussion of work-incentive issues.

83. Jack A. Meyer, "Budget Cuts in the Reagan Administration: A Question of Fairness," in Bawden, *Social Contract Revisited*, p. 41.

84. Report to President Reagan by the White House Domestic Policy Council Low Income Opportunity Working Group, *Up from Dependency: A New National Public Assistance Strategy* (Washington, D.C.: GPO, December 1986).

85. CBO estimates cited in Lawrence M. Mead, "The New Welfare Debate," *Commentary* (March 1988), 51.

86. States that did not have an AFDC-UP program prior to passage of the FSA could limit participation of two-parent families to no more than six months of any twelve-month period, but most states are not exercising this option.

87. Wiseman, "Research and Policy," p. 659.

88. *New York Times*, July 26, 1992, p. 18.

89. Bill Clinton and Michael Castle, "The States and Welfare Reform," *Intergovernmental Perspective* (Spring 1991), 16; *New York Times*, July 26, 1992, p. 18.

90. See Christopher Howard, "A Truly Exceptional Program: The Politics of the Earned Income Tax Credit," paper presented at the 1992 annual meeting of the American Political Science Association, Chicago. I rely in large part on Howard's excellent account in the following paragraphs.

91. Ways and Means, *Background Data*, 1991, p. 901.

92. On the dynamic of "solutions" attaching themselves to a variety of "problems" see Kingdon, *Agendas, Alternatives and Public Policies*.

93. *New York Times*, March 24, 1981, p. A1.

94. Howard, "Politics of the Earned Income Tax Credit," p. 39.

6. THE IMPACT OF CONSERVATIVE GOVERNMENTS

1. For background on the NHS, see Rudolf Klein, *The Politics of the National Health Service* (London: Longman Group, 2d ed., 1989).
2. Tessa Blackstone and William Plowden, *Inside the Think Tank: Advising the Cabinet, 1971–1983* (London: Heinemann, 1988), pp. 95–6.
3. For a more complete discussion, see Rudolf Klein, "The Politics of Ideology vs. the Reality of Politics: The Case of Britain's NHS in the 1980s," *Milbank Memorial Fund Quarterly* (1984), 82–109; Beth C. Fuchs, "Health Policy in a Period of Resource Limits and Conservative Politics," in Waltman and Studlar, eds., *Political Economy*, pp. 207–32; Rudolf Klein, "Why Britain's Conservatives Support a Socialist Health Care System," *Health Affairs* (Spring 1985), 41–58.
4. John Lister, "Shattuck Lecture – The Politics of Medicine in Britain and the United States," *New England Journal of Medicine*, 315 (July 17, 1986), 169.
5. Edwin Griggs, "The Politics of Health Care Reform in Britain," *Political Quarterly*, 62 (1991), 423–7.
6. Department of Health, *Working for Patients* (London: HMSO, Cmnd 555, 1989); Griggs, "Politics of Health Care Reform"; Nicholas Barr, Howard Glennerster, and Julian Le Grand, "Working for Patients? The Right Approach?" *Social Policy and Administration*, 23, no. 2 (August 1989), 117–27; Klein, *Politics of the NHS*, pp. 228–44.
7. *Hansard*, House of Commons Debates, vol. 125, col. 872, January 19, 1988 (Sir Rhodes Boyson).
8. C. Duncan, K. I. Sams, and P. J. White, "The House of Commons and the NHS," *Political Quarterly*, 60 (1989), 365–73.
9. On the development of the health-care system in the United States see Theodore R. Marmor, *The Politics of Medicare* (Chicago: Aldine, 1973); and Paul Starr, *The Social Transformation of American Medicine* (New York: Basic, 1982).
10. As scholars have noted, the weak arsenal of cost controls was the price paid for the passage of Medicare and Medicaid. See Marmor, *Politics of Medicare*; and Starr, *Social Transformation*. For a comparative analysis that lucidly outlines the flaws in America's hybrid system, see Robert G. Evans, "Finding the Levers, Finding the Courage: Lessons from Cost Containment in North America," *Journal of Health Politics, Policy and Law*, 11, no. 4 (1986), 585–615.
11. Jack A. Meyer and Rosemary Gibson Kern, "The Changing Structure of the Health Care System," in Phillip Cagan, ed., *Essays in Contemporary Economic Problems 1986: The Impact of the Reagan Program* (Washington, D.C.: American Enterprise Institute, 1986), p. 196; Congressional Research Service, *1988 Budget Perspectives*, Tables 2.2 and 4.2.
12. Mark A. Peterson, "Momentum Toward Health Care Reform in the U.S. Senate," *Journal of Health Politics, Policy and Law*, 17, no. 3 (1992), 553–73.
13. See Thomas R. Oliver, "Health Care Market Reform in Congress: The Uncertain Path from Proposal to Policy," *Political Science Quarterly*, 106, no. 3 (1991), 453–77; *National Journal*, September 12, 1981, pp. 1616–20; *Congressional Quarterly Almanac 1982*, p. 474; *National Journal*, January 22, 1983, pp. 170–3.
14. Oliver, "Health Care Market Reform," 471–3.
15. *1983 Congressional Quarterly Almanac*, p. 392.

16. *National Journal*, April 2, 1983, pp. 704–7.
17. General Accounting Office, *An Evaluation of the 1981 AFDC Changes: Initial Analysis* (Washington, D.C.: GAO, 1984). For more details on the changes at the federal and state level see Diane Rowland, Barbara Lyons, and Jennifer Edwards, "Medicaid: Health Care for the Poor in the Reagan Era," *American Review of Public Health*, 9 (1988), 427–50.
18. General Accounting Office, *Medicaid Expansions: Coverage Improves but State Fiscal Problems Jeopardize Continued Progress*, GAO/HRD–91–78 (Washington, D.C.: GPO, 1991).
19. Carol M. McCarthy, "DRGs – Five Years Later," *New England Journal of Medicine*, 318 (June 23, 1988), 1683; House Ways and Means Committee, *Background Material and Data on Programs Within the Jurisdiction of the Committee on Ways and Means* (Washington, D.C.: GPO, 1988), pp. 144–9.
20. *Congressional Quarterly Weekly Report*, October 6, 1990, pp. 3217–22; October 13, 1990, pp. 3416–18; and November 3, 1990, p. 3700.
21. See for example Louis B. Russell, *Medicare's New Hospital Payment System: Is it Working?* (Washington, D.C.: Brookings Institution, 1989). Russell's research suggests that the DRG reform has moderated health-care cost increases without spurring significant cost shifting to patients. See also Allen Shick, "Controlling the 'Uncontrollables': Budgeting for Health Care in an Age of Mega-Deficits," in Jack A. Meyer and Marion Ein Lewin, eds., *Charting the Future of Health Care* (Washington, D.C.: American Enterprise Institute, 1987), pp. 13–34.
22. D. Lee Bawden and John L. Palmer, "Social Policy: Challenging the Welfare State," in Palmer and Sawhill, eds., *Reagan Record*, p. 185.
23. *Background Data*, 1991, p. 1515. For a skeptical note on the magnitude of Medicare cuts see Allen Schick, *The Capacity to Budget* (Washington, D.C.: Urban Institute, 1990), pp. 190–3.
24. Report prepared by Ed Roybal, chair, House Select Committee on Aging, "An Assault on Medicare and Medicaid in the 1980s: The Legacy of an Administration" (Washington, D.C.: GPO, 1988).
25. See Theodore R. Marmor, "Coping with a Creeping Crisis," in Marmor and Mashaw, eds., *Social Security*, pp. 177–99.
26. This pressure is certain to continue in the future. See John Holahan and John L. Palmer, "Medicare's Fiscal Problems: An Imperative for Reform," *Journal of Health Politics, Policy and Law*, 13, no. 1 (Spring 1988), 53–81.
27. Shick, "Controlling the 'Uncontrollables' " pp. 30–1.
28. Ibid., p. 30. Carol S. Weissert, "Medicaid in the 1990s: Trends, Innovations, and the Future of the 'PAC-Man' of State Budgets," *Publius*, 22 (Summer 1992), 93–109.
29. Robert Pear, "Deficit or No Deficit, Unlikely Allies Bring About Expansion of Medicaid," *New York Times*, November 4, 1990, p. 24.
30. Michael O'Higgins, "Social Welfare and Privatization: The British Experience," in Sheila B. Kamerman and Alfred J. Kahn, eds., *Privatization and the Welfare State* (Princeton, N.J.: Princeton University Press, 1989), p. 172. See also idem, "Income During Initial Sickness: An Analysis and Evaluation of a New Strategy for Social Security," *Policy and Politics*, 9, no. 2 (1981), 151–71; and A. R. Prest, "The Social Security Reform Minefield," *British Tax Review*, no. 1 (1983), 44–53.
31. Nicholas Barr and Fiona Coulter, "Social Security: Solution or Problem?" in John

Hills, ed., *The State of Welfare: The Welfare State in Britain since 1974* (Oxford University Press, 1990), p. 281.

32. Mordechai E. Lando, Alice V. Farley, and Mary A. Brown, "Recent Trends in the Social Security Disability Insurance Program," *Social Security Bulletin*, 45, no. 8 (1982), 5. The following account draws particularly on Jerry L. Mashaw, "Disability Insurance in an Age of Retrenchment: The Politics of Implementing Rights," in Marmor and Mashaw, eds., *Social Security*, pp. 151–75; and Martha Derthick, *Agency Under Stress: The Social Security Administration in American Government* (Washington, D.C.: Brookings Institution, 1990).

33. Mashaw, "Disability Insurance," pp. 160–5.

34. Subcommittee on Social Security of the House Committee on Ways and Means, *Status of the Disability Insurance Program*, Ninety-seventh Congress, first session (Washington, D.C.: GPO, 1981), p. 4.

35. Derthick, *Agency Under Stress*, p. 36.

36. *Congressional Quarterly*, May 26, 1984, p. 1253.

37. Derthick, *Agency Under Stress*, pp. 42–6, 138–51, 157–72.

38. Mashaw, "Disability Insurance," pp. 166–75.

39. Ways and Means, *Background Data*, 1991, pp. 65–6.

40. Dunleavy, "Urban Basis of Political Alignment"; V. Duke and S. Edgell, "Public Expenditure Cuts in Britain," *International Journal of Urban and Regional Research*, 8 (1984), 177–99; Taylor-Gooby, "Consumption Cleavages and Welfare Politics."

41. On some of the difficulties of researching public opinion on the welfare state see Elim Papadakis, "Public Opinion, Public Policy and the Welfare State," *Political Studies*, 40 (1992), 21–37.

42. Taylor-Gooby, *Social Change*, pp. 111, 132.

43. Peter Taylor-Gooby, "The Politics of Welfare – Public Attitudes and Behavior," in Klein and O'Higgins, eds., *Future of Welfare*, p. 78.

44. The evidence is persuasively evaluated in Peter Taylor-Gooby, "The Future of the British Welfare State: Public Attitudes, Citizenship and Social Policy under the Conservative Governments of the 1980s," *European Sociological Review*, 4, no. 1 (May 1988), 1–19. See also Dennis Kavanagh, *Thatcherism and British Politics: The End of Consensus?* (Oxford University Press, 1987), pp. 292–7.

45. John Hills and Beverley Mullings, "Housing: A Decent Home for All at a Price within their Means?" in Hills, ed., *State of Welfare*, p. 171; Taylor-Gooby, *Social Change*, pp. 125–6.

46. Taylor-Gooby, *Social Change*, pp. 111–32.

47. Anthony Heath with Geoff Garrett, "The Extension of Popular Capitalism," in Anthony Heath et al., *Understanding Political Change: The British Voter, 1964–1987* (Oxford: Pergamon Press, 1991), pp. 126–35.

48. Hugh Heclo, "Reaganism and the Search for a Public Philosophy," in John L. Palmer, ed., *Perspectives on the Reagan Years* (Washington, D.C.: Urban Institute, 1986), pp. 31–61; Morris P. Fiorina, "The Reagan Years: Turning to the Right or Groping for the Middle?" in Barry Cooper, Allan Kornberg, and William Mishler, eds., *The Resurgence of Conservatism in Anglo-American Democracies* (Durham: University of North Carolina Press, 1988), pp. 430–59; Thomas Ferguson and Joel Rogers, *Right Turn: The Decline of the Democrats and the Future of American Politics* (New York: Hill & Wang, 1986), ch. 1.

49. Robert J. Shapiro and John T. Young, "Public Opinion and the Welfare State: The

United States in Comparative Perspective," *Political Science Quarterly*, 104, no. 1 (1989), pp. 73–5.

50. Hugh Heclo, "Poverty Politics," paper presented at Institute for Research on Poverty, Conference on Poverty and Public Policy, May 1992, p. 9.

51. James A. Stimson, *Public Opinion in America* (Boulder, Colo.: Westview, 1991); Fay Lomax Cook, *Support for the American Welfare State* (New York: Columbia University Press, 1992).

52. Edmund M. Gramlich and Daniel L. Rubinfeld, "Voting on Public Spending: Differences Between Public Employees, Transfer Recipients and Private Workers," *Journal of Policy Analysis and Management*, 1, no. 4 (1982), 516–33.

53. Skocpol, "Bringing the State Back In," p. 16.

54. HM Treasury, *Public Expenditure Analyses to 1994–95: Statistical Supplement to the 1991 Autumn Statement* (London: HMSO, 1992), Table 2.3. Social expenditure includes the following functions: employment and training, housing, health and personal social services, and social security.

55. One aspect of government tax policy has served to restrict revenues. As noted in Chapter 4, the government's decision to introduce a poll tax to replace domestic rates is likely to impede the ability of local governments to fund their programs. Given central government's dominant role in funding the welfare state, however, this change is unlikely to offset the increasing flow of revenues created by Thatcher's other tax policies.

56. Office of Management and Budget, *Historical Tables, Budget of the United States Government* (Washington, D.C.: Executive Office of the President, 1989), Table 3.2.

57. Stockman, *Triumph of Politics*, p. 289. Chapter 9 of Stockman's book gives a vivid account of the fight over ERTA, and an astute evaluation of its long-term implications.

58. On indexation's enactment see Weaver, *Automatic Government*, ch. 9.

59. Stockman, *Triumph of Politics*, pp. 274–6. See also Kenneth J. Kies, "The Current Political, Budgetary and Tax Policy Environment Suggests the Possibility of Major Federal Tax Legislation in the 100th Congress," *Tax Notes*, 35, no. 2 (April 12, 1987), 179–91.

60. Ways and Means, *Background Data*, 1988, p. 966.

61. For a detailed account of the events that led to enactment of the Tax Reform Act of 1986, see Jeffrey H. Birnbaum and Alan S. Murray, *Showdown at Gucci Gulch: Lawmakers, Lobbyists, and the Unlikely Triumph of Tax Reform* (New York: Random House, 1987).

62. Henry Aaron, "The Impossible Dream Comes True: The New Tax Reform Act," *Brookings Review* (Winter 1987), 3–10.

63. Aaron Wildavsky, "President Reagan as a Political Strategist," in Kay Lehrman Schlozman, ed., *Elections in America* (Boston: Allen & Unwin, 1987), pp. 221–38; Joe White and Aaron Wildavsky, *The Deficit and the Public Interest: The Search for Responsible Budgeting in the 1980s* (Berkeley and Los Angeles: University of California Press and Russell Sage Foundation, 1989).

64. Here I follow the persuasive arguments of White and Wildavsky, *Deficit and the Public Interest*.

65. See, for example, Peter Riddell, *The Thatcher Decade* (Oxford: Blackwell Publisher, 1989), pp. 177–8.

66. George E. Peterson, "Federalism and the States: An Experiment in Decentralization," in Palmer and Sawhill, eds., *Reagan Record*, pp. 217–59.

67. The literature on Reagan's federalism initiatives is extensive. See especially Conlan, *New Federalism*; David R. Beam, "New Federalism, Old Realities: The Reagan Administration and Intergovernmental Reform," in Salomon and Lund, eds., *Reagan and the Governing of America*, pp. 415–42; John E. Chubb, "Federalism and the Bias for Centralization," in Chubb and Peterson, eds., *New Direction*, pp. 273–306; and Richard P. Nathan, "Institutional Change Under Reagan," in Palmer, ed., *Perspectives on the Reagan Years*, pp. 121–45. For a less skeptical interpretation see Helen F. Ladd, "Federal Aid to State and Local Governments," in Mills and Palmer, eds., *Federal Budget Policy*, pp. 165–202.

68. Paul E. Peterson and Mark Rom, "Lower Taxes, More Spending, and Budget Deficits," in Charles O. Jones, ed., *The Reagan Legacy: Promise and Performance* (Chatham, N.J.: Chatham House, 1988), pp. 228–33.

69. McCarthy, *Campaigning for the Poor*, chs. 12–13; Peter Riddell, "Successful Pressures?" *Poverty* (Spring 1986), 13–14.

70. Leonard Rico, "The New Industrial Relations: British Electricians' New-Style Agreements," *Industrial and Labor Relations Review*, 41, no. 1 (October 1987), 64; David Marsh, "British Industrial Relations Policy Transformed: The Thatcher Legacy," *Journal of Public Policy*, 11, no. 3 (July–September 1991), 301; Riddell, *Thatcher Government*, p. 191.

71. For statements of this perspective, see Stephen McBride, "Mrs. Thatcher and the Post-War Consensus: The Case of Trade Union Policy," *Parliamentary Affairs* 39 (July 1986), 330–40; and John H. Goldthorpe, "Problems of Political Economy after the Postwar Period," in Charles S. Maier, ed., *Changing Boundaries of the Political* (Cambridge University Press, 1987), especially pp. 376–82. An excellent discussion by an analyst less optimistic about the prospects for union revival is Frank H. Longstreth, "From Corporatism to Dualism? Thatcherism and the Climacteric of British Trade Unions in the 1980s," *Political Studies*, 36 (1988), 413–32.

72. Rico, "New Industrial Relations."

73. Theodore J. Lowi, *The End of Liberalism* (New York: Norton, 1969); Grant McConnell, *Private Power and American Democracy* (New York: Random House, 1966).

74. Harold Wolman and Fred Teitelbaum, "Interest Groups and the Reagan Presidency," in Salamon and Lund, eds., *Reagan Presidency*, p. 315. Charles H. Levine and James A. Thurber, "Reagan and the Intergovernmental Lobby: Iron Triangles, Cozy Subsystems, and Political Conflict," in Allan J. Cigler and Burdett A. Loomis, eds., *Interest Group Politics* (Washington, D.C.: Congressional Quarterly Press, 2d ed., 1986), pp. 202–20.

75. See Mark A. Peterson and Jack L. Walker, "Interest Groups and the Reagan Presidency," in Jack L. Walker, *Mobilizing Interest Groups in America: Patrons, Professions, and Social Movements* (Ann Arbor: University of Michigan Press, 1991), pp. 141–56. See also Douglas Rowley Imig, "Resource Mobilization and Survival Tactics of Poverty Action Groups," *Western Political Quarterly* (1992), 501–20.

76. J. David Greenstone, *Labor in American Politics* (University of Chicago Press, 1969); Richard B. Freeman and James L. Medoff, *What Do Unions Do?* (New York: Basic, 1984), pp. 191–206; Vernon Coleman, "Labor Power and Social Equality: Union Politics in a Changing Economy," *Political Science Quarterly*, 103, no. 4 (1988), 687–705.

77. Marick F. Masters and John Thomas Delaney, "Union Legislative Records During

President Reagan's First Term," *Journal of Labor Research*, 8, no. 1 (Winter 1987), 1–17.

78. Marick F. Masters, Robert S. Atkin, and John Thomas Delaney, "Unions, Political Action, and Public Policies: A Review of the Past Decade," *Policy Studies Journal*, 18, no. 2 (Winter 1989–90), 474.

79. Masters et al., "Unions," p. 475. On the sources of union decline see Thomas A. Kochan, Harry C. Kate, and Robert B. McKersie, *The Transformation of American Industrial Relations* (New York: Basic, 1987); and Michael Goldfield, *The Decline of Organized Labor* (University of Chicago Press, 1987). See also Donna Sockell and John Thomas Delaney, "Union Organizing and the Reagan NLRB," *Contemporary Policy Issues* (October 1987), 28–45.

80. On the relatively low priority of social programs, see the comments of union lobbyists in Bill Keller, "Special Treatment No Longer Given Advocates for the Poor," *Congressional Quarterly Weekly Report*, 39, no. 16 (April 18, 1981), 659–64.

81. Quoted in Stephen V. Roberts, "Budget Axe Becomes a Tool of Social Change," *New York Times*, June 21, 1981, p. 2.

82. On this see especially Paul E. Peterson, "The Rise and Fall of Special Interest Politics," *Political Science Quarterly*, 105 (1990), 539–57.

83. Theodore Lowi, "American Business, Public Policy Case Studies, and Political Theory," *World Politics*, 16 (1964), 667–715.

84. Wolman and Teitelbaum, "Interest Groups," pp. 305–9.

85. Ibid.

7. SOCIAL POLICY IN AN ERA OF AUSTERITY

1. On these broad trends see John H. Goldthorpe, ed., *Order and Conflict in Contemporary Capitalism* (Oxford University Press, 1984). For a discussion of the rise of Reagan and Thatcher see Joel Krieger, *Reagan, Thatcher and the Politics of Economic Decline* (Oxford: Polity, 1986).

2. The seminal work in this vein is Mancur Olson, *The Rise and Decline of Nations* (New Haven, Conn.: Yale University Press, 1982). For a critique see David R. Cameron, "Distributional Coalitions and Other Sources of Economic Stagnation: On Olson's *Rise and Decline of Nations*," *International Organization*, 42, no. 4 (1988), 561–603.

3. See Weir et al., eds., *Politics of Social Policy*; and Immergut, "Veto Points." For a perspective that is more ambivalent on the relationship between state centralization and welfare state expansion see Banting, *Welfare State and Canadian Federalism*.

4. R. Kent Weaver and Bert A. Rockman, "Assessing the Effects of Institutions," and "When and How Do Institutions Matter?" in Weaver and Rockman, eds., *Do Institutions Matter?*

5. Of course, Thatcher had to retain the loyalty of her parliamentary party as well, and she was ultimately ousted by her colleagues rather than by the electorate. Concern that Mrs. Thatcher had become an electoral liability, however, appears to have been paramount in the thinking of those who forced her resignation.

6. Compare this account with the analysis of Thatcherism in Garrett, "Politics of Structural Change."

7. As Weaver and Rockman note, it is necessary to distinguish two "regime types" within the system of separation of powers that may operate quite differently: unified

party control of Congress and the presidency, and divided government. Weaver and Rockman, "Assessing the Effects of Institutions."

8. The skeptics' position is forcefully advanced in David R. Mayhew, *Divided We Govern: Party Control, Lawmaking, and Investigations, 1946–1990* (New Haven, Conn.: Yale University Press, 1991). For a range of views see James L. Sundquist, "Needed: A Political Theory for the New Era of Coalition Government in the United States," *Political Science Quarterly*, 103, no. 4 (1988), 613–35; John E. Chubb and Paul E. Peterson, eds., *Can the Government Govern?* (Washington, D.C.: Brookings Institution, 1989); and Gary W. Cox and Samuel Kernell, eds., *The Politics of Divided Government* (Boulder, Colo.: Westview, 1991).

9. For comparative discussions see Fritz W. Scharpf, "The Joint-Decision Trap: Lessons from German Federalism and European Integration," *Public Administration*, 66 (1988), 239–78; and Banting, *Welfare State and Canadian Federalism*.

10. Robert Kuttner, "Reaganism, Liberalism, and the Democrats," in Sidney Blumenthal and Thomas Byrne Edsall, eds., *The Reagan Legacy* (New York: Pantheon, 1988), p. 113.

11. See for example Korpi, "Social Policy and Distributional Conflict"; idem, *Democratic Class Struggle*; Esping-Andersen, *Three Worlds of Welfare Capitalism*; Skocpol, "Targeting Within Universalism"; Mishra, *Welfare State in Capitalist Society*; and Sara A. Rosenberry, "Social Insurance, Distributive Criteria and the Welfare Backlash: A Comparative Analysis," *British Journal of Political Science*, 12, no. 4 (October 1982), 421–47. For a view similar to the one advanced here see Greenstein, "Universal and Targeted Approaches to Relieving Poverty."

12. William A. Niskanen, *Bureaucracy and Representative Government* (Chicago: Aldine, 1971).

13. This argument is used by Peter Taylor-Gooby in explaining the relative durability of education and health-care programs in Britain; Taylor-Gooby, "Future of the British Welfare State."

14. Lowi, "American Business," 677 715; idem, "Four Systems of Policy, Politics, and Choice," *Public Administration Review*, 32 (1972), 298–310; James Q. Wilson, *Political Organizations* (New York: Basic, 1973), pp. 33–7; and idem, *American Government* (Lexington, Mass.: Heath, 4th ed., 1989), pp. 422–47, 590–604.

15. See for example O'Higgins, "Public/Private Interplay"; and Beth Stevens, "Blurring the Boundaries: How the Federal Government Has Influenced Welfare Benefits in the Private Sector," in Weir et al., eds., *Politics of Social Policy*, pp. 123–48.

16. Weaver, *Automatic Government*.

17. Pre-Reagan examples of retrenchment also reflect this dynamic. Trust-fund difficulties forced congressional responses in both Social Security and disability insurance during the late 1970s. On Social Security, see Derthick, *Policymaking for Social Security*, pp. 381–411. On disability insurance see Mashaw, "Disability Insurance," pp. 160–5.

18. Robert D. Behn, "Cutback Budgeting," *Journal of Policy Analysis and Management*, 4, no. 2 (1985), 163, 170.

19. Ferejohn and Kuklinski, *Information and Democratic Processes*; Keith Krehbiel, *Information and Legislative Organization* (Ann Arbor: University of Michigan Press, 1991); Mathew M. McCubbins and Terry Sullivan, eds., *Congress: Structure and Policy* (Cambridge University Press, 1987).

20. By the early 1990s, however, a substantial budget deficit had emerged in Britain.

This resulted largely from increases in spending and a fall in revenues linked to a deep recession, rather than to changes in taxation policy.

21. The ensuing discussion of economic and budgetary policy draws mainly on the following sources. For Britain: Peter Hall, *Governing the Economy*, ch. 5; Peter Riddell, *Thatcher Government*, chs. 4 and 5; and Peter Jenkins, *Mrs. Thatcher's Revolution*, pp. 98–100, 152–6, 277–83. For the United States: Isabel V. Sawhill, "Reaganomics in Retrospect," in Palmer, ed., *Perspectives on the Reagan Years*, pp. 91–120; Stockman, *Triumph of Politics*; Herbert Stein, *Presidential Economics* (Washington, D.C.: American Enterprise Institute, 2d rev. ed., 1988), pp. 235–411; Paul E. Peterson and Mark Rom, "Macroeconomic Policymaking: Who is in Control?" in Paul E. Peterson and John E. Chubb, eds., *Can the Government Govern?* (Washington, D.C.: Brookings Institution, 1989), pp. 139–82; and White and Wildavsky, *Deficit and the Public Interest*.

22. There has been endless dispute about the extent to which the 1981 tax cuts were simply a Trojan horse to aid the rich and undermine the welfare state. The evidence of the motivations of various administration figures is mixed. Perhaps the fairest judgment is that supply-side prescriptions were initially adopted because they offered the only approach that could reconcile the various pieces of Reagan's ambitious budgetary agenda with political realities. Certainly many within the administration were skeptical from the outset. Once the deficits became a reality, however, key figures were quick to identify and utilize this tremendous new leverage over domestic spending. See Stockman, *Triumph of Politics*; White and Wildavsky, *Deficit and the Public Interest.*

23. Peter Hall, "Conclusion: The Politics of Keynesian Ideas," in Peter Hall, ed., *The Political Power of Economic Ideas: Keynesianism Across Countries* (Princeton, N.J.: Princeton University Press, 1989), pp. 361–91.

24. Peterson and Rom, "Macroeconomic Policymaking," p. 179.

25. Hall, *Governing the Economy*, ch. 4.

26. Even here, however, possible adverse effects on work incentives resulting from reduced reliance on universal benefits or tightened eligibility for means testing complicate the picture.

Index